C000319035

"I've mastered HTML. I know all about optimizing images for the We
hundreds of pages—sites that are visited daily by thousands of people. I

I hear questions like this one every time I talk about the Web in front of a group of people. HTML is easy, and you can go a long way in Web design simply by knowing HTML. But the next step, breaking free of the limitations HTML imposes and staying competitive with other Web developers out there, usually involves a technical leap much more complicated than HTML. Neither CGI nor Java programming is simple to learn, particularly if you have no programming experience. The intermediate Web developer needs a stepping stone between HTML and the more advanced Web programming skills.

One excellent example of that stepping stone is Netscape's JavaScript. JavaScript is a programming language, but its syntax and framework are easy to learn. JavaScript requires no special tools; JavaScript programs are embedded inside HTML code and executed when the page is viewed. Despite its simplicity, however, JavaScript can be used in sophisticated ways to create Web pages that are dynamic, based on the context, and that can perform actions based on user input. Once you learn the basics of JavaScript, you have a toehold for learning more complex and general-purpose programming languages for the Web, such as Java, and CGI programming languages, such as Perl or C.

What should you do to start learning JavaScript? You should pick up this book, of course. Most books about programming are either too technical (assuming you know something about programming already) or kind of dull (assuming you'll just magically understand how to program once you know the syntax, which is sort of like assuming you'll know philosophy once you know French). This book is not one of those. Like all the Web Workshop books in this series, *Laura Lemay's Web Workshop: JavaScript* teaches you JavaScript from the ground up, starting with very simple programs and working through more and more complex topics. All along the path, this book uses plenty of real-life examples that you can use in your own Web pages. By the time you finish this book, you'll be far ahead on the curve from other Web developers who know only HTML.

Good luck and enjoy!

Laura Lemay

lemay@lne.com
http://www.lne.com/lemay/

LAURA LEMAY'S
WEB WORKSHOP

JavaScript™

LAURA LEMAY'S
WEB WORKSHOP

JAVASCRIPT™

Laura Lemay

Michael G. Moncur

201 West 103rd Street
Indianapolis, Indiana 46290

President, Sams Publishing:	Richard K. Swadley
Publishing Manager	Mark Taber
Managing Editor:	Cindy Morrow
Director of Marketing:	John Pierce
Assistant Marketing Managers:	Kristina Perry
	Rachel Wolfe

Acquisitions Editor
Mark Taber

Development Editor
Fran Hatton

Software Development Specialist
Bob Correll

Production Editor
Nancy Albright

Indexer
Charlotte Clapp

Technical Reviewer
Jeff Shockley

Editorial Coordinator
Bill Whitmer

Technical Edit Coordinator
Lorraine Schaffer

Resource Coordinator
Deborah Frisby

Editorial Assistants
Carol Ackerman
Andi Richter
Rhonda Tinch-Mize

Cover Designer
Alyssa Yesh

Book Designer
Alyssa Yesh

Copy Writer
Peter Fuller

Production Team Supervisor
Brad Chinn

Production
Stephen Adams
Debra Bolhuis
Mona Brown
Bruce Clingaman
Jason Hand
Daniel Harris
Ayanna Lacey
Clint Lahnen
Laura Robbins
Susan Van Ness

Dedication

This book is dedicated to my wife, Laura, and to my parents, Gary and Susan Moncur.

Overview

Contents

Acknowledgments

I'd like to thank everyone involved in the production of this book. Mark Taber at Sams.net helped fine-tune the initial proposal and got the project off the ground, and he's been involved at every stage. Mark always has time for my questions and has been a great help. Kelly Murdock and Fran Hatton were very helpful in fine-tuning the outline.

Fran also made many helpful comments in the editing stage. I'd like to thank the editor, Nancy Albright, for her comments and edits, which made things much more readable. Deborah Frisby helped to keep the editing process moving along.

I'd like to thank the Software Specialist for this book, Bob Correll, who was very helpful in putting together the content of the CD-ROM. I'd also like to thank the rest of the staff at Sams.net for their help in publishing this book.

Laura Lemay deserves mention for writing the great HTML books that launched the Web Workshop series.

Thanks to Netscape for giving me something to write about, and specifically to Brendan Eich, who goes above and beyond the call of duty in answering questions. I'd also like to thank all the participants in the JavaScript newsgroups and mailing lists; their answers helped me learn JavaScript, and their questions helped me know what to write about.

Finally, personal thanks go to my wife, Laura, my parents, Gary and Susan Moncur, the rest of my family, and my friends, particularly Chuck Perkins, Matt Strebe, Cory Storm, Robert Parsons, Dylan Winslow, James Chellis, Curt Siffert, and Henry J. Tillman. I couldn't have done it without your support.

About the Author

Michael Moncur is the owner of Starling Technologies, a consulting firm specializing in networking and the Internet. He is also a freelance webmaster and author, and has worked with the Internet since 1989. He has written several bestselling books about Novell networks.

Tell Us What You Think!

As a reader, you are the most important critic and commentator of our books. We value your opinion and want to know what we're doing right, what we could do better, what areas you'd like to see us publish in, and any other words of wisdom you're willing to pass our way. You can help us make strong books that meet your needs and give you the computer guidance you require.

Do you have access to CompuServe or the World Wide Web? Then check out our CompuServe forum by typing **GO SAMS** at any prompt. If you prefer the World Wide Web, check out our site at `http://www.mcp.com`.

NOTE: If you have a technical question about this book, call the technical support line at (800) 571-5840, ext. 3668.

As the team leader of the group that created this book, I welcome your comments. You can fax, e-mail, or write me directly to let me know what you did or didn't like about this book—as well as what we can do to make our books stronger. Here's the information:

FAX: 317/581-4669

E-mail: `newtech_mgr@sams.mcp.com`

Mail: Mark Taber
         Sams Publishing
         201 W. 103rd Street
         Indianapolis, IN 46290

Introduction

The World Wide Web began as a simple repository for information, but it has grown into much more—it entertains, teaches, advertises, and communicates. As the Web has evolved, the tools have also evolved. Simple markup tools such as HTML have been joined by true programming languages—including JavaScript.

Now don't let the word "programming" scare you. For many, the term conjures up images of long nights staring at the screen, trying to remember which sequence of punctuation marks will produce the effect you need. (Don't get me wrong. Some of us enjoy that sort of thing—and that's fine too.)

Although JavaScript is programming, it's a very simple language. As a matter of fact, if you haven't programmed before, it makes a great introduction to programming. It requires very little knowledge to start programming with JavaScript—you'll write your first program in Chapter 1, "Creating Simple JavaScript Programs."

If you have programmed in other languages, you'll find JavaScript interesting—it's a language with very few solid rules. The syntax is easy to master, and programming with JavaScript can actually be fun. I've programmed in many languages, and I've found that I can write a truly useful, rewarding application in JavaScript in only an hour or two—with other languages, it often takes days before you see the first actual result of the program.

JavaScript can do all sorts of things to liven up Web pages, and you can even create entire applications that span multiple pages. This book covers them all—serious business applications, gadgets such as scrolling messages, and even games.

Of course, every language has its limitations, and JavaScript is no exception—if it could do everything, it wouldn't be easy to learn. Throughout this book I've pointed out the areas where JavaScript falls short. I also introduce the tools you can use to fill the gaps in JavaScript—CGI, SSI, and Java.

If you've spent much time developing pages for the Web, you know that the Web is constantly changing, and it can be hard to keep up with the latest features. This book will help you add JavaScript to your Web development toolbox, and I think you'll enjoy learning it.

I really had fun writing this book—and believe it or not, writing isn't always fun. I hope you'll have as much fun as you experiment with JavaScript and its capabilities.

Who Should Read This Book

If you want to learn how to enhance your Web pages with JavaScript, this book is for you. I have made a few assumptions, though:

- ❏ You are familiar with the World Wide Web and the basics of creating Web pages with HTML.
- ❏ You have a 100-percent JavaScript-compatible browser handy—at the moment, that means the latest version of Netscape. If you don't, see Appendix C, "Online JavaScript Resources," for the site from which to download it.
- ❏ Of course, you'll need a computer on which to run the browser. Netscape is available for Windows, Windows 95, Macintosh, and UNIX, and the examples in this book should work on any of those platforms. A few of the examples require graphics or other files on the CD-ROM accompanying this book.
- ❏ You'll also need a text editor—a simple one such as Windows Notepad will work fine.
- ❏ To view the examples online, you'll need a connection to the Internet, and you'll need a provider with a Web server to publish your pages. However, most of the examples in this book will work equally well offline.

NOTE: Although they're often confused, JavaScript and Java are very different languages. Although we introduce Java and explain how to connect it with JavaScript, this is primarily a book about JavaScript.

How to Read This Book

This book is divided into six parts, roughly organized according to the complexity of their subjects:

- ❏ Part I, "Fast Track to JavaScript Programming," gives you a quick start with JavaScript programming, and introduces a few basic concepts.
- ❏ Part II, "Using JavaScript Objects and Forms," explains objects and forms—the foundations of building JavaScript applications.
- ❏ Part III, "Creating Smart Web Pages," looks at some of the more complicated issues of JavaScript, with a focus on adding intelligent, interactive features to your Web pages.

❏ Part IV, "Advanced JavaScript Concepts," includes more advanced concepts, including graphics, multimedia, and debugging.

❏ Part V, "JavaScript Alternatives and the Future," examines some of the other popular Web languages and explains how they can be combined with JavaScript in your pages. The last chapter looks at the changes and other issues that may affect JavaScript programming in the future.

❏ Part VI includes four appendixes. These give a concise reference for JavaScript and a list of online resources.

Although this book is organized so that it can be read from cover to cover, you don't need to. You'll want to read Chapter 1 to understand the basic concepts of JavaScript, but you can then skip around as you please. At the end of each chapter you'll find a list of next steps—other chapters to continue your learning, not necessarily in order.

Throughout this book you'll find Tasks, which show you how to use a particular JavaScript feature and include a working example application. The applications range from simple gadgets to business applications to games and graphics.

A Note About Software

JavaScript—like most Web-related languages and products—is constantly evolving. As it has grown in popularity, features have been added and changes have been made. Because of this, which browser you use can affect how well things work.

The examples in this book were developed with Netscape 3.0, and have all been tested on the final version of 3.0. Where possible, I've made every effort to ensure that they'll work on earlier versions, but I recommend that you download the latest version to be sure everything will work.

You may also run into problems if you use a newer browser—needless to say, I wasn't able to test the examples on programs that didn't exist at this writing. Don't download an earlier version, though—my recommendation is to keep the latest version, but consult this book's Web site (see address later in this Introduction) to find out how things have changed.

Keeping in Touch

I can't update your copy of this book each time JavaScript changes, but I've done the next best thing. I've set up a Web site devoted to this book. Here's the URL:

`http://www.starlingtech.com/books/javascript/`

At this site, you'll find online versions of all the examples in this book and a variety of additional examples demonstrating JavaScript's features. You will also find information about the latest new JavaScript features and how you can adapt the examples or your own programs to use them.

If you have any questions or comments about this book and its content, check the Web site for additional information. If you don't find what you need there, feel free to contact me directly via e-mail at this address:

`jsbooks@starlingtech.com`

If you have trouble getting one of the programs in this book to work, or with your own programs, first check out the online resources in Appendix C. If that doesn't help, feel free to contact me and I'll try to help; be warned, though, that it may take me a week or two to dig myself out from my current pile of e-mail to reply.

Last but not least, if you've created a JavaScript application that you're proud of, I'd like to see it. Send the URL to the e-mail address above. I'll post links to some of the best applications created by readers on the Web site.

PART

I

Fast Track to JavaScript Programming

ONE

Creating Simple JavaScript Programs

You're about to begin a journey into the depths of JavaScript, one of the hottest new languages for Web page development. JavaScript enables Web pages to be interactive and intelligent, and can add excitement to an otherwise dreary page.

If you've worked with HTML—the language of the Web—and have a basic idea of the concepts of programming, you should have no trouble understanding JavaScript. It's a simple and flexible language. This chapter starts with an introduction to JavaScript: its history, its features, and its limitations.

What Is JavaScript?

An explanation of exactly what JavaScript is has to begin with Java. Java is a new kind of Web programming language developed by Sun Microsystems. A Java program, or *applet*, can be loaded by an HTML page and executed by the Java Interpreter, which is embedded into the browser.

Java is a complex language, similar to C++. Java is object-oriented and has a wide variety of capabilities; it's also a bit confusing and requires an extensive development cycle. That's where JavaScript comes in.

JavaScript is one of a new breed of Web languages called *scripting languages*. These are simple languages that can be used to add extra features to an otherwise dull and dreary Web page. While Java is intended for programmers, scripting languages make it easy for nonprogrammers to improve a Web page.

JavaScript was originally developed by Netscape Corporation for use in its browser, Netscape Navigator. It includes a convenient syntax, flexible variable types, and easy access to the browser's features. It can run on the browser without being compiled; the source code can be placed directly into a Web page.

You can program in JavaScript easily; no development tools or compilers are required. You can use the same editor you use to create HTML documents to create JavaScript, and it executes directly on the browser (currently, Netscape or Microsoft Internet Explorer).

The single most useful aspect of JavaScript is the capability of adding interactive features to a Web page.

JavaScript was originally called LiveScript, and was a proprietary feature of the Netscape browser. JavaScript has now been approved by Sun, the developer of Java, as a scripting language to complement Java. Support has also been announced by several other companies.

Although useful in working with Java, you'll find that JavaScript can be quite useful in its own right. It can work directly with HTML elements in a Web page, something Java can't handle. It is also simple to use, and you can do quite a bit with just a few JavaScript statements. You'll see examples of the power of JavaScript throughout this book.

NOTE: At this writing, JavaScript is still under development. Although I made every effort to include all the latest features, there may be changes to the language before it becomes final. To keep track of the latest changes, watch Netscape corporation's JavaScript Web pages at the following address:

```
http://home.netscape.com/comprod/products/navigator/version_3.0/script/
```

History of JavaScript

As mentioned before, the history of JavaScript begins with Java. Java was originally developed by Sun Microsystems for use in "real-time embedded systems"—in other words, consumer electronics. Java has now become the de facto standard for advanced Internet programming, but you may still see it running your cellular phone someday.

Java was designed to operate on a *virtual machine*—a piece of software that interprets the Java code and acts on it as if it were a computer in itself. The virtual machine was designed to be simple so it could be implemented easily in a device. This is what makes it easy to implement in Web browsers.

NOTE: Several companies, including Oracle and Apple, have proposed designs for *network computers*—simplified PCs designed to work online, getting their software over the net. Most of these machines will use Java, or a variation of it, as an operating system.

Java's potential for the Internet was clear to Netscape almost immediately.

Java was originally supported only by HotJava, an experimental Web browser developed by Sun for that purpose. Recognizing its potential, Netscape integrated it into its Web browser, Netscape Navigator. Because Navigator is the most popular browser, this greatly increased the publicity for Java.

In 1995, Java became the hottest new buzzword for the Internet, but few people actually knew how to program it. Netscape Communications recognized the need for a simple, clear language for Web pages and introduced LiveScript, the first of the Web scripting languages.

LiveScript had a syntax based on Java, but was more concise and easier to learn. It was also a directly interpreted language rather than a compiled language like Java. Netscape built LiveScript into the beta versions of Netscape Navigator. Support for LiveScript began with version 2.0b1, released in June 1995.

LiveScript was renamed JavaScript to capitalize on Java's popularity.

Later in 1995, Netscape reached an agreement with Sun. Sun also recognized that a simple scripting language was a good idea, so they officially endorsed LiveScript. Thus, the connection with Java became official, and the name changed to the one you're familiar with: JavaScript.

See Chapter 18 for more information about MSIE and VBScript.

At this writing, JavaScript is still being developed and continues to improve. Netscape's support for JavaScript is expected to be finalized by the end of 1996, and other companies—most notably, Microsoft—are rushing to release competing products. Microsoft Internet Explorer (MSIE) 3.0, currently in beta, supports basic JavaScript, along with Microsoft's answer to JavaScript, VBScript.

JavaScript Versus Java

JavaScript is not only simpler than Java; it also includes several unique features.

The process of writing a Java applet can be complicated—writing the source code, compiling, and making the applet available on the server. JavaScript provides a much simpler alternative for small projects. The JavaScript source code is interpreted directly by the browser. The source can either be included directly within an HTML page or referenced in a separate file.

Although JavaScript doesn't really have any features that eclipse Java, it adds some conveniences, simplifies programming, and provides better integration with the browser. The key differences include the following (explained in the following sections):

❏ JavaScript can be combined directly with HTML.

❏ The JavaScript language structure is simpler than that of Java.

❏ The JavaScript interpreter is built into a Web browser.

❏ JavaScript is supported on more platforms than Java.

Combining JavaScript with HTML

Java applets are compiled and stored on the server as byte codes, but JavaScript programs are simple ASCII text files. You can keep them as separate files or include the JavaScript functions within an HTML page.

The <SCRIPT> tag, an extension of HTML supported by Netscape, enables you to include one or more JavaScript functions in the page. Listing 1.1 is a very small JavaScript script embedded directly within HTML. You take a more detailed look at the syntax of these tags later in this chapter.

Listing 1.1. (SIMPLE.HTM) A simple JavaScript program within an HTML document.

```
<HTML><HEAD>
<TITLE>Simple JavaScript Example </TITLE>
</HEAD>
<BODY>
HTML Text goes here.
<SCRIPT LANGUAGE="JavaScript">
document.write("Here is my output.")
</SCRIPT>
</BODY></HTML>
```

Event handlers are explained in detail in Chapter 3.

An alternate option called an *event handler* enables you to specify a JavaScript action that will be performed when an event occurs. For example, a button on the page might have an action performed when it is pressed. This provides a more dynamic method of accessing JavaScript.

Instead of the <SCRIPT> tag, an event handler is added as an attribute to an HTML tag. As an example, the following HTML code defines a link with an event handler:

```
<A HREF="www.netscape.com" onClick="alert('This will take you to Netscape's
home page.');">
```

In this case, the name of the event is `onClick`. This particular event happens when the user clicks on the link. The JavaScript code to perform when the link is clicked is enclosed within double quotation marks.

Simplified Language Structure

The limitations of JavaScript also make it much easier for the programmer. The syntax of the JavaScript language is more relaxed than that of Java, and variables (names used to store values) are easier to use. Here are the specifics:

❏ The JavaScript language is interpreted rather than compiled. Changing a script is as simple as changing an HTML page.

❏ Rather than creating objects and classes, you can do quite a bit by simply accessing existing objects in JavaScript.

❏ Variables are *loosely typed*: You do not need to declare variables before their use, and most conversions (such as numeric to string) are handled automatically.

❏ Event handlers enable a JavaScript function to execute whenever an action is performed on part of the HTML document. For example, a form's input field can be checked for certain values whenever it is modified.

Web Browser Integration

JavaScript is an *object-oriented* language. This simply means that it can use objects. An object is a more complicated version of a variable. It can store multiple values and can also include actual JavaScript code. You can create your own objects to represent just about anything.

The various objects available in JavaScript are described in Chapter 5, "Accessing Window Elements as Objects."

JavaScript also includes objects that enable you to access features of the browser directly. These objects represent actual elements of the browser and the Web page, such as windows, documents, frames, forms, links, and anchors.

You can access information about the links, anchors, and form elements in the current page. You can also control the browser with JavaScript. For example, it's possible to include a "back" button on your page that will send the user back to the previous page—just like the browser's back-arrow button.

Of course, when I say "browser" here, I'm talking about browsers that support JavaScript. Netscape Navigator began supporting it in version 2.0b1, and at this writing, version 3.0b6 is the latest version. It will also be supported by Microsoft Internet Explorer.

Supported on More Platforms

Because JavaScript is supported by Netscape on all the available platforms, it is supported more widely than Java. Until Java becomes more widely supported, using JavaScript for simple applications enables you to reach a wider audience on a wide variety of platforms. Currently, the only browser that fully supports JavaScript is Netscape Navigator. This functionality is provided on the following platforms:

- ❏ Windows 3.1, using the 16-bit version of Navigator
- ❏ Windows 95 or Windows NT, using the 32-bit version of Navigator
- ❏ Macintosh System 7 or higher, using the Macintosh version
- ❏ Most versions of UNIX, using the X Window version of Navigator

NOTE: At the time of this writing, Microsoft has released a beta version of its Web browser, Microsoft Internet Explorer version 3.0, which includes support for JavaScript. However, it is still under development and currently has trouble with some JavaScript programs.

Although this is a wide range of support and should enable about 90 percent of the Web's audience to use your script, but don't forget the other 10 percent. Whenever possible, be sure to provide an alternative for non-JavaScript browsers.

CAUTION: Although JavaScript is supported on these platforms, full support is provided by a beta version of Navigator at this writing. This means that it is still subject to bugs. See Chapter 14, "Debugging JavaScript Programs," for further information.

Uses for JavaScript

You've learned some technical details as to why JavaScript is important, but what's it really good for? What will it do for your Web pages? The following sections present some of the most important uses for JavaScript.

Including Dynamic Information

See Chapter 7, "Real-Life Examples I," for some examples of dynamic Web pages.

JavaScript can be used to add a bit of life to a Web page by making some of the text dynamic. As a simple example, you could display an appropriate greeting—"good morning" or "good evening", depending on the time. Because you can use and control the HTML itself, you can extend this by dynamically choosing graphics or links using JavaScript. Thus, depending on the user, the time, or any factor, you can present the appropriate page.

Validating Forms

Chapter 6, "Using Interactive Forms," will show you how to use JavaScript with interactive forms.

You've seen forms at many Web pages, and probably used them yourself. The user enters data into the form, then presses the Submit button, and the server, using a CGI program, responds to the information. This is useful, but it isn't very interactive—before you can receive a response, you have to wait for the data to travel to the server and back.

NOTE: The biggest difference between JavaScript and CGI is that CGI works on the server and JavaScript works on the user's own machine (the client). CGI is most useful for sending data to the server and sending server data back to the user.

JavaScript can add instant gratification to a Web form. You still can't send the data to the server until the Submit button is pressed, but JavaScript can act on the data in the meantime. For example, you could fill out a loan application online and, as you fill it out, instantly get feedback about the kind of payments the loan will require. After you're satisfied with the application, you can then submit it to the server.

Making Pages Interactive

See Chapter 8, "Improving a Web Page with JavaScript," for examples of adding interactive features with JavaScript.

Finally, JavaScript can be used to remove some of the drudgery from a normal Web page by giving the user some control of the page. For example, you could have a background on/off button to control the display of the background, or a button to toggle the display of a table of contents.

Getting Started with JavaScript

The process of developing a JavaScript application is simple. The following sections introduce the tools you need to create and execute JavaScript scripts and describe the process of combining a script with an HTML page. Finally, you'll learn about the hardware and software platforms that currently support JavaScript.

Required Software and Hardware

Currently, the only requirement in this area (and the only option) is Netscape Navigator, version 2.0b or higher. The available hardware platforms are discussed later in this section. Several other browser manufacturers plan to support JavaScript in the near future, however.

Development Tools

You need no special tools to create a JavaScript program.

Provided you have a version of Netscape to view your creations on, there are no tools that are specifically required in order to develop a JavaScript script. All you need to create the scripts is a text or HTML editor—probably the same one that you use to develop HTML pages.

NOTE: So far, none of the dedicated HTML editors have announced support for JavaScript; however, you can still use them to create JavaScript programs. Several HTML editors are included on the CD-ROM accompanying this book.

Testing a Simple JavaScript Program

A JavaScript program can be simple—even as small as a single statement—or much more complicated. Take a look at the simple example in Listing 1.2.

Listing 1.2. (ALERT.HTM) A script that displays a message in the text and in an alert box.

```
<HTML><HEAD>
<TITLE>Another JavaScript Test </TITLE>
</HEAD>
<BODY>
<SCRIPT LANGUAGE="JavaScript">
document.write("Hello!");
window.alert("Hello again!");
</SCRIPT>
</BODY>
</HTML>
```

The alert() statement is technically a method of the Window object. This is explained in Chapter 5.

This example displays the "Hello!" message as part of the HTML document. In addition, it uses the alert() statement to display a message to the user in a dialog box.

What happens when you load this Web page in Netscape? Let's take a quick look at the inner workings of JavaScript. Once you understand what happens and in what order, you'll find it easy to learn the specifics—such as the JavaScript language itself.

Receiving the Web Page

Let's start with a review of the basics: What happens when you request a Web page from a server? This is an important process to understand. Here are the steps involved:

These steps might be slightly different with non-Netscape browsers, but the idea is the same.

1. You enter a URL into your browser, or select a bookmark.
2. The browser sends an HTTP request for the URL to the appropriate server (known as a GET request).
3. The server sends back the contents of the Web page at the URL.
4. The browser sends additional requests for each of the graphics included in the Web page.
5. After receiving enough information about the graphics to devote the correct amount of space to them, the browser displays the page.
6. The remaining graphics are displayed as they are received.

Processing the Script

When JavaScript is involved, the process is slightly different. After the full HTML document is received, as in step 3 in the last section, it is examined for the <SCRIPT> tag. If a script is included, it is processed; however, the processing depends on the type of script:

❏ If the script is included in the header, it is ignored unless a script later calls it.

❏ If the script is included directly in the body, its output will be included in the Web page—thus, it can affect the display of the page.

❏ If the script is an event handler for a specific part of the page, it will be processed only when the event happens.

All three of these are useful ways of implementing a JavaScript program; you choose one of these methods depending on your needs. In a complicated JavaScript application, you will probably use all three.

Potential Problems with JavaScript

In this section, you learn some of the problems you might encounter when using JavaScript in your Web pages. Because these concerns might affect the security of your source code and data, you should also carefully consider them while developing JavaScript applications.

Security Considerations

All of JavaScript's security problems are relatively minor.

As JavaScript has been developed, there have been several concerns about security—most of them legitimate. The Computer Incident Advisory Committee (CIAC), an agency of the Department of Energy that monitors computer security problems, has reported several minor problems with JavaScript.

Because JavaScript is limited in its capabilities, there are no major problems—such as a method for a wayward script to erase your hard drive. All the potential problems involve the owner of the script or Web page being able to access information on your system. Here are the incidents the CIAC has reported:

❏ A JavaScript script can read your URL history and report it to the remote site.

❏ The browser's disk cache can be read and transmitted.

❏ Your e-mail address can be read—and used to send an e-mail without your knowledge.

❏ A list of files on your hard disk can be obtained.

❏ URLs you visit can be logged by a script and transmitted.

All these problems are specific to Netscape's implementation of JavaScript. The good news is that they have all been fixed by later versions of Netscape. The first two were fixed by version 2.0; the remaining ones are fixed by versions 2.01 and 2.02.

If you have the latest version of Netscape, you should be safe from these problems. However, considering that this many problems have been discovered, there is always a chance there will be more.

Your Source Code Is Accessible

Another problem with JavaScript is that, currently, there is no way to use a JavaScript on your Web page without making the script source available to anyone who wishes to copy it.

This means that you might spend hours working on a script, only to find that people have copied it onto their own Web pages. You may be programming in JavaScript for fun and not mind this, but it might be a serious consideration if you are making a JavaScript for pay or specifically for your own Web page.

Remember that even though your source code is accessible, that doesn't mean it's free to be copied. You legally have a copyright on any script you write.

The issue of copyright also affects HTML and Java applets.

If someone does copy your scripts, often the best solution is to send that person a friendly note pointing out your copyright and saying that you do not want anyone else using it. You should also clearly state this in the source code and on the Web page that contains it.

NOTE: If you've developed many HTML pages, you will recognize that HTML itself has this same problem. Although there's usually no harm in copying an HTML technique from a Web page—such as using <UL> for a list—some unscrupulous users have copied entire Web pages and labeled them as their own. For this reason, it's always a good idea to place a copyright notice on important Web pages—with or without JavaScript.

Overcoming JavaScript's Limitations

Limitations aren't always bad; because JavaScript is limited to simple functions, it's easy to learn.

Although the JavaScript language has many features, it's far from perfect and has many limitations. Some of these may be fixed as the language matures, but others may never be—because JavaScript is meant to be an easily understood scripting language, some features just don't belong.

Luckily, there are ways around most of the limitations in JavaScript. These include programming a solution "the long way," and combining JavaScript with other powerful languages, such as Java, CGI, and SSI.

Missing Features

JavaScript is still being developed, so there are still a few missing features. These might be fixed by a future version, but some may never be fixed. The following sections describe some of the most important features that are missing from JavaScript.

Working with Entire HTML Pages

A convenient use for JavaScript is to make a Web page interactive—for example, displaying the current time or date or including information that depends on the user's input. Unfortunately, there is no way for a JavaScript program to replace part of the currently loaded HTML page. You can reload the page with different contents, but you can't change the text on a page in place.

There are some elements of the page you can change: the images, and anything in a form element. You can also display the information you need to change in a separate frame. You can also get around this by using Java, which has no such limitations.

Lack of Network Communication

JavaScript cannot access any data on the server or send data to the server.

JavaScript has no facilities for communicating between the Web browser and the HTTP server. This means that although you can use JavaScript to manipulate data the user enters in a form, you can't send the resulting data back to the server. You can combine JavaScript with another Web language to solve this problem; CGI is the easiest way to do this.

TIP: Netscape has created a server-side version of JavaScript called Livewire. Unfortunately, it works only with Netscape server software. You'll look at Livewire in Chapter 20, "The Future of JavaScript."

Limited Graphics and Multimedia Capabilities

JavaScript does have some graphics capabilities, which you'll look at in Chapter 12, "Working with Graphics in JavaScript."

JavaScript is a scripting language, so you should hardly expect it to be a multimedia powerhouse. You can include graphics in a Web page and use JavaScript to specify which ones, but you cannot create graphics—for example, draw a graph. Currently, Java is the best solution when you need to do this.

Limited Size of Scripts

The early implementations of JavaScript (in Netscape Navigator) required that the scripts you use for a Web page be included in the HTML for that page. This means that there was a practical limitation of about 32K for the page and all scripts, because the browser must download the entire page before executing the script.

The JavaScript specification includes an SRC attribute to the <SCRIPT> tag, and this is supported by Netscape's latest version. This will enable you to embed a JavaScript script in the page, similar to an image. This should make much larger scripts practical. To use it, follow these steps:

1. Place the JavaScript program in a file with a .js extension, such as program.js.
2. Include the <SCRIPT> tag to refer to it, such as <SCRIPT SRC="program.js">.
3. Be sure the script and the JavaScript file are in the same directory on the Web server.

Limited Speed

Although JavaScript is slow, it's much faster than Java for simple applications.

The current implementation of JavaScript is a bit slow. Any complex calculation or manipulation of HTML tends to run at a slow creep. I assume that Netscape is aware of this and will improve the speed in future versions. Unfortunately, complex Java applets also run quite slowly, so there is no clear solution at this time.

Don't let this scare you away from JavaScript—many of the most powerful things you can do with JavaScript are simple and execute incredibly fast. It's only complex applications that suffer from this limitation.

Combining JavaScript with Other Languages

There are some situations where JavaScript really shines—and as you've learned, there are some where it doesn't even come close. Although JavaScript may be improved in the future, the current solution is to use the right tool for the job. Several Web languages can be used in combination with JavaScript.

JavaScript and Java

Java, the "big brother" of JavaScript, is the most obvious choice to use if you need to fill in some of the holes in JavaScript. Java includes many features, including communication across the network and graphics capabilities.

You will learn more about Java, and integrating it with JavaScript, in Chapter 16, "Integrating JavaScript with Java."

Java is harder to learn than JavaScript, but you may not need to learn it. Many ready-to-use Java applets are available. You will find several of these on the CD that comes with this book.

Best of all, JavaScript includes features that enable it to be tightly integrated with Java. You can use a Java applet and use JavaScript to control its features. See Chapter 16 for an example of this technique.

TIP: Remember that JavaScript can do many things Java can't do—including modifying HTML during its display, validating forms, and handling user-generated events.

JavaScript and CGI

Common Gateway Interface (CGI) has been a standard almost as long as the Web has, and it can be used to make Web pages interactive. You encounter CGI all over the Web—anywhere you fill in a form and press a Submit button, you've accessed a CGI script.

CGI is not actually a language, but rather a standard interface. You can write CGI programs in any language. The most commonly used languages for the task are Perl and C.

Chapter 17, "Combining JavaScript, CGI, and SSI," takes a closer look at the use of JavaScript with CGI and SSI.

CGI is different from Java or JavaScript in that it executes entirely on the server. Your client sends information to it in the request and then receives the results in the form of a Web page. You cannot have instant results—such as a total that automatically updates as you change the numbers entered. Combining JavaScript with CGI gives you the best of both worlds.

JavaScript and SSI

SSI enables you to control the Web page dynamically as it is sent from the server to the browser.

An alternative to CGI is Server-Side Include, or SSI. This enables you to include dynamic data in a page, similar to JavaScript's capability, but it happens on the server side.

Like CGI, SSI is a standard, and you can use any language to program SSI. You can combine SSI and JavaScript to make a truly dynamic page. You can even use SSI to change the JavaScript code included in the page based on certain factors. You'll find examples of this in Chapters 17 and 19.

Unfortunately, although most Web servers support SSI, not all systems (or system administrators) allow their use. The main reason for this is that each Web page has to be parsed for SSI instructions, which slows down the server. There are also security concerns. Ask your system administrator whether you are allowed to use SSI.

Writing a Simple JavaScript Application

In this section, you explore the process of JavaScript development with a simple JavaScript application. This application doesn't do much, but it will help you understand the steps required to develop and test a script. You'll find much more sophisticated examples throughout this book.

Creating the Script

You'll learn more about the JavaScript language in Chapter 2, "Working with Larger Programs and Variables."

First, let's look at a very simple JavaScript application. The following script simply displays the location of the current page and a brief message. This script will be combined with an HTML page and its use demonstrated.

```
document.write("<B> location: </B>" + document.location + "<br>")
document.write("This is a test of JavaScript." + "<br>")
```

After you've created the script, you need to do two things:

1. Embed the script in the HTML page. You can use the <SCRIPT> tag to do this, or use an event handler.
2. Test the script by viewing the document with Netscape.

Embedding the Script in an HTML Page

There are two ways to embed a JavaScript script in your HTML page. Each has its advantages and disadvantages. In a complex JavaScript application, you'll end up using both of these methods several times.

Using the <SCRIPT> tag

The simplest method of including a JavaScript script in an HTML page is to use the <SCRIPT> tag, as described earlier in this chapter. This tag is usually used as a container, and the script is included directly after it. Listing 1.3 adds the necessary opening and closing <SCRIPT> tags to the script:

Listing 1.3. A simple example of the <SCRIPT> tag.

```
<!-- <SCRIPT language=JAVASCRIPT>
document.write("<B> location: </B>" + document.location + "<br>")
document.write("This is a test of JavaScript." + "<br>")
</SCRIPT> -->
```

Notice the strange syntax. The extra brackets and exclamation marks indicate a comment; the entire script is marked as a comment so that older browsers will not attempt to display it. JavaScript-aware browsers will execute it correctly.

If you use this method within the body of a Web page, the script will be executed immediately when the page loads, and the output of the script will be included at that point in the page. You can also use the <SCRIPT> tag within the header of a page to prevent it from executing immediately. This can be useful for subroutines that you will call later.

Creating an Event Handler

An alternate approach is to use an event handler to perform a script when a certain event occurs. This is best used when you want to act on the press of a button or the entry of a field.

Rather than use the <SCRIPT> tag, an event handler is inserted as an attribute to an HTML tag. Tags that support event handlers include <LINK>, <IMG>, and the form element tags.

As a basic example of an event handler, here's a common use for JavaScript: creating a back button in a page that performs just like the browser's back button. You can easily accomplish this with an event handler, as in Listing 1.4.

Listing 1.4. A simple JavaScript event handler.

```
<INPUT TYPE="button" VALUE="Back!" onClick="history.go(-1); return true;">
```

You'll find more examples of event handlers in Chapter 3.

This defines a button with an event handler. The event handler is defined as an attribute of the <INPUT> tag. The attribute name is the event name—in this case, onClick. This is an event that occurs when the user clicks the mouse on an object.

In this example, a button is used to send the user back to the previous page. You could also use this technique with an image, or a simple link to the word `"back!"`.

NOTE: Because an event handler is inserted between double quotation marks, be sure to use single quotation marks to delimit any strings within the event handler.

Viewing Your Script's Output

The main tool you'll use to view the script's output is a Web browser. Currently, you should use Netscape to view the output, but other browsers may support JavaScript in the future. There's nothing special you need to do to view a script's output—just load the Web page that contains the script. You can even test JavaScript on your local computer, without uploading anything to the Web server.

NOTE: Be sure you have the latest version of Netscape. Because JavaScript is still being developed, there may be major differences in the results between versions of the browser. All the examples in this book are meant to use version 3.0 or later of Netscape Navigator, although they may work with older versions.

Hiding JavaScript from Older Browsers

Of course, any JavaScript you write will be intended for JavaScript-compatible browsers; however, the last thing you want is for someone using an ancient version of Mosaic to load your page and see the actual JavaScript code all over their screen.

Although 90 percent of users on the Web use Netscape, there are still many non-JavaScript browsers.

You can avoid this by enclosing JavaScript within HTML comments. This hides the code from older browsers; JavaScript-aware browsers, such as Netscape, will interpret it as JavaScript. Here's an example of a `<SCRIPT>` tag with HTML comments:

```
<!-- <SCRIPT language=JAVASCRIPT>
document.write("I lost a buttonhole. ");
</SCRIPT> -->
```

The key elements here are the comment begin and end tags: `<!!` and `—>`. These are standard HTML 2.0, and define the start and end of a comment.

Unfortunately, things aren't always that simple. Here are a few things to watch out for:

❑ Some browsers will treat any greater-than sign (>) as the end of the comment. The decrement operator (−) can also cause problems.

❑ Some browsers still won't recognize comments correctly, so your script may be displayed.

Because of problems like these, there is no ideal solution. The best way to avoid these problems is to use the <SCRIPT SRC> tag instead, although it isn't always the best solution. Another solution is the <NOSCRIPT> tag, which indicates content that will be ignored by JavaScript browsers. For example, this HTML will display only on non-JavaScript browsers:

```
<NOSCRIPT>
You're using a non-JavaScript browser. Please use the
<a href="nojs.html">Non-JavaScript version.</a> of this document.
</NOSCRIPT>
```

For clarity, I won't use HTML comments in the examples through this book. If you use these techniques on a Web page of your own, you may wish to add comments to support older browsers.

Workshop Wrap-Up

Although limited and still under development, JavaScript is a powerful tool to enhance a Web page. It offers features that are available to no other Web language. You've learned the following terms and concepts in this chapter:

❑ What JavaScript is, and where it came from

❑ The key differences between JavaScript and Java

❑ How to include a JavaScript program within an HTML document, and keep it from displaying on older browsers

❑ The key limitations and problems of JavaScript

❑ The basics of writing a JavaScript application

Next Steps

Your next task is to learn more of the specifics of the JavaScript language:

❑ To move on to larger JavaScript programs, see Chapter 2, "Working with Larger Programs and Variables."

❑ To learn more about JavaScript's object-oriented features, turn to Chapter 3, "Working with Objects and Events."

❑ To learn to manipulate and use parts of the Web page with JavaScript, see Chapter 5, "Accessing Window Elements as Objects."

❏ To see some real-life examples of JavaScript in action, see Chapter 7, "Real-Life Examples I."

❏ To learn more about Java, turn to Chapter 16, "Integrating JavaScript with Java".

Q&A

Q: If JavaScript and Java are so different, why are they named similarly? Some people even seem to use the words interchangeably.

A: It all comes down to marketing. Java was a publicity phenomenon at the time, and simply including the word Java (or any other coffee-related word) in a product's name was enough to get instant attention. Netscape got permission from Sun to do so, and the rest was history. Unfortunately, this has caused many beginners—and many columnists—to consider them identical, or at least much more similar than they really are.

Q: Will learning JavaScript give me a head start in learning to program with Java?

A: Yes. Although the languages have significant differences, many of the basic structures, functions, and concepts are the same. Be sure not to assume that things will work exactly the same, though.

Q: I already know some Java. Will this make it easier to learn JavaScript?

A: Yes—many of the objects and properties in JavaScript are based on Java, and the syntax is similar. However, don't make any assumptions that things will work exactly the same as Java—they rarely do.

Q: Is there a way to hide my JavaScript code without forcing myself to jump through hoops, avoiding greater-than and other essential symbols?

A: Not if the JavaScript program is embedded in an HTML file. If you keep your JavaScript separate and use `<SCRIPT SRC>` to include it, you can avoid these issues.

Q: Is there a way to hide JavaScript code from all browsers, so nobody can steal my programs? Can `<SCRIPT SRC>` do this?

A: There's no way to hide JavaScript source code. Using `<SCRIPT SRC>` makes it a bit more difficult to look at it, but anyone can still download your code and do so.

TWO

Working with Larger Programs and Variables

Without a way of storing data and using it repeatedly, a programming language isn't much better than a pocket calculator. In this chapter, you explore the types of data you can use in JavaScript, and how to define and use variables to store data. You'll also learn a bit about the structure of the JavaScript language.

JavaScript Language Structure

JavaScript has a simple, relaxed structure. You can include a single line of JavaScript in an HTML document, and it will act as a JavaScript program in itself. No specific statements are required to begin or end a JavaScript script, except for the <SCRIPT> and </SCRIPT> tags in HTML. For example, this is a simple JavaScript program to print a message:

```
<SCRIPT LANGUAGE="JavaScript">
document.write("The eagle has landed. The fat man walks
alone.");
</SCRIPT>
```

A JavaScript program can be as small as a single statement.

This script includes a single JavaScript statement. The `document.write()` command is actually part of the `document` object, which you will learn about in detail later; however, you don't need to understand objects to know that this statement simply prints the text, as if it were part of the HTML.

A wide variety of statements are available to perform different types of tasks. A statement can also assign a value to a variable, as you'll see later in this chapter.

Statements or functions that require a parameter, such as `document.write()` in the last example, use parentheses to surround their parameters. If more than one parameter is required, they are separated by commas. For example, this statement sends three numbers to a function called `total`:

```
result = total(12,36,14.5);
```

Notice the semicolon at the end of the example statement. This is a common feature of many languages, such as C and Java, to indicate the end of a statement. However, JavaScript isn't as picky as those languages; you can leave out the semicolons if you desire. You may want to include them for clarity, or to avoid developing a bad habit if you routinely program in C, Java, or Perl.

JavaScript is easy to use because it has few solid rules for punctuation.

The final punctuation marks you will need for JavaScript programs are the left and right braces: { and }. If you're familiar with C or Perl, you know that those languages use brackets to enclose blocks of statements, and that all statements must be inside a set of brackets. Once again, JavaScript isn't as strict as other languages. The only time braces are needed is when you are defining a block of statements for a specific purpose, such as a function.

NOTE: JavaScript keywords, function and object names, and variable names are case-sensitive. Be sure you use the correct combination of upper- and lowercase when entering JavaScript statements.

Next, let's take a look at the various components that can be included in a JavaScript program. You will learn about these in detail in this chapter and in Chapters 3, "Working with Objects and Events," and 4, "Using Built-In Objects and Custom Objects."

Statements

In general, any line in a JavaScript program can be considered a statement.

Statements are simply commands that perform a certain purpose. Several statements are built into JavaScript; these are used to test variables, control the flow of the program, and perform actions.

The term *statement* is also used to refer to any line of JavaScript code. For example, the document.write() statement used in the examples is technically an object method, which you'll explore in detail in Chapter 3.

Functions

A *function* accepts *parameters* and returns a value. You explore three built-in functions in the section titled Converting and Evaluating Variables and Expressions later in this chapter:

- ❏ parseInt converts strings to integers.
- ❏ parseFloat converts strings to floating-point numbers.
- ❏ eval evaluates JavaScript expressions.

You can also define your own functions with the function keyword. This example defines a very simple function that adds two numbers:

```
function Add(a,b){
   var result = a + b;
   return result;
}
```

Functions provide a way to simplify JavaScript code. You'll look at them further in Chapter 3.

To use a function, you simply include the function's name, followed by the parameters in parentheses. For example, here is a simple script that uses the Add() function to print a result:

```
var test = Add(2,4);
document.write("Two plus four equals:",test);
```

Variables

A variable is a container you can use to hold a value.

A *variable* is simply a name given to a value. Variables can be given different values throughout the course of a JavaScript program. In the previous example, a variable called test is used to store the result returned by the Add() function. You learn about variables in detail in the section titled Data Types and Variables later in this chapter.

Expressions

An *expression* is something that JavaScript interprets before using it in a statement. For example, this statement assigns a number to the variable total, using an expression:

```
total = result1 + result2;
```

The expression result1 + result2 is interpreted; in this case, the values are simply added together. This value is then used as the value to assign to the total variable.

Along with mathematical expressions, expressions can include function results and conditional expressions (explained in Chapter 3).

Objects, Properties, and Methods

Recall from Chapter 1, "Creating Simple JavaScript Programs," that JavaScript is an object-oriented language. This means that it supports objects. *Objects* are custom data types that combine data with functions. An object includes *properties*, which hold the data. In addition, it can include *methods,* functions to act on the data. You'll learn about objects in detail in Chapter 3.

Using Comments

A final element you can include in a JavaScript program is a *comment*. These are items of text that can be included for your information, or for others who might try to understand the script. Comments are ignored by the JavaScript interpreter.

JavaScript supports two types of comments:

- ❏ A single-line comment begins with two slashes (//) and ends at the end of the line.
- ❏ A multiple-line comment begins with the /* delimiter and ends with the */ delimiter. This type of comment can include any number of lines. These work like the comments in the C language.

You can use whichever type of comment is the most convenient. The /* and */ comments are useful for "commenting out" a block of JavaScript code to prevent it from executing temporarily. Single-line comments are handy to provide descriptions of particular lines of code. The following short JavaScript example includes both types of comments:

```
//function to return total number of cars
function total(compact, subcompact, luxury) {
   var temp = compact + subcompact + luxury;
   // we don't want to print right now, so these are commented out.
   /*document.write("Compacts: ",compact, " Subcompacts: ", subcompact);
   document.write("Luxury cars: ",luxury, "\n");
   document.write("Total number of cars: ", temp);*/
   //above lines are commented out; nothing will be printed.
   return temp;
}
```

As you can see, comments can help make your JavaScript code readable—and in some cases, they can make it more confusing. It's generally a good idea to avoid making excessive comments, but rather to label major sections of the program and statements that may be confusing.

Pay special attention to the comments in listings in this book; they are used to make some statements more clear, and occasionally to illustrate a point in the text.

NOTE: Do not confuse JavaScript comments with HTML comments. You can use HTML comments to hide JavaScript commands from non-JavaScript browsers, and they cannot be used within the script. JavaScript comments are part of the script, and they can be used only between the <SCRIPT> tags.

Programs and Applications

The concept of just what a program is can be confusing in JavaScript, because it's tightly integrated with HTML—two languages in the same file. Programs and applications are not technical JavaScript terms, but I'll define them here, because they are used frequently throughout this book:

❑ A JavaScript *program* consists of all of the functions, event handlers, and variable declarations included in a single HTML file. These might not execute in the order they are defined, but the browser reads and interprets them all at the same time.

❑ Consider a JavaScript *application* to be a set of HTML files and scripts that work together to form a useful purpose. A complete application might involve several JavaScript programs in several different HTML files, and may even include additional functionality through different languages, such as CGI or Java.

Data Types and Variables

One of the most important features of a programming language is the capability of working with data. JavaScript includes flexible support for most types of data with which you will need to work.

You can use data in a JavaScript program in two ways:

❑ As a *literal* or constant value, which is included directly in the JavaScript code. For example, 54, 6.17, and "This" are all literal values.

❑ As a *variable*. As mentioned earlier in this chapter, variables are named containers that can hold a value. You can assign them different values during the course of the program. Variable names might include total, tax_amt, or data1.

A variable can hold a value of any type.

JavaScript includes support for relatively few types of data, but you can use these to create other types. In fact, using JavaScript's object-oriented features, you can create a wide variety of custom types.

The four fundamental data types used in JavaScript are the following:

❏ *Numbers*, such as 3, 25, or 1.4142138. JavaScript supports both integers and floating-point numbers.

❏ *Boolean*, or logical values. These can have one of two values: true or false.

❏ *Strings*, such as "This is a string". These consist of one or more characters of text.

❏ *The null value*, represented by the keyword null. This is the value of an undefined variable.

Some programming languages, such as C and Java, are *strongly typed*. This means that variables can hold a very specific type of value. You have to declare the type of data a variable can hold when you define it, and you must use conversion functions when you wish to change a variable's type. This works fine for in-depth, structured programming, but isn't really ideal for the quick jobs for which JavaScript can be used.

There is no need to specify a variable's type when you define it.

By contrast, JavaScript is a *loosely typed* language. This means that when you declare a variable, you don't have to define its type. You can store any allowable type of data in a variable. Conversions between different types of data happen automatically.

NOTE: Another example of a loosely typed language is Perl, a popular choice for CGI scripts and other Internet applications. Perl variables, like JavaScript, can hold different types of data.

Because JavaScript is loosely typed, you don't need to give much thought to the type of data a variable will hold. Nevertheless, there are special considerations for each type of data, which are discussed in detail in the following sections.

Integers

An integer is simply a number that does not include a decimal. Integers in JavaScript can be only positive numbers. You can use an integer as a literal in JavaScript simply by including the number. For example, this statement prints the number 47:

```
document.write(47);
```

JavaScript considers any number without a leading zero to be a decimal (base 10) number. You can also use data in hexadecimal (base 16) and octal (base 8). Here is a summary of the syntax you use to specify different types of numbers with examples:

❏ Decimal: no leading zero (`57`, `5000`)

❏ Hexadecimal: prefix with `0x` (`0x56`, `0xFE`)

❏ Octal: leading `0` (`045`, `013`)

You can include integers in your programs in whichever base is convenient. For example, 42, 052, and 0x2A are all different ways of listing the decimal number 42. Because you probably think best in base 10, decimal numbers are the easiest to use in most cases; however, there are some situations when another format is more convenient. For example, the color codes used to specify background and text colors in an HTML page are usually given in hexadecimal.

NOTE: Base 10 numbers can also use decimal fractions, as you will learn later. Hexadecimal and octal numbers are limited to integer values.

Floating-Point Numbers

You can also use floating-point decimal numbers in your JavaScript programs. These can be used to represent just about any number conveniently. A simple floating-point value consists of an integer followed by a decimal point and a fractional value, such as 2.01.

Unlike integers, floating-point values can be either positive or negative. You can specify negative values for floating-point numbers by adding the negative sign to the beginning of the number, as in `-3.1`. Any number without a negative sign is assumed to be positive.

You can also use a form of scientific notation to refer to floating-point numbers. This makes it easy to specify very large numbers. To use this notation, you include the letter E (either upper- or lowercase) followed by the exponent, either positive or negative.

Positive exponents move the decimal point to the right or make the number larger; negative exponents make the number smaller. Here are a few examples of exponent notation and the decimal numbers they represent:

❏ 1E6: One million (1,000,000)

❏ 1.5E9: 1.5 billion (1,500,000,000)

❏ 25E-2: One-quarter (.25)

❏ 1E-6: One-millionth (.000001)

❏ 4.56E5: 456,000

Boolean Values

Boolean values are most often used in conditional statements, which you'll explore in Chapter 3.

Boolean values are the simplest data type. They can contain one of two values: `true` or `false`. Because they can represent an on/off or 1/0 state, these are sometimes called *binary* values.

Boolean values are most commonly used as *flags*; variables that indicate whether a condition is true or not. For example, you might set a Boolean variable called `complete` to `true` to indicate that the user has completed all the needed information in a form. You can then easily check this value and act on it later.

NOTE: You can use the numbers `0` and `1` as synonyms for `false` and `true` in many cases in JavaScript; however, it's best to treat Boolean values as strictly Boolean.

Strings

Another important type of value you can work with in a JavaScript program is a *string*. Strings are simply groups of characters, such as `"Hello"` or `"I am a jelly doughnut."`.

You can work with strings using the `String` object, explained in Chapter 4.

You can include strings as literals in JavaScript by enclosing them in double or single quotation marks. Here are some examples of values that JavaScript will treat as strings:

- ❏ `"This is a string."`
- ❏ `'A'`
- ❏ `'25 pounds'`
- ❏ `"200"`

You can use the two types of quotes interchangeably. However, you must use the same type of quote to end the string that you used to begin it.

TIP: HTML uses double quotation marks to indicate values for some tags. Because you will be using JavaScript within HTML documents, and especially in event handlers, you may want to get into the habit of using single quotation marks within JavaScript statements. This will avoid conflicts with the HTML codes.

Special Characters

Along with alphanumeric characters, you can use a variety of special characters in JavaScript strings. These include carriage returns, tabs, and other nonprintable characters.

To use one of these special characters, include a backslash (\) followed by the code for that character. The codes are as follows:

- ❑ \a: Alert (bell) character (produces a bell sound)
- ❑ \b: Backspace character (moves the cursor back one character)
- ❑ \f: Form-feed character (indicates a new page on a printer)
- ❑ \n: New line character (indicates a new line of text)
- ❑ \r: Carriage return character (moves the cursor to the beginning of the line)
- ❑ \t: Tab character (advances the cursor to the next tab stop)

You can include special characters directly in a string. For example, the following statement prints out three separate lines of text:

```
document.write(" this is line 1\n this is line 2\n this is line 3");
```

Depending on what you're using the string for, some of these characters may or may not have a meaning. For example, this line will only work in a predefined portion of the HTML page. Tab and form-feed characters will not affect HTML output to the browser, but they may be useful for other applications.

Another use for the backslash is to include quotation marks within a string. This is known as *escaping* a character. For example, the following statement won't work, because it uses quotation marks incorrectly:

You must escape any quotation mark or backslash if you wish to include it in a string.

```
document.write("Jane said, "Have you seen my wig around?"");
```

This is invalid because quotation marks can be used only at the beginning and end of the string. You can escape the quotation marks within the string with the backslash character to make a correct statement:

```
document.write("Jane said, \"Have you seen my wig around?\"");
```

The escaped quotation marks are considered as part of the literal string, so this will print the correct result, including quotation marks. You can also use the backslash character twice to include an actual backslash character in a string:

```
document.write("The DOS files are in the C:\\DOS\\FILES directory.");
```

TIP: Single quotation marks, double quotation marks, and backslashes are the only characters you need to escape with the backslash character. You can include any other punctuation character inside the quotation marks, and it will be considered part of the string.

Creating an Array

Arrays are built-in JavaScript objects. Chapter 4 explains arrays and other built-in objects in detail.

Many languages support *arrays*—numbered sets of variables. For example, scores for 20 different students might be stored in a scores array. You could then refer to scores[1] for the first student's score, scores[5] for the fifth student, and so on. This makes it easy to define a large number of variables without having to give each one a name. The number in the brackets is called an *index* into the array.

JavaScript does not support arrays as variables. Instead, they are handled as objects. You can create an array by using the Array object. As an example, this statement creates an array called scores with 20 values:

```
scores = new Array(20);
```

Once you define the array, you can access its elements by using brackets to indicate the index. For example, you can assign values for the first and tenth scores with these statements:

```
scores[0] = 50;
scores[9] = 85;
```

As you learn more about JavaScript objects, you'll learn that you can create much more complicated structures than mere arrays. In the meantime, you can use arrays to store any numbered set of values.

TIP: In the previous example, notice that the first student's score is referred to as scores[0]. As in many other computer languages, JavaScript array indices begin with 0. A five-element array would have indices from 0 to 4.

Working with Numbers and Text

To get an idea of how data typing works in JavaScript, let's look at some examples of using numbers and text in variables. To begin, consider these statements:

```
total = 22;
description = " large polar bears";
```

These variables are now declared; `total` is an integer, and `description` is a string. Suppose this statement happened next:

```
total += .025;
```

This adds a fraction to `total`. The type for `total` is changed to floating-point, and its value is now `22.025`. Now add to `total` again:

```
total += .975;
```

This brings `total` up to `23`—an integer once again.

```
total = total + description;
```

Now things get a bit tricky. You might think this statement would cause an error—not in JavaScript. The values are automatically converted to match. They are treated as strings, so instead of addition, concatenation (combining strings) is used.

As a result, `total` is now a string variable, and its value is `"23 large polar bears"`. You should now see how easy JavaScript is to work with—much easier than actual polar bears.

Naming and Declaring Variables

By now, you should have a good understanding of what variables are for, and what types of data you can store in them. Next, let's take a quick look at the rules you must follow when using variables: how to name them, and how and where to declare them.

Rules for JavaScript Variable Names

As mentioned earlier in this chapter, each variable has a name. In technical terms, JavaScript calls the variable name an *identifier*. There are specific rules you must follow when choosing a variable name:

Longer variable names make for more readable JavaScript programs.

❏ Variable names can include letters of the alphabet, both upper- and lower-case. They can also include the digits 0-9 and the underscore (_) character.

❏ Variable names cannot include spaces or any other punctuation character.

❏ The first character of the variable name must be either a letter or the underscore character.

❏ Variable names are case-sensitive; `totalnum`, `Totalnum`, and `TotalNum` are separate variable names.

❏ There is no official limit on the length of variable names, but they must fit within one line.

Using these rules, the following are examples of valid variable names:

```
total_number_of_students
LastInvoiceNumber
temp1
a
_var39
```

Obviously, it's possible to use friendly, easy-to-read names or completely cryptic ones. Do yourself a favor: use longer, friendly names whenever possible. One exception is temporary variables that are used in a small section of code; one-letter names or single words work well for these and save a bit of typing.

Assigning Values to Variables

You've already seen several examples of assigning a value to a variable. The syntax for an assignment is simply an equal sign (=). For example, the following statement assigns the value 18 to the variable wheels:

```
wheels = 18;
```

This is a good time to explain more about the loosely typed nature of JavaScript. After assigning the integer value 18 to the wheels variable, the following assignment is perfectly valid:

```
wheels = "round rolling things";
```

JavaScript now converts the wheels variable to a string type, and it becomes valid in expressions that require a string. Although this is one of JavaScript's greatest strengths, it can also be a weakness. For example, later in your program you might have the following statement:

```
document.write("The vehicle has ",wheels, " wheels.\n");
```

In this case, a statement that would have produced sensible output with one value now produces nonsense. Even worse, consider the following statement:

```
total_wheels = wheels * NumberOfVehicles;
```

If the wheels variable has been assigned a string, you now have a statement that will cause an error, or at least cause the data to be corrupt.

Although you can probably remember which type to use in your variables, don't count on the user to remember. Because situations like this can happen, you'll need to be careful any time the user enters a value.

Variable Declarations and Scope

JavaScript variables can be declared automatically or explicitly.

In some languages, you must declare each variable you will use. JavaScript does not require this; the first time you assign a value to a variable, it is automatically declared. You may also need to use the var keyword to declare a variable, depending on where you will use it.

Any variable in JavaScript has a *scope*—a section of code in which it is valid. There are generally two types of scope possible in JavaScript:

- ❏ A variable declared within a function with the var keyword is *local* to that function; other functions cannot access it. Variables used to store the function's parameters are also local to the function.

- ❏ A variable declared outside a function, or without the var keyword in a function, is *global*; all JavaScript statements in the current HTML or script file can access the value.

This means that if you define a variable called temp with the var keyword in a function, it can't be accessed by other functions. In fact, another function can declare a local variable with the same name, and it will have its own separate storage area. There will be no conflict between the two temp variables.

You may wish to use var to declare all variables to avoid confusion.

By using the var keyword, you can make it clear that you are declaring a variable—either local (within a function) or global (outside a function). The following example declares a variable called keys and sets its initial value to 88:

```
var keys=88;
```

In many cases, local variables are convenient—such as for holding parameters passed to a function or calculating a result to be displayed. You will want to declare global variables for values that several functions within the HTML file will use.

A global variable's declaration must occur in the HTML file before any statements that use it. The most common place to declare global variables is in the <HEAD> section of the HTML document. This ensures that they'll come first, and also conveniently hides the JavaScript code from non-JavaScript browsers.

Declaring Variables

To make it clear how to use variables and scope, let's look at a few examples. First of all, an important thing to remember is that a variable is declared the first time you use it. Consider the example in Listing 2.1.

Listing 2.1. (DECLARE.HTM) Variable declarations.

```
<HTML>
<HEAD><TITLE>Variable Declarations</TITLE>
<SCRIPT LANGUAGE="JavaScript">
var teeth = 30;
var arms = 2;
legs = 2;
function init() {
   teeth = teeth - 4;
   var heads = 1;
   eyes = heads * 2;
}
</SCRIPT>
</HEAD>
<BODY>
Text here.
</BODY>
```

This example includes quite a few variable declarations. (In fact, it does little else.) Let's take a look at each one:

❏ teeth and arms are declared as global in the header with the var keyword.

❏ legs does not use the var keyword, but is still declared as global because the declaration is outside any function.

❏ heads is declared as local by using the var keyword within the init function.

❏ eyes is declared without var, so it is global, although declared within the init function.

This should give you a good understanding of which variables will be local and global. Be sure to use the correct syntax with your variables; incorrect syntax is one of the most common JavaScript programming errors.

Using Expressions and Operators

You can combine variables and literal values to form a complex expression. The tools you use to create an expression are *operators*. A simple example of an operator is the plus sign in the expression students + 1. JavaScript supports the following types of operators:

❏ *Assignment operators* are used to assign a value to a variable, or change its current value.

❏ *Arithmetic operators* are used to perform addition, subtraction, and other math on numeric literals or variables.

❏ *String operators* are used to manipulate string values.

❏ *Logical operators* deal with Boolean values, and are mainly used for testing conditions.

❑ *Bitwise operators* are used to manipulate individual bits of a numeric value in a Boolean fashion.

❑ *Comparison operators* are used to test the relationship between two numeric values.

You'll learn about the various operators of each type provided by JavaScript in the next sections. You will also explore *operator precedence,* the system used to determine which operation will be performed first in a complex expression.

Assignment Operators

One assignment operator has already been used in this chapter: the equal sign (=). This is the simplest assignment operator. It assigns the value (or expression) to the right of the equal sign to the variable on the left. Here are some examples:

❑ `test_score` = 199 assigns the number 199 to the variable `test_score`.

❑ `a` = `b` + 1 adds 1 to variable `b` and stores the result in `a`.

❑ `a` = `Results(12)` sends the number 12 to a function called `Results()` and stores the returned value in `a`.

❑ `a` = `a` + 1 adds 1 to the variable `a` and stores the new value in `a`.

In the last example, an operation is performed on a variable and stored in the same variable. Because this is a common task, there are several assignment operators that make it easier:

❑ += adds the number on the right to the variable on the left.

❑ -= subtracts the number on the right from the variable on the left.

❑ *= multiplies the variable by the number on the right.

❑ /= divides the variable by the number on the right.

❑ %= uses the modulo operator, described in the next section.

The statement used as an example earlier, `a` = `a+1`, thus can be written in a shorter form: `a` += 1. Addition is a particularly common use for these operators, because you routinely need to add one (or another number) to a counter variable. Here are a few final examples:

❑ `count` += 1 adds 1 to, or *increments,* the `count` variable.

❑ `a` *= `b` multiplies `a` by `b` and stores the result in `a`.

❑ `a` /= 2 divides the value of `a` by 2 and stores the result in `a`.

There are also several assignment operators for bitwise operations, described in the section Bitwise Operators, later in this chapter.

Arithmetic Operators

Arithmetic operators are used to perform mathematical operations on variables and literals. You're already familiar with the basic arithmetic operators: addition (+), subtraction (-), multiplication (*), and division (/). These work the way you would expect them to, and each has an equivalent assignment operator. There are several other operators, explained in the next sections.

The Modulo Operator

The term *remainder* is sometimes used to refer to a modulo operation.

You may have encountered the modulo (%) operator in a different programming language; it works the same way in JavaScript. In case you haven't seen it before, let's look at the following example:

```
b = a % 2;
```

This would be read as "b equals a modulo 2." Technically speaking, *modulo* is the remainder when two numbers are divided. Thus, the example could be explained as "the remainder when you divide x by 2." Here are a few literal examples:

- ❏ 100 % 2 = 0 (2 divides into 100 evenly; there is no remainder)
- ❏ 100 % 3 = 1 (100 divided by 3 is 33, with a remainder of 1)
- ❏ 20 % 7 = 6 (20 divided by 7 is 2, with a remainder of 6)

Right now the modulo operator may seem useless, but you'll run into many uses for it throughout this book. Just to prove that it's worth something, note that the result of the first example is 0. If a modulo operation returns 0, this means the number is evenly divisible, so this is an easy way to test whether a number is even or odd, or whether it is divisible by some other number. This example:

```
If (a % 2 == 0) document.write("a is an even number.\n");
```

also uses a comparison operator, which is described later in this section.

The Negation Operator

Only floating-point values can be negative.

You've already seen the negation operator used with numbers. The minus sign at the beginning of the number -3.11 indicates that the number is negative. You can also use this *unary negation* operator with variables. For example, look at this statement:

```
temp = -temp;
```

This replaces the value of temp with its negative equivalent, or complement. If temp had a value of 17, its new value would be -17. Negating a number that is already negative results in a positive number. If the value of temp was -25, the new value would be 25.

Incrementing and Decrementing Variables

Recall from the section on assignment operators that short versions exist for commands that operate on one variable and store the result in the same variable. For example, the following statements are equivalent:

```
a = a + 1;
a += 1;
```

Both add 1 to the value of a, and store the result in a. Because it's very common to add 1 to the value of a number, or subtract 1 from its value, JavaScript provides an even shorter method of doing so with the *increment* and *decrement* operators:

❏ Increment (++) adds 1 to the variable's value.

❏ Decrement (--) subtracts 1 from the variable's value.

Thus, the statements could be written in an even shorter way:

```
a++;
```

The increment and decrement operators can be used as either a *prefix* or a *postfix*; in other words, they can be before or after the variable name, respectively. For example, both of these statements decrement the variable count:

```
count--;
--count;
```

The difference between these two methods is when the increment or decrement operation actually happens. If you use prefix notation, the variable is incremented before it is used in an expression; if you use postfix notation, it is incremented after. This example should help make this clear:

```
total = count++;
```

This assigns the value of count to the variable total, and *then* increments the count. For example, if count is 25 before this statement, total will receive a value of 25, and count will then be incremented to 26. Now look what happens when you use a prefix:

```
total = ++count;
```

In this case, count is incremented *before* using it in the expression. If count starts with a value of 25, it will be incremented to 26, and total receives a value of 26. Obviously, you need to choose carefully which method to use, depending on when you need the incrementing or decrementing to happen.

String Operators

You can concatenate strings with numeric values; the result will be a string.

There is only one dedicated string operator in JavaScript: the *concatenation* operator (+). This takes the string on the right and tacks it onto the string on the left. Here are three examples:

```
text = header + " and so forth.";
sentence = subject + predicate;
chars = chars + "R";
```

In the first example, if the `header` string variable contained the text `"This is a test"`, the value assigned to `text` would be "This is a test and so forth." This makes it easy to combine strings.

The last example uses the same variable on both sides of the equal sign. Like arithmetic operators, you can shorten this type of statement with the += operator. The following statement does the same thing:

```
chars += "R";
```

There are actually several operations you can perform on strings, including extracting portions of their values and comparing them. You'll look at those in detail in Chapter 4.

CAUTION: Because addition and concatenation use the same syntax, be sure you know with which data type you are working. For example, if you attempt to add numbers to a non-numeric string, they will be concatenated instead—probably not what you intended.

Logical Operators

Just as the arithmetic operators work on numeric values, *logical operators* work with Boolean values. The following logical operators are available:

- ❏ && (And) returns true if both of the operands are true.
- ❏ ¦¦ (Or) returns true if either of the operands is true.
- ❏ ! (Not) returns the opposite of the variable it prefixes. This takes only one operand, similar to the negation operator for numbers.

The main use for these logical operators is in conditional expressions. You'll learn more about conditionals in Chapter 3.

Bitwise Operators

Bitwise operators are a category of operators that are used with binary numbers. Each of the operands is converted into a binary number, then manipulated bit by bit. These are mostly useful for manipulating values that have an individual meaning for each bit.

The following bitwise operators are available:

- ❏ And (&) returns one if both of the corresponding bits are one.
- ❏ Or (¦) returns one if either of the corresponding bits is one.
- ❏ Xor (Exclusive Or) (^) returns one if either, but not both, of the corresponding bits is one.
- ❏ Left shift (<<) shifts the bits in the left operand a number of positions specified in the right operand.
- ❏ Right shift (>>) shifts to the right, including the bit used to store the sign.
- ❏ Zero-fill right shift (>>>) fills to the right, filling in zeros on the left.

NOTE: You might think you'll have little use for binary options in JavaScript—and you're right. One area in which they do come in handy is working with color values.

Comparison Operators

Comparison operators are used to compare two numbers. They return a Boolean value (either true or false) based on whether the operands match the condition. The simplest comparison operator is the equality (==) operator; it returns true if the numbers are equal. For example, this expression evaluates to true if a has a value of 17:

```
(a == 17)
```

NOTE: Be sure not to confuse the equality operator (==) with the assignment operator (=). This is one of the most common mistakes in JavaScript programming. You'll learn more about this and other common mistakes in Chapter 14, "Debugging JavaScript Programs."

You can also use the *inequality* operator (!=), which returns true if the numbers are not equal. There are also several other comparison operators to examine the relationship between two values:

- ❑ Less than (<)
- ❑ Greater than (>)
- ❑ Greater than or equal to (>=)
- ❑ Less than or equal to (<=)

The main use for conditional expressions is in conditional statements, such as the `if` statement. You'll learn about those statements in detail in the next chapter.

Understanding Operator Precedence

You can use several operators in the same statement. For example, consider the following statement:

```
a = b + x * 25;
```

JavaScript's operator precedence is based on Java and C.

As you can see, this statement could mean more than one thing. Should b be added to x before multiplying by 25, or after? Will a be assigned to b or to the entire expression b + x * 25? A programming language keeps a set of rules to explain situations like this. These rules are known as *operator precedence*.

To explain JavaScript's operator precedence, here is a list of all the operators, with the lowest precedence on top. Operators at the bottom of the list are evaluated first, so operators on the bottom are considered more important:

- ❑ Comma (,), used to separate parameters
- ❑ Assignment operator (=)
- ❑ Conditional operators (?, :)
- ❑ Logical OR (¦¦)
- ❑ Logical AND (&&)
- ❑ Bitwise OR (¦)
- ❑ Bitwise XOR (^)
- ❑ Bitwise AND (&)
- ❑ Equality (==) and inequality (!=)
- ❑ Comparison operators (<, <=, >, >=)
- ❑ Bitwise shift (<<, >>, >>>)
- ❑ Addition and subtraction (+, -)
- ❑ Multiplication, division, and modulo (*, /, %)

❏ Negation (!, ~, -), increment (++), and decrement (--)

❏ Function call or array index ((), [])

Using Variables in Expressions

To explain operators and precedence further, let's look at a few examples using variables and values. First, here's a simple expression:

```
a = b * 5;
```

There is no confusion about what this statement does; it multiplies b by 5, and stores the result in a. Now look at this:

```
a = b * 5 + 1;
```

This is where operator precedence comes into play. Because multiplication has a higher precedence than addition, b is multiplied by 5 before adding 1.

```
a = b * (5 + 1);
```

In this case, operator precedence is overridden by the use of parentheses, which have a very high precedence. The numbers 5 and 1 are now added, then b is multiplied by the result (6). One more example:

```
a = (b * 5) + 1;
```

This works exactly like the first example: b is multiplied by 5, then added to 1. In this particular case, the parentheses don't do anything. I've included this example to make a point: when in doubt, use parentheses. You won't get an error by using unnecessary parentheses, so you can use them whenever you're unsure about precedence, or simply to make your code more readable.

Converting and Evaluating Variables and Expressions

As discussed earlier, JavaScript is a loosely typed language. You don't need to declare a variable's type when you define it, and you don't need to do anything special to store a different type of data in a variable.

There are also many built-in functions as methods of built-in objects, which you'll look at in Chapter 4.

Even in a loosely typed language, there are some cases when you want to convert data to a specific type. You can use several built-in functions of JavaScript, described in the next sections, to handle these conversions.

The `parseInt` Function

The `parseInt()` function looks for an integer number as the first part of the string. It ignores the decimal portion, if found. For example, this statement assigns the variable a to the value 39:

```
a = parseInt("39 steps");
```

You can specify an optional second parameter to `parseInt()` that specifies the base of number you're looking for in the string. This can be 8 (octal), 10 (decimal), or 16 (hexadecimal)—in fact, you can use any numeric base. The following statement reads a hexadecimal number from the `text` string variable:

```
a = parseInt(text,16);
```

`parseInt()` returns a special value, `"NaN"`, (Not a Number) if it encounters a non-numeric character at the beginning of the string. On Windows platforms, zero may be returned instead. See Chapter 14 for specifics about this and other platform-specific issues.

The `parseFloat` Function

The `parseFloat()` function is similar to `parseInt()`, but works with floating-point values. It attempts to find a decimal floating-point number in the string, and returns it. For example, the following statement assigns the value 2.7178 to the variable a:

```
a = "2.7178 is the base of a natural logarithm.";
```

This statement can handle all the components of a floating-point number: signs, decimal points, and exponents. Like `parseInt()`, if it encounters any other character before it has determined the value, it returns `"NaN"` or zero, depending on the platform.

The `eval` Function

The `eval()` function has many uses in sophisticated programming techniques, and you'll see it many times throughout this book. Rather than looking for a number in a string, `eval()` looks for any valid JavaScript expression. A simple example assigns 25 to the a variable:

```
a = eval("20 + 1 + 4");
```

You can use `eval()` to create a JavaScript program "on the fly."

The use of `eval()` can be much more complicated than this. You can use any JavaScript expression in the string passed to `eval()`—numeric operations, comparison operations, statements, multiple statements, and even entire JavaScript functions. For example, the following statements define a variable called `Fred` and set its value to 31. The value of the `text` variable is used as the variable's name:

```
var text = "Fred";
var statement = text + "= 31";
eval(statement);
```

Because `eval()` can work with any expression, you can use it to perform calculations based on data entered by the user. You'll use it many times for similar purposes. You can even construct a JavaScript statement or function "on the fly" and execute it. This is one of the most powerful operations available in JavaScript.

CAUTION: Because `eval()` will execute any statement in the string, be very careful when using it with user-entered strings. A clever user could enter JavaScript statements in the string and cause problems with your program.

Workshop Wrap-Up

In this chapter, you learned more about the JavaScript language and the basic foundations of JavaScript's structure. You also learned the following concepts:

❑ The components that make up a JavaScript program or application

❑ The way JavaScript handles various data types, whether included as a literal value or stored in a variable

❑ The basics of JavaScript objects and properties

❑ The techniques for declaring variables, storing data in them, and using them in expressions

Next Steps

To continue your exploration of the JavaScript language, continue with one of the following chapters:

❑ To review the basics of JavaScript, see Chapter 1, "Creating Simple JavaScript Programs."

❑ To learn more about JavaScript's object-oriented features, turn to Chapter 3, " Working with Objects and Events."

❑ To learn more about the built-in objects and functions in JavaScript, along with custom objects of your own, see Chapter 4, "Using Built-In Objects and Custom Objects."

❑ To see some applications of the techniques in this chapter, see Chapter 7, "Real-Life Examples I."

Q&A

Q: Can I use more than one JavaScript program in the same HTML page?

A: Yes. Just enclose each program within its own set of <SCRIPT> tags. Note that variables you define in one program will be available to others in the same file.

Q: What is the importance of the var keyword? Should I always use it to declare variables?

A: You only need to use var to define a local variable in a function. Outside a function, things work the same whether you use var or not.

Q: In Perl, using the eval statement on data entered by the user can be a serious security risk. Is this also true with JavaScript?

A: Yes and no. Although the user could enter statements and make your program behave strangely, there would be no way to do real damage, because JavaScript has no access to the server. The worst they could do is crash Netscape on their own machine.

P A R T

II

Using JavaScript Objects and Forms

Working with Objects and Events

This chapter continues the discussion of JavaScript programming with some of the more advanced aspects of the language. You will learn some of the tools you can use to create complete, complex JavaScript applications—objects, functions and methods, forms, loops and conditionals, and event handlers.

Using JavaScript Objects

As mentioned in the previous chapter, JavaScript is an object-oriented language. An object is a custom data type that can combine data with functions to act upon it. The data items in an object are its *properties*, and the functions are its *methods*.

With some languages, such as C++, the term "object-oriented" sends many people running for cover. Object-oriented programming can be confusing with these languages. However, JavaScript's implementation of objects is very basic and easy to understand—in fact, you've used objects already—every array or string in JavaScript is an object.

Object properties can be named using the same rules as for variables.

Objects can include both data and functions to work with it.

Using Object Properties

Recall also that the bits of data stored in an object are called properties of the object. Properties can be numbers, strings, or even other objects. Each property has a name associated with it, which you must use to refer to that property.

To illustrate object properties, let's look at an object you've already used—the `String` object. Any variable that contains a string in JavaScript is actually a `String` object. This is an object built into the JavaScript language; you don't have to refer to it explicitly as an object.

TIP: You'll learn more about the `String` object, including its methods, in the Built-In Objects section of Chapter 4, "Using Built-In Objects and Custom Objects."

The `String` object has a single property called `length`. As you might have guessed, the `length` property indicates the current length of the string. You can use two different types of notation to refer to an object's property. The first and most common method is to separate the object name and property name with a period. For example, the following statement sets the variable `len` to the length of the `address` string variable:

```
len = address.length;
```

The second method is the one you use to refer to array elements, which are actually properties of an array object. This uses brackets around the property name. This example sets the `len` variable to the length of the `address` string, just as the previous example does:

```
len = address["length"];
```

Because this method can be used effectively to create an array with names instead of numbers for indices, it is also referred to as an *associative array*. This is an array with named values, which makes it very easy to deal with things such as database entries.

You can use either the bracket or period syntax interchangeably in most cases. The exception is when you are using a variable to hold the name of a property. For example, the following statements refer in a roundabout way to a string's `length` property:

```
x = "length";
len = address[x];
```

In this case, you have to use brackets for the property name. If you simply used `address.x`, the interpreter would look for a property called `x`, resulting in an error.

> **NOTE:** You may be familiar with associative arrays if you have done any programming in Perl. The named properties in a JavaScript object provide a similar capability. Chapter 10, "Working with Multiple Pages and Data," includes an example of using associative arrays.

Assigning Values to Properties

Object properties can be read-only or writable.

In the previous examples, you've read the properties of the object, rather than writing to them. The string object's length property is a *read-only* property; you cannot set it to a value. However, other objects enable you to do this.

As another example, let's create an imaginary type of object called Card, which will store business cards. The Card object has the following properties:

- ❏ name
- ❏ address
- ❏ work_phone
- ❏ home_phone

Assuming you had created a Card object called card1, you could define its properties using these statements:

```
card1.name = "Sherlock Holmes";
card1.address = "221B Baker Street";
card1.work_phone = "555-2345";
card1.home_phone = "555-3456";
```

Later in this chapter, you'll work with the Card object more, and learn how to define and create objects.

Functions and Methods

As you can see, by using objects and properties you can easily store any type of data in JavaScript. Objects aren't just groups of data, though—they can also include ways of using the data, the methods. Methods are functions dedicated to the object.

Declaring a Function

Not all functions return values, and not all functions need parameters.

Recall that a function is a set of JavaScript statements that accept one or more parameters and return a value. Even without using objects, you can use a function in JavaScript to perform a specific task. Chapter 2, "Working with Larger Programs and Variables," defined a function to add two numbers. This was a simple function, and a useless one—the addition operator does the same thing.

Let's try a more complex (and more useful) function. One handy use for functions is to avoid repetitive use of complex HTML codes to output information. For example, consider the <TABLE> tag in HTML 3.0. This example shows the HTML code to define a table of names, ages, and birthdays for several people:

```
<TABLE>
<TR> <TD>Fred</TD> <TD>27</TD> <TD>June 17</TD> </TR>
<TR> <TD>Tom</TD> <TD>24</TD> <TD>March 13</TD> </TR>
<TR> <TD>Rebecca</TD> <TD>25</TD> <TD>November 30</TD> </TR>
</TABLE>
```

The <TABLE> tag is required to start and end the table, the <TR> tag starts and ends table rows, and the <TD> tag starts and ends each cell within the row. As you can see, this can make for some complicated HTML.

If your JavaScript program is producing this information as output, it becomes that much more difficult, because you have to print each of the tags carefully in the right order. Listing 3.1 shows a JavaScript program to print the table shown previously.

Listing 3.1. A JavaScript program to print the table.

```
document.write("<TABLE>\n");
document.write("<TR> <TD>Fred</TD> <TD>27</TD> <TD>June 17</TD> </TR>\n");
document.write("<TR> <TD>Tom</TD> <TD>24</TD> <TD>March 13</TD> </TR>\n");
document.write("<TR> <TD>Rebecca</TD> <TD>25</TD> <TD>November 30</TD> </
➡TR>\n");
document.write("</TABLE>");
```

As you can see, this isn't exactly the most readable JavaScript program. A much better method is to use a function to perform the repetitive task—in this case, printing the <TR> and <TD> tags in the right order with each row of data. Listing 3.2 shows the definition for a PrintRow() function to perform this task:

Listing 3.2. The **PrintRow** function, for printing a table row.

```
function PrintRow(name, age, birthday) {
   document.write("<TR> <TD>", name, "</TD> <TD>", age, "</TD> <TD>", birthday,
➡"</TD> </TR>\n");
}
```

All functions begin with the function keyword and are surrounded by braces.

The first line of the function definition includes the function keyword, which is required to begin a function definition. The function name, PrintRow, is then given. The parameters the function will expect are in the parentheses; these are also the names of variables, local to the function, which will be defined to store the parameters passed.

The statements that comprise the function begin with the left brace. In the second line, the document.write function is used to output the parameters, with the proper HTML table tags between them. Because this is the final statement in the function, it ends with a right brace.

TIP:
Not all functions have parameters. You can define a function that doesn't require any parameters by using an empty parameter list: ().

Calling a Function

You now have a function that can be used to print a row of the table. In order to use it, you need to call the function. A function call is simply the name of the function and the parameters to send it.

Using function calls to the PrintRow() function defined in Listing 3.2, you can easily create the table of names, ages, and birthdays without unnecessary repetition:

```
document.write("<TABLE>\n");
PrintRow("Fred", 27, "June 17");
PrintRow("Tom", 24, "March 13");
PrintRow("Rebecca", 25, "November 30");
document.write("</TABLE>\n");
```

As you can see, although it's a simple one-line function, the PrintRow() function can save quite a bit of typing—especially if the table has more than three rows. It also creates more readable, clear JavaScript code. Compare this to the first program to print the table (Listing 3.1) and you'll see the difference.

Returning a Value

Use the return keyword to return a value in a function.

The function used previously accepted parameters, but did not return a value. A function can send a value back to the calling statement with the return keyword. This can be useful for a function that calculates a result; it can also be used to indicate success or failure.

The value returned by a function can be of any type—a number, a string, or even an object. As a simple example of returning values, let's define a function that returns a string. Once again HTML is used as an example. The function in Listing 3.3 provides a quick way to add boldface on/off (<B> and </B>) HTML tags to a piece of text.

Listing 3.3. A simple function to convert text to boldface HTML.

```
function Bold(text) {
    var temp = "<B>" + text + "</B>";
    return temp;
}
```

This function accepts a string as a parameter and stores it in the `text` variable. It then creates another variable called `temp` and concatenates the required tags to `text`. The `temp` variable is then returned.

NOTE: This function provides a good demonstration of the loosely typed nature of JavaScript. The function would actually accept any type of variable as a parameter; the only thing that implies that a string is required is the concatenation operator used in the second line.

The function call is slightly different for a function that returns a value, because you need to do something with the returned value. For example, you could store it in a variable:

```
boldtext = Bold("This is a test.");
```

Because JavaScript considers a function call to be an expression, you can also use it anywhere that type of data (in this case, a string) is expected. For example, you could print it directly:

```
document.write(Bold("This is a test."));
```

In this case, the `Bold()` function is called to produce a result, and the resulting string is used as the parameter of the `document.write()` function. JavaScript always evaluates expressions like this starting at the innermost level of parentheses.

One final note: You don't actually have to use the value a function returns unless you want to. For example, you have already looked at the `eval()` built-in function, which executes JavaScript commands from a string. The `eval()` function returns the result of the commands, but if you don't need to use the result, you can ignore it by simply using a normal function call:

```
eval("temp = 12");
```

Integrating Functions with HTML

The `function` keyword declares a function but does not execute it.

You should now understand the basics of JavaScript functions and be able to use them in your own programs. At this point, let's look at the best ways of including functions in an HTML document.

First, you should understand one thing: When you declare a function (with the `function` keyword) the JavaScript interpreter stores it and prepares it for use—but it is not executed. No function is executed until a function call is made for it.

An HTML document consists of two main sections: the header section, contained within the <HEAD> tags, and the body section, contained within <BODY> tags. You can include JavaScript commands and functions in either section.

By convention, the proper place to define a function is in the <HEAD> section. The main reason for this is that browsers do not attempt to display any of the information in this section, so it makes it easy to keep your Web page compatible with older browsers.

NOTE: Another method of hiding JavaScript from older browsers is discussed in Chapter 1, "Creating Simple JavaScript Programs."

Another reason to include function definitions in the header is that it is the first part of the HTML document loaded by the browser. This will ensure that when you make the function call, the function is loaded and ready to execute. You cannot call a function that hasn't been defined yet.

The function call, on the other hand, should be included in the <BODY> of the HTML document so that it can display its results. As an example, Listing 3.4 shows an HTML document that includes the PrintRow function, defined in Listing 3.2, and uses calls to the function in the body to display a table.

Listing 3.4. (TABLE.HTM) An HTML document that uses JavaScript to print a table.

```
<HTML>
<HEAD>
<TITLE>JavaScript table test</TITLE>
<SCRIPT language="JAVASCRIPT">
function PrintRow(name, age, birthday) {
    document.write("<TR> <TD>", name, "</TD> <TD>", age, "</TD> <TD>", birthday,
➥"</TD> </TR>\n");
}
</SCRIPT>
</HEAD>
<BODY>
<H1>Table Test Using JavaScript</H1>
<TABLE>
<SCRIPT language="JAVASCRIPT">
PrintRow("Fred", 27, "June 17");
PrintRow("Tom", 24, "March 13");
PrintRow("Rebecca", 25, "November 30");
</SCRIPT>
</TABLE>
End of table.
</HTML>
```

As you can see, the `PrintRow` function is defined in the `<HEAD>` section of the document and called where it is needed, in the `<TABLE>` tags in the document's body. You can see the output of this document, as displayed by Netscape, in Figure 3.1.

Figure 3.1.
Netscape displays the output of the JavaScript table example.

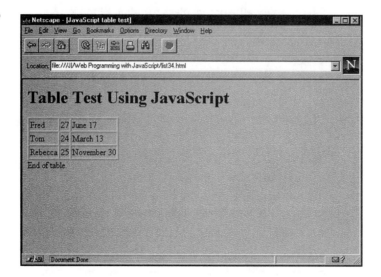

TIP: You may not even need a `<SCRIPT>` tag to call your function. Functions can also be used by event handlers to respond to events. You will explore event handlers in detail in the Event Handlers section, later in this chapter.

Dividing a Task into Functions

Functions eliminate repetition and make programs easier to read.

At this point, you should understand the purpose of functions. As you move into more complicated JavaScript programming, you will find there are very few tasks you can do without using at least one function, and splitting a task into functions makes it easy to understand.

When you are writing JavaScript, you may not know exactly what should be a function and what shouldn't. Here are some tips for determining whether you should use a function:

❑ If you find yourself typing the same (or nearly the same) set of commands repeatedly.

❑ If you expect to use the same commands again for a different purpose, define a function. It will make your job easier when you need to do it again.

❏ Even if you won't use a section of code again, you might want to consider using functions to separate the individual tasks within the program.

❏ If you need to complete a set of statements in a single line—such as in an event handler, described later in this chapter—you'll need to use a function.

In general, any time you end up with more than five to six lines of code, you may want to split parts of it into functions. This makes the main body of code easier to read. As a matter of fact, many programmers use functions almost exclusively, making the main program itself small and very easy to understand.

Communication Between Functions

Functions can communicate with parameters, or by using global variables.

As you create a large JavaScript program with several functions, you may wonder how the functions will work together. There are two ways to keep track of data between functions.

The first method of passing data to and from a function is the one you've already used—function parameters. You can pass a set of parameters to the function, and the function can return a value.

Although this parameter-passing mechanism works well in most cases, you will run into some situations where it just isn't practical. One reason for this is that functions can return only one value. In cases like this, the answer is to use a variable.

As you learned in Chapter 2, variables you declare in a function with the var keyword are local to that function; they can't be accessed from any other function. In order to keep data between functions, you need to use a global variable.

Defining a global variable is easy: just place the variable definition outside any functions. Once you've defined it, you can then use it in all functions in your program. You can also use global variables in statements outside of functions and in event handlers.

This technique is particularly useful for quantities that concern the whole program. For example, in a game program you might use a global variable for the score. This would enable you to add to the score from any function, without having to pass it back and forth.

Understanding Methods

A method is a function that is associated with a certain object.

Now that you understand functions, let's look at how they work with objects. You use a function to define an object, and you can also define methods, or built-in ways of working with the objects.

Methods are simply functions that have been linked to an object and work on the properties of that object. As an example, the built-in string object includes some methods to work with strings. One of them, `toLowerCase()`, converts the string to all lowercase.

To call a method, you use a period to divide the string name and the method name, as with properties. However, because a method is a function, you must include parentheses for the parameters. In the case of the `toLowerCase()` method, there are no parameters. The following JavaScript code demonstrates the use of this method:

```
var text = "THIS IS UPPERCASE";
var ltext = text.toLowerCase();
```

In this example, the `ltext` variable is used to hold the lowercase version of the `text` string. The `toLowerCase()` method does not modify the string itself; instead, it returns a lowercase version.

 # Defining Objects and Methods

To further illustrate methods and objects, let's return to the business card example. As you may recall, the `Card` object you worked with earlier has the following properties:

- ❏ `name`
- ❏ `address`
- ❏ `work_phone`
- ❏ `home_phone`

To define and use this object in a JavaScript program, you need to create a function to create new `Card` objects. This function is referred to as the *object definition* for an object, or the *constructor*. Here is an object definition for the Card object:

```
function Card(name,address,work,home) {
   this.name = name;
   this.address = address;
   this.work_phone = work;
   this.home_phone = home;
}
```

The object definition is a simple function that accepts parameters to initialize a new object and assigns those to the corresponding properties. One thing you haven't seen before is the `this` keyword; this is required for object definitions and refers to the current object—the one that is being created by the function.

Next, let's create a method to work with the `Card` object. Because all `Card` objects will have the same properties, it might be handy to have a function that prints the properties out in a neat format. Let's call this function `PrintCard()`.

Because your `PrintCard()` function will be used as a method for `Card` objects, you don't need to ask for parameters. Instead, you can use the `this` keyword again to refer to the current object's properties. Here is a function definition for the `PrintCard()` function:

```
function PrintCard() {
    document.write("Name: ", this.name, "\n");
    document.write("Address: ", this.address, "\n");
    document.write("Work Phone: ", this.work_phone, "\n");
    document.write("Home Phone: ", this.home_phone, "\n");
}
```

Method functions are defined as functions and assigned in the object's constructor.

This function simply reads the properties from the current object (`this`), prints each one with a caption, and skips to a new line. The last thing you need to do is make `PrintCard()` part of the function definition for `Card` objects. Here is the modified function definition:

```
function Card(name,address,work,home) {
    this.name = name;
    this.address = address;
    this.work_phone = work;
    this.home_phone = home;
    this.PrintCard = PrintCard;
}
```

The added statement looks just like another property definition, but it refers to the `PrintCard()` function. This will work so long as the `PrintCard()` function is defined with its own function definition.

Creating Instances of Objects

A variable of an object type is an *instance* of the object.

Now let's try using the object definition and method. In order to use an object definition, you create a new object. This is done with the `new` keyword. The following statement creates a new `Card` object called `tom`:

```
tom = new Card("Tom Jones", "123 Elm Street", "555-1234", "555-9876");
```

As you can see, creating an object is easy. All you do is call the `Card()` function (the object definition) and give it the required attributes, in the same order as the definition.

Once this statement executes, a new object is created to hold Tom's information. This is called an *instance* of the `Card` object; just as there can be several string variables in a program, there can be several instances of an object you define.

Now that you've created an instance of the card object, you can use the `PrintCard()` method to print it out:

```
tom.PrintCard();
```

Putting It All Together

Now you've created a new object to store business cards and a method to print them out. As a final demonstration of objects, properties, functions, and methods, let's use this object in a Web page to print data for several cards.

The HTML document will need to include the function definition for PrintCard() along with the function definition for the Card object. You will then create three cards and print them out in the body of the document. Listing 3.5 shows the complete HTML document.

Listing 3.5. (ADDRESS.HTM) An HTML document that uses the Card object.

```
<HTML>
<HEAD>
<TITLE>JavaScript Business Cards</TITLE>
<SCRIPT LANGUAGE="JavaScript">
function PrintCard() {
   document.write("<B>Name:</B> ", this.name, "<BR>");
   document.write("<B>Address:</B> ", this.address, "<BR>");
   document.write("<B>Work Phone:</B> ", this.work_phone, "<BR>");
   document.write("<B>Home Phone:</B> ", this.home_phone, "<HR>");
}
function Card(name,address,work,home) {
   this.name = name;
   this.address = address;
   this.work_phone = work;
   this.home_phone = home;
   this.PrintCard = PrintCard;
}
</SCRIPT>
</HEAD>
<BODY>
<H1>JavaScript Business Card Test</H1>
Script begins here.<HR>
<SCRIPT LANGUAGE="JavaScript">
// Create the objects
sue = new Card("Sue Suthers", "123 Elm Street", "555-1234", "555-9876");
phred = new Card("Phred Madsen", "233 Oak Lane", "555-2222", "555-4444");
henry = new Card("Henry Tillman", "233 Walnut Circle", "555-1299", "555-1344");
// And print them
sue.PrintCard();
phred.PrintCard();
henry.PrintCard();
</SCRIPT>
End of script.
</BODY>
</HTML>
```

Notice that I have modified the PrintCard() function slightly to make things look good with HTML line breaks, boldface, and horizontal rules. The Netscape output of this document is shown in Figure 3.2.

Figure 3.2.
Netscape displays the output of the business card example.

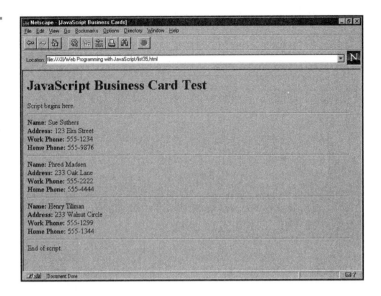

Conditionals and Loops

Conditionals and loops are used to control the flow of a JavaScript program.

Next, let's look at two types of statements you'll need in just about any large program: *conditionals,* which enable you to test data, and *loops,* which execute a block of code multiple times.

The `if...else` Construct

The `if` statement is the main conditional statement in JavaScript. You can use it to check for certain values and act accordingly. You will find that just about every large program uses conditionals, whether to act on data the user enters or to check for errors. Here is an example of a basic `if` statement:

```
if (a == 1) document.write("Found a 1!");
```

This statement checks the variable `a`, and if it has a value of `1`, prints a message. Otherwise, it does nothing. You can also use multiple statements by enclosing them in braces:

```
if (a == 1) {
   document.write("Found a 1!");
   a = 0;
}
```

This block of statements checks the variable a once again. If it finds a value of 1, it prints a message and sets a back to zero.

The `if` statement has an optional `else` keyword, which can specify a block of statements to execute if the condition is *not* true. You could modify Listing 3.5 to print an alternative message if the value of a is not 1:

```
if (a == 1) {
    document.write("Found a 1!");
    a = 0;
}
else {
    document.write("Incorrect value: " + a);
    a = 0;
}
```

You can use several `else` statements with `if` statements to check for multiple values.

As you can see, you can follow the block of statements after the `if` keyword with an `else` keyword and a second block of statements. Only one of the blocks will be executed, depending on the condition.

You can use any of the conditional expressions and operators introduced in Chapter 2 as the conditional in the `if` statement. You can also use a nonconditional expression, such as a variable assignment; the condition will be true if the assignment is successful.

NOTE:
One of the most common errors is to use the assignment (=) operator in a conditional instead of the equality (==) operator. This can be especially confusing because the assignment will evaluate as a true condition. Be sure to check your conditions for this.

Conditional Expressions

In addition to the `if` statement, JavaScript provides a shorthand type of conditional expression that you can use to make quick decisions. This uses a peculiar syntax, which is also found in other languages, such as C. Here is an example of a conditional expression:

```
value = (a == 1) ? 1 : 0;
```

This statement may look confusing, but it is equivalent to this `if` statement:

```
if (a == 1)
    value = 1;
else
    value = 0;
```

In other words, the value after the question mark (?) will be used if the condition is true, and the value after the colon (:) will be used if the condition is false. The colon represents the `else` portion of the statement, and like the `else` portion of the `if` statement, is optional.

You can think of a
conditional expression
as a question and an
answer.

These shorthand expressions can be used anywhere JavaScript is expecting a value. They provide an easy way to make simple decisions about values. As an example, here's an easy way to display a grammatically correct message about the `counter` variable:

```
document.write("Found ", counter, (counter == 1) ? " word." : " words.");
```

This will print the message `"Found 1 word"` if the counter has a value of 1, and `"Found 2 words"` with a value of 2 or greater. This is one of the most common uses for a conditional expression.

Using the for Keyword

One of the main reasons for computer programs is to perform repetitive tasks. JavaScript includes several keywords that make it easy to repeat blocks of code in a loop. There are several different types of loops, each with its own keyword.

Loops with for in
JavaScript work much
the same as in Java or C.

The `for` keyword is the first tool to look at for creating loops. A `for` loop typically uses a variable (called a *counter* or *index*) to keep track of how many times the loop has executed, and it stops when the counter reaches a certain number. A basic `for` statement looks like this:

```
for (var = 1; var < 10; var++) {
```

There are three parameters to the `for` loop, separated by semicolons:

- ❏ The first parameter (`var = 1` in the example) specifies a variable and assigns an initial value to it. This is called the *initial expression*, because it sets up the initial state for the loop.
- ❏ The second parameter (`var < 10` in the example) is a condition that must remain true to keep the loop running. This is called the *condition* of the loop.
- ❏ The third parameter (`var++` in the example) is a statement that executes with each iteration of the loop. This is called the *increment expression*, because it is usually used to increment the counter.

After the three parameters are specified, a left brace is used to signal the beginning of a block. All the statements between the braces will be executed with each iteration of the loop.

This may sound a bit confusing, but once you're used to it, you'll use `for` loops frequently. Let's take a look at a simple example of this type of loop, shown in Listing 3.6.

Listing 3.6. A loop using the `for` keyword.

```
for (i=1; i<10; i++) {
    document.write("This is line ",i,"\n");
}
```

This example displays a message including the loop's counter during each iteration. The output of Listing 3.6 would look like this:

```
This is line 1
This is line 2
This is line 3
This is line 4
This is line 5
This is line 6
This is line 7
This is line 8
This is line 9
```

Notice that the loop was executed only nine times. This is because `i<10` is the conditional. When the counter (`i`) is incremented to `10`, the expression is no longer true. If you need the loop to count to `10`, you could change the conditional; either `i<=10` or `i<11` will work fine.

NOTE: You might notice that the variable name `i` is often used as the counter in loops. This is a programming tradition that began with an ancient language called Fortran. There's no need for you to follow this tradition, but it is a good idea to use one consistent variable for counters.

The structure of the `for` loop in JavaScript is based on Java, which in turn is based on C. Although it is traditionally used to count from one number to another, you can use just about any statement for the initialization, condition, and increment. However, there's usually a better way to do other types of loops with the `while` keyword, described in the next section.

Using `while` Loops

while loops are often easier to use than `for` loops.

The other keyword for loops in JavaScript is `while`. Unlike `for` loops, `while` loops don't necessarily use a variable to count. Instead, they execute as long as (while) a condition is true. In fact, if the condition starts out as false, the statements might not execute at all.

The `while` statement includes the condition in parentheses, and it is followed by a block of statements within braces, just like a `for` loop. As an example, here is a simple `while` loop:

```
while (total < 10) {
n++;
total += values[n];
}
```

This loop uses a counter, n, to iterate through the values array. Rather than stopping at a certain count, however, it stops when the total of the values reaches 10.

You might have noticed that you could have done the same thing with a for loop:

```
for (n=0;total < 10; n++) {
total += values[n];
}
```

As a matter of fact, the for loop is nothing more than a special kind of while loop that handles an initialization and an increment for you. You can generally use while for any loop; however, it's best to choose whichever type of loop makes the most sense for the job, or takes the least amount of typing.

The for...in Construct

The for...in loop is used strictly for working with object properties.

There's a third type of loop available in JavaScript. The for...in loop is not as flexible as ordinary for or while loops; instead, it is specifically designed to perform an operation on each property of an object.

For example, remember that the elements of an array are actually properties of an array object. You can use a for...in loop to access each element of the array in turn. This simple loop adds one to each of the members of the counters array:

```
for (i in counters) {
counters[i]++;
}
```

Like an ordinary for loop, this type of loop uses an index variable. (i in the example). For each iteration of the loop, the variable is set to the next property of the object. This makes it easy when you need to check or modify each of an object's properties.

Remember that this doesn't just work with arrays—the previous example would work with an array with indices 1 through 5, but it would also work if the object had properties such as hits and misses. The index variable would be set to each of the property names.

Infinite Loops

The for and while loops allow you quite a bit of control over the loop. In some cases, this can cause problems if you're not careful. Take this loop, for example:

```
while (j < 10) {
n++;
values[n] = 0;
}
```

Most often, an infinite loop is created by accident.

I've made a mistake in the previous example. The condition of the `while` loop refers to the j variable, but that variable doesn't actually change during the loop. This creates an *infinite loop*. The loop will continue executing until it is stopped by the user, or until it generates an error of some kind.

Obviously, infinite loops are something to avoid. They can also be difficult to spot, because JavaScript won't give you an error that actually tells you there is an infinite loop. Thus, each time you create a loop in your JavaScript programs, you should be careful to make sure there's a way out.

Occasionally, you may want to create an infinite loop deliberately. This might include situations when you want your program to execute until the user stops it or if you are providing an escape route with the `break` statement, introduced below. Here's an easy way to create an infinite loop:

```
while (true) {
```

Because the value `true` is the conditional, this loop will always find its condition to be true.

The `break` Statement

The `break` statement can exit any loop— whether infinite or not.

There is one way out of an infinite loop. The `break` statement can be used during a loop to exit the loop immediately and continue with the first statement after the loop:

```
while (true) {
n++;
if (values[n] == 1) break;
}
```

Although the `while` statement is set up as an infinite loop, the `if` statement checks the corresponding value of an array, and if it finds a 1, it exits the loop.

When a `break` statement occurs, the rest of the loop is skipped, and execution continues with the first statement after the loop's ending right brace. You can use the `break` statement in any type of loop, whether infinite or not. This provides an easy way to exit if an error occurs, or if you've found what you're looking for.

The `continue` Statement

One more statement is available to help you control the execution of statements in a loop. The `continue` statement skips the rest of the loop, but unlike `break`, it continues with the next iteration of the loop:

```
for (i=1; i<21; i++) {
if (score[i]==0) continue;
document.write("Student number ",i, " Score: ", score[i], "\n");
}
```

This program uses a `for` loop to print out scores for 20 students, stored in the `score` array. The `if` statement is used to check for `0` scores. You assume that a score of `0` means that the student didn't take the test, so you continue the loop without printing the score.

Using Multiple Parameters in Functions

As a practical example of looping, let's look at a program that deals with multiple values in an array. When dividing your program into functions, you may run into a need for a function that can accept a variable number of parameters. For example, imagine a `Total()` function that would add together all the parameters it receives. You could call it using these statements:

```
a = Total(2,3,4);
document.write(Total(a, 17));
b = Total (a, b, c, d, e);
```

To return the correct result in all of these cases, the `Total()` function needs to accept a variable number of parameters. JavaScript supports multiple-parameter functions through a special array, `arguments`, which is a property of the function. You can define a function without a parameter list, then use this array to read the parameters.

Using this feature, you can easily create the `Total()` function:

```
function Total() {
   var tot = 0;
   for (i=0;i<Total.arguments.length;i++) {
      tot += Total.arguments[i];
   }
   return tot;
}
```

You use a `for` loop to read all the arguments. The `arguments.length` property gives us the total number of arguments. Each is added to the local `tot` variable, which is returned.

Events and Event Handlers

Event handlers usually respond to the user's actions.

The final concept you will look at in this chapter is one of the strengths of JavaScript: event handlers. These enable you to integrate JavaScript with a Web page in ways possible with no other language.

In an object-oriented environment, *events* are often used to trigger portions of a program. In JavaScript, events pertain to the Web page containing the script. When the user clicks on a link, selects or enters text, or even moves the mouse over part of the page, an event occurs.

You can use JavaScript to respond to these events. For example, you can have custom messages displayed in the status line (or somewhere else on the page) as the user moves the mouse over links. You can also update fields in a form whenever another field changes.

TIP: Because one of the main uses for event handlers is in HTML forms, you will explore them in much more detail in Chapter 6, "Using Interactive Forms."

Types of Events

You will explore the different events available for use in JavaScript, and the objects they correspond with, in Chapter 5, "Accessing Window Elements as Objects." For now, take a quick look at Table 3.1, which lists the types of events and their use.

Table 3.1. Available events in JavaScript.

Event Name	Description
onAbort	Occurs when the user aborts the loading of an image
onBlur	Occurs when an object on the page loses focus
onChange	Occurs when a text field is changed by the user
onClick	Occurs when the user clicks on an item
onError	Occurs when a document or image can't load correctly
onFocus	Occurs when an item gains focus
onLoad	Occurs when the page (or an image) finishes loading
onMouseOver	Occurs when the mouse pointer moves over an item
onMouseOut	Occurs when the mouse pointer moves off an item
onSelect	Occurs when the user selects text in a text area
OnSubmit	Occurs when a submit button is pressed
OnUnload	Occurs when the user leaves the document or exits

As you can see, you can respond to a wide variety of events. This makes it possible to interact with the user instantaneously—something CGI programmers have wanted for years.

Creating an Event Handler

An HTML tag can include event handlers for more than one event.

Event handlers are not defined with <SCRIPT> tags. Instead, they are an attribute of individual HTML tags. For example, here is a link that includes an event handler:

```
<A HREF="http://www.starlingtech.com/books/javascript/"
    onMouseOver="window.status='An amazingly useful link'; return true">
Click here</A>
```

Note that this is all one <A> tag, although it's split into multiple lines. This specifies two statements to be used as the onMouseOver event handler for the link. The first statement displays a message in the status bar; the second returns a true value to keep the message from being erased.

NOTE: The previous example uses single quotation marks to surround the text. This is necessary in an event handler, because double quotation marks are used by HTML. The event handler itself is surrounded by double quotes.

You can use JavaScript statements like the previous one in an event handler, but if you need more than one statement, it's a good idea to use a function instead. Just define the function in the <HEAD> of the document, then call the function as the event handler:

```
<a href="#bottom" onMouseOver="DoIt();">Move to the bottom</A>
```

This example calls the DoIt() function when the user moves the mouse over the link. Using a function is convenient because you can use longer, more readable JavaScript routines as event handlers.

How Event Handlers Interact

Using event handlers leads to nonsequential programming.

As a final note about event handlers, you need to know a bit of programming philosophy. If you've programmed in a language such as BASIC, C, or Perl, you're used to creating a program that executes in a logical order, and you control that order.

With graphical environments, such as Windows and the Macintosh, came the need for *event-based* programming. This type of programming uses events to trigger sections of the program, so you don't really know what order it will execute in—that depends on what the user does.

On the other hand, event-based programming can make things much easier. In traditional programming, you typically interact with the user with a series of `if` statements, checking for each thing the user might have done. In event-based programming, this part is done for you—all you have to do is write the functions for each event you wish to handle.

If you've programmed in other environments, the event-based nature of JavaScript might take a bit of getting used to, but it's worth it—it makes programming simple. If JavaScript is the first language you're learning, you'll find it easy to learn to use events. Event handlers are used in several useful ways in Chapter 5 and throughout this book.

Workshop Wrap-Up

In this chapter, you learned many of the more advanced aspects of JavaScript, including the following:

- ❑ The basics of object-oriented programming: objects, properties, and methods
- ❑ Functions, which can be used to separate tasks in JavaScript
- ❑ Using loops for executing repetitive statements
- ❑ Using conditionals for reacting to data
- ❑ How to use event handlers in JavaScript
- ❑ The differences between traditional and event-based programming

Next Steps

Next, you can learn more about objects in JavaScript, or move on to creating more complex programs:

- ❑ To learn more about the built-in objects and functions in JavaScript, along with custom objects of your own, see Chapter 4, "Using Built-In Objects and Custom Objects."
- ❑ To learn about the specific events you can use with each of the objects in an HTML page, see Chapter 5, "Accessing Window Elements as Objects."
- ❑ To see how you can use objects with HTML forms, see Chapter 6, "Using Interactive Forms."
- ❑ To see some applications of the techniques in this chapter, see Chapter 7, "Real-Life Examples I."

Q&A

Q: There are many books that go into more complicated detail about object-oriented programming. Do these apply to JavaScript?

A: Only partially. JavaScript uses a basic implementation of objects, and does not fully support features, such as encapsulation and inheritance, which are considered traits of "true" objects. JavaScript's objects are simple, and you should learn all you need to know about them in this book.

Q: Some languages, such as C, have a `switch` or `case` statement, which enables me to test several conditions conveniently. Does JavaScript have anything like this?

A: Not exactly. You can use a sequence of `if` and `else if` statements to do the same thing, though.

Q: If I use the `onSelect` method, how can I tell what part of the text was selected?

A: Unfortunately, you can't. This may be resolved in a future version of JavaScript. Even then, writing a complete text editor in JavaScript may be a bit ambitious.

FOUR

Using Built-In Objects and Custom Objects

You learned about the basic principles of object-oriented JavaScript programming in Chapter 3, "Working with Objects and Events." This chapter goes into detail about the techniques used in object-oriented programming. You will also explore the built-in objects you can use to make JavaScript programming easier, and learn about these objects using several example programs.

Techniques for Object-Oriented Programming

To continue the discussion of object-oriented JavaScript programming, let's look at the keywords and terms JavaScript uses to represent objects and other object-oriented concepts, and the ways you can use them. This will give you a foundation to understand the built-in objects, which are introduced in the next section.

In this chapter, you

- ❏ Learn the keywords for JavaScript object-oriented programming
- ❏ Learn to use String object for working with strings
- ❏ Use the Date object for date-related functions
- ❏ Use the Math object for math functions
- ❏ Get information about the browser with the navigator object
- ❏ Create your own objects and learn to customize existing ones

Tasks in this chapter:

- ❏ Using Objects, Properties, and Methods
- ❏ Looping Through an Object's Properties
- ❏ Creating an Array
- ❏ Customizing the String Object

Using Objects, Properties, and Methods

The basic component of object-oriented programming is, of course, an object. You can define objects by creating a function to define them, as you learned in Chapter 3. For example, this function defines the Card object, which you worked with in Chapter 3:

```
function Card(name,address,work,home) {
    this.name = name;
    this.address = address;
    this.work_phone = work;
    this.home_phone = home;
    this.PrintCard = PrintCard;
}
```

This function simply defines the name of the object type and assigns values to each of its functions. It also assigns the name of a function (PrintCard) as a method of the Card object.

You can use any variable as a property of an object—in fact, you can use another object as a property. For example, suppose you defined an Address object to hold the different components of an address:

```
function Address(street1, street2, city, state, zip) {
    this.street1 = street1;
    this.street2 = street2;
    this.city = city;
    this.state = state;
    this.zip = zip;
}
```

Because JavaScript doesn't require that you specify variable types, you don't need to change the definition for the Card object. It already expects an address and assigns it to the address property. You can assign an object to this property just as easily. Here is an example:

```
tomaddr = new Address("123 Elm Street", "Apartment 312", "Ogden", "UT",
➡"84404");
tom = new Card("Tom Smith", tomaddr, "555-1239", "555-2394");
```

Here you have defined an Address object called tomaddr to hold Tom's address. Next, you create the Card object called tom. As the address parameter, you specify the name of the Address object.

You now have an object within an object—the tomaddr Address object is a property, or child object, of the tom Card object. The syntax for accessing these properties is simply to list both objects separated by periods. For example, if you need to assign a variable to Tom's zip code, you could use this statement:

```
z = tom.address.zip;
```

An object used as a property can have methods also. For example, you could define a PrintAddress() method for the Address object that prints each field of the address:

```
function PrintAddress() {
    document.write("Address:\n");
    document.write(this.street1, "\n");
    document.write(this.street2, "\n");
    document.write(this.city, "\n");
    document.write(this.state, "\n");
    document.write(this.zip, "\n");
}
```

You would then link this function as a method of the Address object by adding this statement to the Address object's definition:

```
this.PrintAddress = PrintAddress;
```

You could then access this method for Tom's address:

```
tom.address.PrintAddress();
```

Methods can also be used within other methods. For example, you could expand the PrintCard() method to print all the address fields by calling the PrintAddress() method:

```
function PrintCard() {
    document.write("Name: ", this.name, "\n");
    this.address.PrintAddress();
    document.write("Work Phone: ", this.work_phone, "\n");
    document.write("Home Phone: ", this.home_phone, "\n");
}
```

This is the syntax you will use any time an object is used as a property of another object. You will see in Chapter 5, "Accessing Window Elements as Objects," that the built-in objects used to represent parts of the browser's display and the Web page use this technique frequently.

The new Keyword

The new keyword creates a new instance, or copy, of an object.

I used the new keyword several times in the previous examples to create new objects. In object-oriented terms, you are actually creating an instance of an *object class*. Any variable you create with the new keyword is an instance of that object. The object definition itself is referred to as the object class, or the object type.

With some built-in objects, such as the String object, you don't need to use the new keyword; you simply define a string variable, and JavaScript creates a String object automatically. There are other built-in objects with which you can use new.

The this Keyword

The this keyword has appeared in most of the examples. It is simply a shorthand for "the current object." This is usually used in object definitions, where it refers to the object being defined, and in method definitions, where it refers to the object the method is acting on. It can also be used in event handlers, as you'll see in Chapter 5.

The with Keyword

The with keyword is one you haven't seen before. You can use it to make JavaScript programming easier—or at least easier to type.

You can use with any time you use the same object several times in a row.

The with keyword specifies an object, and it is followed by a set of statements enclosed in braces. For each statement in the set, any properties you mention without specifying an object are assumed to be for that object.

As an example, suppose you used the Address object definition given earlier to create an address object called Fred. You could then use the following statements to assign values to the Address object's properties:

```
with (Fred) {
    street1= "12 E 400 S";
    street2= "Suite 200";
    city="Beverly Hills";
    state="CA";
    zip="90210"
}
```

This enables you to avoid typing the object's name (Fred) at the beginning of each property name: Fred.street1, Fred.street2, and so forth.

Obviously, the with keyword only saves a bit of typing in situations like this. However, you will find it very useful when you're dealing with an object throughout a large procedure, or when you are using a built-in object, such as the Math object.

Creating a Generic Object

Because JavaScript objects are so flexible, you may wonder why the constructor function is necessary at all. As a matter of fact, you can create an object without one by using the Object() constructor. For example, this statement creates an object called data:

```
data = new Object();
```

Because it isn't any particular kind of object yet, I call it a *generic object*. You can add properties to the object in the usual fashion. This is particularly handy when you are using the object as an associative array; you'll look at this technique in Chapter 10, "Working with Multiple Pages and Data."

Looping Through an Object's Properties

The final statement used for object-oriented work in JavaScript is the `for...in` loop, which you looked at briefly in Chapter 3. This loop executes once for each property of an object, assigning the index variable to the property name. For example, you could make a simple function to list the properties of an object and their values, as in Listing 4.1.

Listing 4.1. A simple example of a `for...in` loop.

```
function list(object) {
   for (var i in object) {
      document.write("Property: ",i," Value: ",object[i], "<BR>");
   }
}
```

This function uses the variable `i` to iterate through the object's properties and uses the `document.write()` function to display the property name and the value.

NOTE: Notice that I used the syntax `object[i]` to refer to the property of the object in the previous example. It may seem more obvious to use `object.i` to refer to the property, but this won't work—JavaScript will interpret this as asking for a property called `i`. In order to use the *value* of `i`, you need to use brackets.

Using Built-In Objects

Other objects are part of the *object hierarchy*, which describes Web page elements; this is explained in Chapter 5.

JavaScript includes several built-in objects. They are not part of the object hierarchy, and they do not represent any part of a Web page. Instead, they are used for programming functions. These include the following:

❑ You can use *array objects* to store numbered variables.

   ❑ You can use `String` objects to manipulate strings of characters.

   ❑ `Date` objects enable you to store and work with dates.

   ❑ The `Math` object includes methods and properties for mathematical functions.

   ❑ The `navigator` object stores information about the user's browser and its capabilities.

You will look at each of these types of objects in detail in the next sections.

Using Array Objects

Chapter 2, "Working with Larger Programs and Variables," introduced the Array object briefly. The original version of JavaScript did not include arrays, but they are now a built-in feature. You can create a new Array object to define an array. (Unlike other variables, arrays must be declared.) Use the new keyword to define an array:

```
students = new Array(30);
```

The indices in JavaScript arrays begin with 0.

This example creates an array with 30 elements, numbered 0 through 29. You can use these values by addressing their array index:

```
students[29]="Phred Madsen";
```

This refers to the last element of the array, index 29.

Array objects have a single property, length. This provides the number of elements in the array, usually the same number with which you declared the array. In the array declared in the previous example, students.length would return 30.

NOTE: When you define an array, its elements are filled with null, or undefined values, up to the length you specify. You can dynamically change an array's size by assigning to the length property.

In addition, the array object has three methods:

- ❏ join() quickly joins all the array's elements, resulting in a string. The elements are separated by commas or by the separator you specify.
- ❏ reverse() returns a reversed version of the array: the last element becomes the first, and the first element becomes the last.
- ❏ sort() returns a sorted version of the array. Normally, this is an alphabetical sort; however, you can use a custom sort method by specifying a comparison routine.

You will see examples of these methods throughout this book; for example, in Chapter 15, "Real-Life Examples III," the sort() method is used to score poker hands. You will also look at a simple example in the next section.

Creating an Array

Before continuing, let's explore an example of using an Array object with some of the array methods. Look at the JavaScript program shown in Listing 4.2.

Listing 4.2. Use of the `Array` object and its methods.

```
// Room for 3 items (0-2)
groceries = new Array(3);
groceries[0]="dental floss";
groceries[1]="baby powder";
groceries[2]="clam chowder";
document.writeln(groceries.join());
document.writeln(groceries.reverse().join());
document.writeln(groceries.sort().join());
```

All arrays must be defined with the **new** keyword.

This defines an array called `groceries`, able to hold 3 items. Next, you assign values to three of the items. You can then observe the `Array` object methods in action with three `document.writeln` statements:

- ❏ `groceries.join()` displays the items separated by commas: `"dental floss,baby powder,clam chowder"`.
- ❏ `groceries.reverse().join()` reverses the items, then joins and displays them: `"clam chowder,baby powder,dental floss"`.
- ❏ Finally, `groceries.sort().join()` alphabetically sorts the items before displaying them: `"baby powder,clam chowder,dental floss"`.

Using `String` Objects

Any string variable—or a literal, quoted string—is a `String` object.

You've already used `String` objects; any string variable in JavaScript is actually a `String` object. You learned about this object briefly in Chapter 3. `String` objects have a single property, `length`. They also have a variety of methods that you can use to perform string functions.

The `String` object methods return a modified copy of the string; they do not change the string itself.

The methods of the `String` object enable you to convert strings, work with pieces of strings, search for values, control the string's appearance on the HTML page, and control HTML links and anchors. You'll look at these by category in the next sections.

NOTE: You don't have to create a string variable to use the `String` object methods; you can use them on any object with a string value. This includes the text-valued properties of any of the objects in the Web page object hierarchy.

String Conversions

Two methods of the `String` object enable you to convert the contents of the string easily to all uppercase or all lowercase:

❏ `toUpperCase()` converts all characters in the string to uppercase.

❏ `toLowerCase()` converts all characters in the string to lowercase.

For example, the following statement displays the value of the `text` string variable in lowercase:

```
document.write(text.toLowerCase());
```

Note that the statement doesn't change the value of the `text` variable. These methods return the upper- or lowercase version of the string, but they don't change the string itself. All of the methods of the `String` object work in this manner.

One other conversion method is the `toString()` method. This one is a bit odd—it can be used with non-string objects. It is used to explicitly convert them to strings. For example, if a is a numeric variable containing the number 500, `a.toString()` would return the string `"500"`.

Working with Substrings

A substring is a section of a string, starting with one character and ending with another.

Three important `String` object methods enable you to work with *substrings*, or portions of strings. These methods are useful when you need to split a string into components or test portions of the string one at a time.

The first of these is the `substring()` method. This returns a string consisting of a portion of the original string between two index values, which you must specify in parentheses. For example, the following displays the fourth through sixth characters of the `text` string:

```
document.write(text.substring(3,6));
```

So where do the 3 and the 6 come from? No, there is no typo. There are three things you need to know about the index parameters:

❏ Indexing starts with 0 for the first character of the string, so the fourth character is actually index 3.

❏ The second index is noninclusive. A second index of 6 includes up to index 5 (the sixth character).

❏ You can specify the two indexes in either order; the smaller one will be assumed to be the first index. In the previous example, (6,3) would have produced the same result.

As another example, suppose you defined a string called `alpha` to hold the alphabet:

```
alpha = "ABCDEFGHIJKLMNOPQRSTUVWXYZ";
```

The following are examples of the `substring()` method using this string:

- ❏ `alpha.substring(0,4)` returns `"ABC"`.
- ❏ `alpha.substring(10,12)` returns `"KL"`.
- ❏ `alpha.substring(12,10)` also returns `"KL"`. Because it's smaller, `10` is used as the first index.
- ❏ `alpha.substring(6,7)` returns `"G"`.
- ❏ `alpha.substring(24,26)` returns `"YZ"`.
- ❏ `alpha.substring(0,26)` returns the entire alphabet.
- ❏ `alpha.substring(6,6)` returns the null value, an empty string. This is true whenever the two index values are the same.

If you need to use a single-character substring, the `charAt()` method is more efficient.

The second method for working with substrings is the `charAt()` method. This method is simpler: it takes a single index, and returns a single character. Here are a few examples using the `alpha` string defined previously:

- ❏ `alpha.charAt(0)` returns `"A"`.
- ❏ `alpha.charAt(12)` returns `"M"`.
- ❏ `alpha.charAt(25)` returns `"Z"`.
- ❏ `alpha.charAt(27)` returns an empty string, because there is no character at that index.

The final method for working with parts of strings is probably the most powerful. The `split()` method splits a string into an array of strings, based on a separator you specify. For example, the following statement splits the components of a name divided by spaces:

```
nn = "John Q. Public".split(" ");
```

After this statement, the `nn` array will contain three elements: `nn[0]` is `"John"`, `nn[1]` is `"Q."`, and `nn[2]` is `"Public"`. This method is useful any time you need to process a list of items.

Searching a String

The `indexOf()` method searches for a string within another string. Use the string you wish to search for the method call and specify the string to be searched for in the parentheses. This example searches for `"text"` in the `temp` String object:

```
location = temp.indexOf("text");
```

The value returned to the location variable is an index into the string, similar to the first index in the `substring()` method. The first character of the string is index zero.

You can specify an optional second parameter to indicate the index value to begin the search. For example, this statement searches for the word `"fish"` in the `temp` string, starting with the 20th character:

```
location = temp.indexOf("fish",19);
```

TIP:
One use for the second parameter is to search for multiple occurrences of a string. After finding the first occurrence, you search starting with that location for the second one, and so on.

`indexOf()` searches forward through a string, and `lastIndexOf()` searches backward.

A second method, `lastIndexOf()`, works the same way, but finds the *last* occurrence of the string. It searches the string backwards, starting with the last character. For example, this statement finds the last occurrence of `"Fred"` in the `names` string:

```
location = names.lastIndexOf("Fred");
```

As with `indexOf()`, you can specify a location to search from as the second parameter. In this case, the string will be searched backward starting at that location.

Changing a String's Appearance

These methods are useful only when displaying the string in an HTML page.

Several methods of the `String` object are available for displaying the string in various formats. These simply return a string consisting of the string enclosed by certain HTML tags. They do not modify the string itself. Here are the available attributes, and their equivalent HTML tags:

❏ `String.big()` displays big text, using the `<BIG>` tag in HTML 3.0.

❏ `String.blink()` displays blinking text, using the `<BLINK>` tag in Netscape.

❏ `String.bold()` displays bold text, using the `<B>` tag.

❏ `String.fixed()` displays fixed-font text, using the `<TT>` tag.

❏ `String.fontcolor()` displays the string in a colored font, equivalent to the `<FONTCOLOR>` tag in Netscape.

❏ `String.fontsize()` changes the font size, using the `<FONTSIZE>` tag in Netscape.

❏ `String.italics()` displays the string in italics, using the `<I>` tag.

❏ `String.small()` displays the string in small letters using the `<SMALL>` tag in HTML 3.0.

- ❏ `String.strike()` displays the string in a strike-through font, using the `<STRIKE>` tag.
- ❏ `String.sub()` displays subscript text, equivalent to the `<SUB>` tag in HTML 3.0.
- ❏ `String.sup()` displays superscript text, equivalent to the `<SUP>` tag in HTML 3.0.

TIP: There are also two JavaScript functions, `escape()` and `unescape()`, which convert strings to URL encoding and back. These are explained in Chapter 17, "Combining JavaScript, CGI, and SSI."

Links and Anchors

The `link()` and `anchor()` methods of `String` objects can be used to produce HTML for links and anchors. The value of the string is used as the actual link or anchor value, and the parameter specifies the link to jump to or the anchor to set. For example, the following statement sets an anchor called `"test"` using the value `"This is a Test"`:

```
"This is a Test".anchor("test");
```

Notice that I didn't have to define a string variable in these examples.

and this statement sets a link on the words `"Click Here"` to the anchor defined previously:

```
"Click Here".link("#test");
```

Using `Date` Objects

The `Date` object is a built-in JavaScript object that enables you to conveniently work with dates and times. You can create a `Date` object any time you need to store a date, and use the `Date` object's methods to work with the date.

Strangely, the `Date` object has no properties. To set or obtain values from a `Date` object, you must use the methods described in the next section.

NOTE: JavaScript dates are stored as the number of milliseconds since January 1st, 1970, at midnight. This date is called the *epoch*. Dates before 1970 aren't allowed. This means I can't store my birthday in a `Date` object, and there's a good chance you can't either. Hopefully, this will be fixed in a future version of JavaScript. In the meantime, you can work with dates manually, using strings or numeric variables.

Creating a Date Object

You can create a Date object using the new keyword. You can also optionally specify the date to store in the object when you create it. You can use any of the following formats:

```
birthday = new Date();
birthday = new Date("June 20, 1996 08:00:00");
birthday = new Date(6, 20, 96);
birthday = new Date(6, 20, 96, 8, 0, 0);
```

You can choose any of these formats, depending on which values you wish to set. If you use no parameters, as in the first example, the current date is stored in the object. You can then set the values using the set methods, described in the next section.

Setting Date Values

A variety of set methods enable you to set components of a Date object to values:

- ❏ setDate() sets the day of the month.
- ❏ setMonth() sets the month. JavaScript numbers the months from 0 to 11, starting with January (0).
- ❏ setYear() sets the year.
- ❏ setTime() sets the time (and the date) by specifying the number of milliseconds since January 1st, 1970.
- ❏ setHours(), setMinutes(), and setSeconds() set the time.

Getting Date Values

You can use the get methods to get values from a Date object. This is the only way to obtain these values, because they are not available as properties:

- ❏ getDate() gets the day of the month.
- ❏ getMonth() gets the month.
- ❏ getYear() gets the year.
- ❏ getTime() gets the time (and the date) as the number of milliseconds since January 1st, 1970.
- ❏ getHours(), getMinutes(), and getSeconds() get the time.

Working with Time Zones

A few functions are available to help you work with local time values and time zones:

- ❏ getTimeZoneOffset() gives you the local time zone's offset from GMT (Greenwich Mean Time, also known as UTC).

❏ `toGMTString()` converts the date object's time value to text, using GMT.

❏ `toLocalString()` converts the date object's time value to text, using local time.

Converting Between Date Formats

Two special methods of the `Date` object enable you to convert between date formats. These are not methods of individual `Date` objects; instead, you use them with the built-in object `Date` itself. These include the following:

UTC is an abbreviation for Universal Coordinated Time, formerly Greenwich Mean Time (GMT).

❏ `Date.parse()` converts a date string, such as `"June 20, 1996"` to a `Date` object (number of milliseconds since 1/1/1970).

❏ `Date.UTC()` is the opposite: it converts a `Date` object value (number of milliseconds) to a UTC (GMT) time.

The `Math` Object

In technical terms, the `Math` object is not a first-class object.

The `Math` object is a bit different from the `String` and `Date` objects: it is a built-in object in itself, rather than an object class of which you can create instances. In other words, you can't create your own `Math` objects. The `Math` object exists automatically in any JavaScript program and encapsulates all of JavaScript's math capabilities.

The `Math` object's properties represent mathematical constants, and its methods are mathematical functions.

NOTE: Because you may use the `Math` object's properties and methods throughout an entire group of statements, you may find it useful to use the `with` keyword, introduced earlier in this chapter, to specify the `Math` object for those statements.

I will introduce some highlights of the `Math` object's methods in the following sections. For a complete list of the properties and methods of this object, including trigonometric and logarithmic functions, refer to Appendix A.

Rounding and Truncating

Three of the most useful methods of the `Math` object enable you to round decimal values up and down:

❏ `Math.ceil()` rounds a number up to the next integer.

❏ `Math.floor()` rounds a number down to the next integer.

❏ `Math.round()` rounds a number to the nearest integer.

All these take a single parameter: the number to be rounded. You might notice one thing missing: the ability to round to a decimal place, such as for dollar amounts. You can easily simulate this, though. Here's a function to round to two decimal places:

```
function round(num) {
    return Math.round(num * 100) / 100;
}
```

This function multiplies the value by 100 to move the decimal, then rounds the number to the nearest integer. Finally, the value is divided by 100 to restore the decimal. You'll use this function in an automatic order form in Chapter 6, "Using Interactive Forms."

Generating Random Numbers

One of the most commonly used methods of the `Math` object is the `Math.random()` method, which generates a random number. This method doesn't require any parameters. The number it returns is a random decimal number between 0 and 1.

You usually will want a random number between 1 and a value. You can do this with a general purpose random number function like this:

```
function rand(num) {
    return Math.floor(Math.random() * num) + 1;
}
```

This function multiplies a random number by the value you send it, then converts it to an integer between 1 and the number using the `Math.floor()` method.

The `navigator` Object

The `navigator` object is a special object that stores information about the version of the browser. This is a Netscape-specific tag, and it may or may not be implemented in other browsers. (This may make you question its usefulness.)

The `navigator` object doesn't technically qualify as a built-in object, because it represents a physical entity—the browser in use. In this way it's similar to the objects, such as `window` and `document`, which you will look at in Chapter 5. Because it isn't really part of the object hierarchy either, you'll examine it here.

These are the same formats as the user agent text that appears in Web server logs.

The `navigator` object includes several properties that reflect information about the version of Netscape in use. These are all read-only properties:

❏ `navigator.appCodeName` is the browser's code name, usually `"Mozilla"`.

❏ `navigator.appName` is the browser's name, usually `"Netscape"`.

❏ `navigator.appVersion` is the version of Netscape being used—for example, `"2.0(Win95;I)"`.

TIP: One use for the `navigator` object is to check for a particular version of Netscape; this is most useful if you are using a feature that was recently added and want to include an alternative for users of older versions.

There are also several properties of the `navigator` object that deal with Java, plug-ins, and multimedia documents:

❑ `navigator.javaEnabled` indicates whether Java is enabled in the browser.

❑ `navigator.plugIns` is a list of the currently available plug-ins.

❑ `navigator.mimeTypes` is a list of the currently available MIME types.

❑ `navigator.taintEnabled()` indicates whether data tainting (see Chapter 10) is enabled.

Because these last two properties deal with plug-ins and multimedia, you'll take a closer look at them in Chapter 13, "Working with Multimedia and Plug-Ins." The `navigator.javaEnabled` property is described in detail in Chapter 16, "Integrating JavaScript with Java."

Customizing Objects

Along with the various built-in objects, you can also create objects of your own. You've already seen the basic example of doing this with the `new` keyword:

```
var = new ObjectType(parameters);
```

This assumes you have created an object definition for the object. Once you've done this, you can work with the properties and methods of the object, just like the built-in objects.

You can extend built-in or custom objects with the `prototype` keyword.

In object-oriented terms, the object definition defines a *prototype* for the object. This is the set of rules that govern how an object works. JavaScript provides a `prototype` keyword, which enables you to modify the prototype of all objects of a certain class.

As an example, suppose you defined an object called `lunch` with the following properties:

```
lunch.sandwich
lunch.drink
lunch.fruit
```

You could then create a `lunch` object like this:

```
mylunch = new lunch("bologna","coke","banana");
```

As you saw in other chapters, you could then add a property to the object:

```
mylunch.dessert = "pie";
```

As you saw in other chapters, you could then add a property to the object:

```
mylunch.dessert = "pie";
```

With a prototype, though, you can add a property to the object definition itself. This command will add the `dessert` property to all existing and future `lunch` objects:

```
lunch.prototype.dessert = "cake";
```

Any `lunch` object created after this point will include this property, with a default value of `"cake"`. The property will also be added to existing `lunch` objects. You can also extend the prototypes of the built-in objects, as you'll see in the next example.

You can also extend the **Date** object and the **Array** object.

You can add both properties and methods to an object's prototype.

Customizing the `String` Object

A powerful feature of the `prototype` keyword is the capability of extending the definitions of built-in objects. If you think the `String` object doesn't quite fit your needs, you can extend it, adding a new property or method.

As an example, let's add a method to the `String` object definition. There are a few methods, such as `big()`, `blink()`, and `bold()`, that output HTML tags with the string, but there is no method to work with headers. Listing 4.3 adds a `head()` method to the `String` object definition that will display the string as a heading.

Listing 4.3. Adding a method to the `String` object.

```
//define the function
function addhead (level) {
    html = "H" + level;
    text = this.toString();
    start = "<" + html + ">";
    stop = "</" + html + ">";
    return start + text + stop;
}
//add the method to the String prototype
String.prototype.head = addhead;
//test it
document.write ("This is a test".head(1));
```

First, you define the `addhead()` function, which will serve as the new string method. It accepts a number to specify the heading level. The `start` and `stop` variables are used to store the HTML begin and end header tags, such as `<H1>` and `</H1>`.

After the function is defined, you simply use the `prototype` keyword to add it as a method of the `String` object. You can then use this method on any `String` object; this is demonstrated by the last statement, which displays a quoted text string as a level-one header.

Workshop Wrap-Up

In this chapter, you learned the details of JavaScript's object-oriented capabilities, the various keywords used for working with objects in JavaScript, and techniques for working with objects and properties.

You also learned about the built-in objects that aren't directly related to Web pages:

❏ The String object for working with strings

❏ The Date object for date-related functions

❏ The Math object for math functions

❏ The navigator object for information about the browser

❏ Creating custom objects, and customizing existing ones

Next Steps

You can now learn about the JavaScript object hierarchy and more advanced features:

❏ To learn about the object hierarchy, which enables you to work with Web page elements, see Chapter 5, "Accessing Window Elements as Objects."

❏ To learn to use the objects to work with HTML forms, see Chapter 6, "Using Interactive Forms."

❏ To review the basics of JavaScript objects, see Chapter 3, "Working with Objects and Events."

❏ To see some of the techniques in this chapter in action, see Chapter 7, "Real-Life Examples I."

❏ To learn techniques for perfecting and debugging your JavaScript programs, see Chapter 14, "Debugging JavaScript Programs."

Q&A

Q: Do you really need to use objects within objects? Is there any practical reason to do this?

A: JavaScript programs are usually simple, and you probably won't need data structures that are complicated very often. However, the object hierarchy—which you'll learn about in Chapter 5—uses these techniques heavily.

Q: Most of the string appearance methods, such as `string.big`, take almost as much typing as simply including the appropriate HTML codes. Why would I use these?

A: One reason is that they may be more readable if someone (including you) needs to read through the source code later. Another reason is that the HTML specification may change; presumably, future versions of JavaScript will use the appropriate codes for new versions of HTML, so you won't have to worry about updating your program.

Q: Is there any limit to the length of a string variable in JavaScript?

A: Strictly speaking, no. The only limitation is the memory available on the user's machine. You should keep lengths to a minimum, though, to avoid crashing the browser.

FIVE

Accessing Window Elements as Objects

One of JavaScript's strengths is the capability of working with elements of the Web page directly. This is handled through the JavaScript *object hierarchy*. This hierarchy includes a variety of objects that represent data on the current Web page and in the current browser window.

These objects are organized into a *hierarchy* of parent and child objects. A *child object* is simply an object that is used as a property of another object (the *parent object*).

Each of the objects in the hierarchy includes properties, which are often objects in themselves. It may also include methods to perform functions on the object. Finally, it may include event handlers, which call functions or JavaScript statements when an event happens to that object.

In this chapter, you

- ❏ Learn about the objects in the JavaScript object hierarchy and their properties, methods, and event handlers
- ❏ Use the window object to refer to windows, display dialogs, and open and close windows
- ❏ Use the document object to work with HTML documents
- ❏ Use the location and history objects to send the user to different Web pages
- ❏ Use the link and anchor objects to find out about the links and anchors in a document

Tasks in this chapter:

- ❏ Changing the Status Line
- ❏ Opening and Closing Windows
- ❏ Using Prompts, Alerts, and Confirmation Dialogs
- ❏ Updating a Page with Timeouts
- ❏ Using window Object Event Handlers
- ❏ Implementing BACK and FORWARD Buttons

Each object in the hierarchy corresponds to part of a Web page or window.

A diagram of the object hierarchy is given in Figure 5.1. The hierarchy begins with the window object, which serves as the parent object for most of the other objects. This chapter describes each object in the following sections, beginning with the window object and working downward through the hierarchy.

Figure 5.1.
The JavaScript object hierarchy.

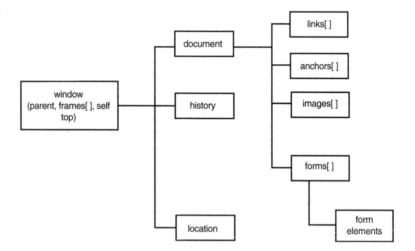

The window Object

Each frame or open browser window has a separate window object.

The window object is at the top of the object hierarchy. A window object exists for each open browser window. The properties of this object describe the document in the window and provide information about the window. Three of the window object's properties are child objects:

- ❏ The location object stores the location (URL) that is displayed in the window.
- ❏ The document object holds the Web page itself.
- ❏ The history object contains a list of sites visited before and after the current site.

Each of these objects is described in detail later in this chapter. In most cases, there is only one window object, so you can omit the window object name when referring to the current script's window. For example, this statement sets the current window's status property:

```
status = "This is a test."
```

There are several terms that refer to `window` objects:

- ❏ `window` refers to the current `window` object.
- ❏ `self` also refers to the current `window` object.
- ❏ `top` refers to the topmost (usually, the first) browser window.
- ❏ `parent` refers to the parent window when frames are used. Frames will be introduced later in this section.
- ❏ `opener` is used for windows you create and refers to the window that opened the current window.

You will now take a closer look at the properties, methods, and event handlers of the `window` object. The child objects (`location`, `document`, and `history`) will be covered in their own sections later in this chapter.

`window` Object Properties

The `window` object has a variety of properties that specify information about the window and its components. The simplest property is the `name` property; this contains the name of the current window.

If you create a window yourself, using the `open()` method described later in this chapter, you give it a name; otherwise, the `name` property remains blank. You will now look at the other properties of the `window` object, which enable you to deal with the status line and with framed documents.

You will learn how to use the status line for a scrolling message in Chapter 8, "Improving a Web Page with JavaScript."

Changing the Status Line

One of the simplest `window` object properties enables you to manipulate the status line—the gray-background line at the bottom of the window. This line is usually used to display URLs of links as you move the mouse over them. With JavaScript, you can display anything you like in this area.

As an example, Listing 5.1 shows an HTML page that uses a JavaScript event handler to enable you to modify the status line when you press a button.

Listing 5.1. (STATUS.HTM) An HTML document that uses JavaScript to change the status line.

```
<HTML>
<HEAD><TITLE>The Amazing Status Line Changer</TITLE>
</HEAD>
<BODY>
<H1>Change the Status Line</H1>
<HR>
Enter the text for the status line in the space below, then
press the CHANGE button to change it.<HR>
```

continues

Listing 5.1. continued

```
<FORM NAME="statform">
<INPUT TYPE="text" SIZE="65" NAME="input1"><BR>
<INPUT TYPE="button" VALUE="CHANGE"
onClick="window.status=document.statform.input1.value;">
</FORM>
<HR>
end.
</BODY>
</HTML>
```

This is an example of how much you can do with a single JavaScript statement. The HTML defines a form called `statform` with two fields: a text field and a button. You enter the text in the text field. Each time you press the button, the `onClick` event handler changes the status line to match the text field. Netscape's display of this page, including a modified status line, is shown in Figure 5.2.

Figure 5.2.

The status line changing program, as displayed by Netscape.

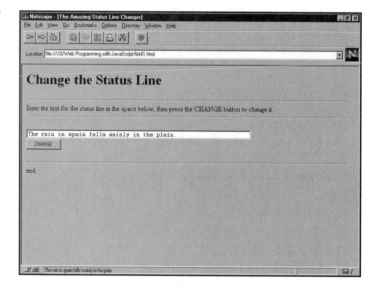

NOTE: Notice the syntax used to refer to the text field: `document.statform.input1.value`. This may be a bit confusing, but this is the syntax required to access an element of a form. You'll learn about forms in detail in Chapter 6, "Using Interactive Forms."

Although this application is an example of how much fun you can have with JavaScript in only one statement, it's not very useful. A more common (and more practical) application is to use the status line for `onMouseOver` event handlers, which enables you to provide useful instructions for links and form elements. You'll learn about this use of the `status` property in Chapter 8.

Using Frames

Frames were introduced by Netscape in Navigator version 1.2, and they are now becoming an accepted standard.

Some browsers (including the latest Netscape and Microsoft browsers) support frames or framesets. These enable you to divide the browser window into multiple panes, called frames. Each frame can contain a separate URL or the output of a script.

When you use frames, there are several window objects: one for the main (parent) window, and one for each frame. The window object has two properties that are used with frame documents:

❏ The frames array is used to store information about each frame. It is made up of frame objects, which work as window objects in themselves. You can also refer to a frame's window object by name.

❏ The parent.frames.length property specifies the number of frames in the window.

Because frames can make for some complicated—and useful—programming, they are described in detail in Chapter 9, "Using Frames, Cookies, and Other Advanced Features."

window Object Methods

Along with the properties you have already looked at, the window object includes a variety of methods. These enable you to perform window-related functions: opening, closing, and manipulating windows and displaying dialog boxes. Methods are also included to set timers to perform an action after a certain time.

The window.open() method enables you to open a new browser window. A typical statement to open a new window looks like this:

```
WindowName=window.open("URL", "WindowName", "Feature List");
```

The following are the components of the window.open() statement:

❏ The WindowName variable is used to store the new window object. You can access methods and properties of the new object by using this name.

❏ The first parameter of the window.open() method is an URL, which will be loaded into the new window. If left blank, no Web page will be loaded.

❏ The second parameter specifies a window name (here, WindowName again). This is assigned to the window object's name property and is used for *targets*, which are explained in Chapter 9.

❏ The third parameter is a list of optional features, separated by commas. You can customize the new window by choosing whether to include the toolbar, status line, and other features. This enables you to create a variety of "floating" windows, which may look nothing like a typical browser window.

The features available in the third parameter of the `window.open()` method include `width` and `height`, to set the size of the window, and several features that can be set to either `yes` (1) or `no` (0): `toolbar`, `location`, `directories`, `status`, `menubar`, `scrollbars`, and `resizable`. You can list only the features you want to change from the default. This example creates a small window with no toolbar or status line:

```
SmallWin = window.open("","small","width=100,height=120,toolbar=0,status=0");
```

 # Opening and Closing Windows

Of course, you can close windows as well. The `window.close()` method closes a window. Netscape doesn't enable you to close the main browser window without the user's permission; its main purpose is for closing windows you have created. For example, this statement closes a window called `updatewindow`:

```
updatewindow.close();
```

As another example, Listing 5.2 shows an HTML document that enables you to open a new window by pressing a button. (I have specified a very small size for the second window so you can tell them apart.) You can then press another button to close the new window. The third button attempts to close the current window; Netscape allows this, but asks for confirmation first.

Listing 5.2. (WINDOWS.HTM) An HTML document that uses JavaScript to enable you to create and close windows.

```
<HTML>
<HEAD><TITLE>Create a New Window</TITLE>
</HEAD>
<BODY>
<H1>Create a New Window</H1>
<HR>
Use the buttons below to test opening and closing windows in JavaScript.
<HR>
<FORM NAME="winform">
<INPUT TYPE="button" VALUE="Open New Window"
onClick="NewWin=window.open('','NewWin',
'toolbar=no,status=no,width=200,height=100'); ">
<P><INPUT TYPE="button" VALUE="Close New Window"
onClick="NewWin.close();" >
<P><INPUT TYPE="button" VALUE="Close Main Window"
onClick="window.close();">
</FORM>
<BR>Have fun!
<HR>
</BODY>
</HTML>
```

Again, this example uses event handlers to do its work, one for each of the buttons. Figure 5.3 shows Netscape's display of this page, with the small new window on top.

Figure 5.3.
*A new Netscape
window opened with
JavaScript.*

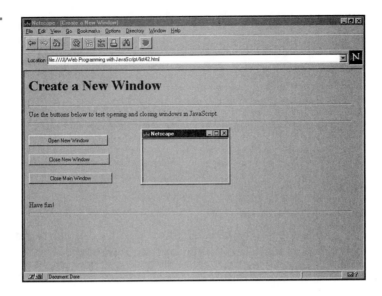

Displaying Dialogs

These dialogs take over
the browser screen until
the user answers them.

The `window` object includes three methods that are useful for displaying messages and
interacting with the user:

❏ The `alert()` method displays an alert dialog box, shown in Figure 5.4. This
dialog simply gives the user a message.

❏ The `confirm()` method displays a confirmation dialog. This displays a
message and includes OK and Cancel buttons. This method returns true if
OK is pressed and false if Cancel is pressed. A confirmation is displayed in
Figure 5.5.

❏ The `prompt()` method displays a message and prompts the user for input. It
returns the text entered by the user.

Figure 5.4.
*A JavaScript alert dialog
displays a message.*

Figure 5.5.
*A JavaScript confirm
dialog asks for
confirmation.*

Using Prompts, Alerts, and Confirmation Dialogs

As a further illustration of these types of dialogs, Listing 5.3 lists an HTML document that uses buttons and event handlers to enable you to test dialogs.

Listing 5.3. (DIALOG.HTM) An HTML document that uses JavaScript to display alerts, confirmations, and prompts.

```
<HTML>
<HEAD><TITLE>Alerts, Confirmations, and Prompts</TITLE>
</HEAD>
<BODY>
<H1>Alerts, Confirmations, and Prompts</H1>
<HR>
Use the buttons below to test dialogs in JavaScript.
<HR>
<FORM NAME="winform">
<INPUT TYPE="button" VALUE="Display an Alert"
onClick="window.alert('This is a test alert.');   ">
<P><INPUT TYPE="button" VALUE="Display a Confirmation"
onClick="temp = window.confirm('Would you like to confirm?');
window.status=(temp)?'confirm: true':'confirm: false'; ">
<P><INPUT TYPE="button" VALUE="Display a Prompt"
onClick="var temp = window.prompt('Enter some Text:','This is the default
value');
window.status=temp;   ">
</FORM>
<BR>Have fun!
<HR>
</BODY>
</HTML>
```

This example displays three buttons, and each uses an event handler to display one of the dialogs. Let's take a detailed look at each one:

❏ The alert dialog is displayed when you click on the button.

❏ The confirmation dialog displays when you press the button, and displays a message in the status line indicating whether true or false was returned. The returned value is stored in the `temp` variable.

❏ The third button displays the prompt dialog. Notice that the `prompt()` method accepts a second parameter, which is used to set a default value for the entry. The value you enter is stored in the `temp` variable and displayed on the status line. Notice that if you press the Cancel button in the prompt dialog, the `null` value is returned.

Figure 5.6 shows the program in Listing 5.3 in action. The prompt dialog is currently displayed and shows the default value, and the status line is still displaying the result of a previous confirmation dialog.

Figure 5.6.

The dialog box example's output, including a prompt dialog.

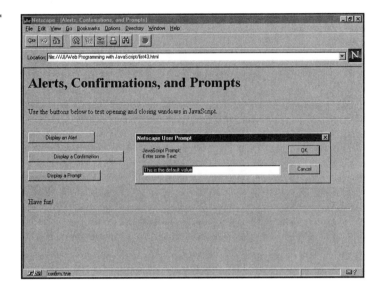

NOTE: Notice that Netscape prefaces each of the dialogs with a message, such as "JavaScript Alert:" or "JavaScript Confirm:". Unfortunately, there is no way to avoid the display of these messages in the present version.

Using Timeouts

Netscape calls them timeouts, but "timers" might be a more appropriate term.

Two more methods of the `window` object enable you to set *timeouts*. These are statements (or groups of statements) that will be executed after a certain amount of time elapses. These are handy for periodically updating a Web page or for delaying a message or function.

You begin a timeout with the `setTimeout()` method. This method has two parameters. The first is a JavaScript statement, or group of statements, enclosed in quotes. The second parameter is the time to wait in milliseconds (thousandths of seconds). For example, this statement displays an alert dialog after 10 seconds:

```
ident=window.setTimeout("alert('Time's up!')",10000);
```

A variable (ident in this example) stores an identifier for the timeout. This enables you to set multiple timeouts, each with its own identifier. Before a timeout has elapsed, you can stop it with the clearTimeout() method, specifying the identifier of the timeout to stop:

```
window.clearTimeout(ident);
```

These timeouts execute only once; they do not repeat unless you set another timeout each time.

Updating a Page with Timeouts

You can make a timeout repeat by issuing the setTimeout() method call again in the function called by the timeout. Listing 5.4 is an HTML document that demonstrates a repeating timeout.

Listing 5.4. (TIMEOUT.HTM) Using the timeout methods to update a page every 2 seconds.

```
<HTML>
<HEAD><TITLE>Timeout Example</TITLE>
<SCRIPT>
var counter = 0;
// call Update function in 2 seconds after first load
ID=window.setTimeout("Update();",2000);
function Update() {
    counter ++;
    window.status="The counter is now at " + counter;
    document.form1.input1.value="The counter is now at " + counter;
// set another timeout for the next count
    ID=window.setTimeout("Update();",2000);
}
</SCRIPT>
</HEAD>
<BODY>
<H1>Timeout Example</H1>
<HR>
The text value below and the status line are being updated every two seconds.
Press the RESET button to restart the count, or the STOP button to stop it.
<HR>
<FORM NAME="form1">
<INPUT TYPE="text" NAME="input1" SIZE="40"><BR>
<INPUT TYPE="button" VALUE="RESET" onClick="counter = 0;"><BR>
<INPUT TYPE="button" VALUE="STOP" onClick="window.clearTimeout(ID);">
<HR>
</BODY>
</HTML>
```

This program displays a message in the status line and in a text field every two seconds, including a counter that increments each time. You can use the RESET button to start the count over and the STOP button to stop the counting.

You must call
`setTimeout()` for each
repetition of a timed
event.

The `setTimeout()` method is used when the page first loads and again at each update. The `Update()` function performs the update, adding one to the counter and setting the next timeout. The RESET button sets the counter to zero, and the STOP button demonstrates the `clearTimeout()` method. Figure 5.7 shows Netscape's display of the timeout example after the counter has been running for a while.

As you can see, timeouts can be useful for performing regular updates to a Web page's fields. You see this further with a scrolling message in Chapter 8 and with a graphical clock display in Chapter 12, " Working with Graphics in JavaScript."

Figure 5.7.

*The output of the
Timeout Example, as
displayed by Netscape.*

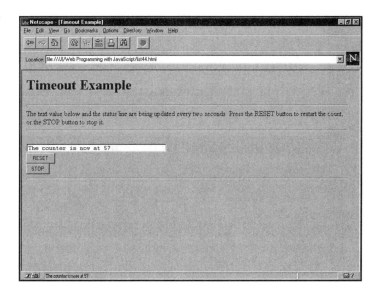

Other `window` Object Methods

The `window` object has three remaining methods, which enable you to manipulate the window itself:

❏ The `scroll()` method scrolls the window, either horizontally or vertically. The parameters are *x* and *y* (column and row) offsets in pixels. For example, `window.scroll(0,10)` scrolls the window down 10 pixels.

❏ The `focus()` method gives a window focus—in other words, brings it to the top. This is handy when you have several windows open.

❏ The `blur()` method is the opposite—it removes focus from the specified window, sending it to the background.

Using window Object Event Handlers

The window object has several event handlers:

❏ The onLoad event occurs when the document in the window is finished loading.

❏ The onUnload event occurs when another document starts to load, replacing the window's current document.

❏ The onFocus event occurs when the window receives focus.

❏ The onBlur event occurs when the window loses focus.

❏ The onError event occurs if the document in the window fails to load properly.

You can specify JavaScript statements or functions for these events using attributes of a Web page's <BODY> tag. For example, Listing 5.5 shows an HTML document that displays an alert message when it is loaded and another when it is unloaded.

Listing 5.5. (ONLOAD.HTM) Using the onLoad and onUnload events to display dialogs.

```
<HTML>
<HEAD><TITLE>onLoad and onUnload Example</TITLE>
</HEAD>
<BODY onLoad="window.alert('Hello, and welcome to this page.');"
onUnload="window.alert('You unloaded the page. Goodbye!');">
<H1>The onLoad and onUnload Methods</H1>
<HR>
This page displays a "hello" dialog when you load it, and a "goodbye"
dialog when you unload it. Annoying, isn't it?
<HR>
This is done through event handlers specified in this document's
&LTBODY&GT tag. Aside from that tag, the rest of the document doesn't
affect the dialogs.
<HR>
</BODY>
</HTML>
```

This document will display a "hello" alert when it loads and a "goodbye" alert when it unloads. You can unload the page by closing the browser window or by loading a different page. Figure 5.8 shows Netscape's display of this document, including the onLoad alert.

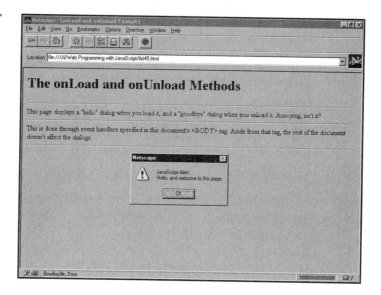

The location Object

The location object is a property of the window object. It contains information about the current URL being displayed by the window. It has a set of properties to hold the different components of the URL, but no methods.

As you know, the URL format is used to specify the location of the Web page. Here is an example of a URL:

```
http://www.starlingtech.com:80/books/javascript/test.html#part2
```

The following are the components of the URL as they correspond with properties of the location object:

- ❏ location.protocol is the protocol (or method) of the URL. This specifies the protocol to be used—world-wide web, gopher, and so forth. In the example, the protocol is http:. The colon is included in the protocol property.

- ❏ location.hostname specifies the host where the resource is located (www.starlingtech.com in the example).

- ❏ location.port specifies the communication port number on the host, usually 80 for the Web (and in the example).

- ❏ location.host is a combination of the host name and port (www.starlingtech.com:80 in the example).

- ❏ location.pathname is the directory to find the document on the host and the name of the file (/books/javascript/test.html in the example).

❏ `location.hash` is the name of an anchor within the document, if specified (`#part2` in the example). You can set this value to different anchor names to jump around the Web page.

❏ `location.target` specifies the TARGET attribute of the link that was used to reach the current location. You will examine this attribute in detail in Chapter 9.

❏ `location.query` specifies a query string; if the location is a CGI program, this string is passed as a parameter to the program.

❏ Finally, `location.href` is the whole URL, including all the parts listed.

You can read the location of the current window by using the properties listed previously. In addition, you can send the user to a new URL by changing the `location` object's properties. For example, this command loads the Sams.net Publishing Web page:

```
window.location.href="http://www.mcp.com/samsnet/"
```

The `location` object has two methods:

❏ `location.reload()` reloads the current document; this is the same as the reload button on Netscape's toolbar.

❏ `location.replace()` replaces the current location with a new one; this is similar to setting the `location` object's properties yourself. The difference is that the new location replaces the current history entry rather than adding to the history.

The document Object

Each window or frame has its own `document` object.

Another child of the `window` object is the `document` object. This object represents the contents of the current HTML Web page. This object includes a wide variety of attributes that specify information about the current page.

In addition, the `document` object includes the `form`, `link`, and `anchor` objects to describe forms, links, and anchors on the page. You will look at each of these later in this chapter. The `document` object has no event handlers of its own.

document Object Properties

The properties of the `document` object represent characteristics of the current HTML page. Many of these are specified in the <BODY> tag of the document, and others are set by the browser when the document is loaded.

NOTE: The only way to modify most of the document object's properties is to change the HTML page itself, or use JavaScript statements within the page to generate HTML dynamically.

Information About the Document

Several properties of the document object include information about the current document in general:

❏ The URL property (formerly location) specifies the document's URL. Don't confuse this with the location object explained earlier: it's a simple text field. You can't change this property; if you need to send the user to a different location, use the window.location.href property.

❏ The title property lists the title of the current page, defined by the HTML <TITLE> tag.

❏ The referrer property is the URL of the page the user was viewing prior to the current page—usually, the page with a link to the current page.

❏ The lastModified property is the date the document was last modified. This date is sent from the server along with the page.

As an example, this is a short HTML document that displays its last-modified date:

```
<HTML><HEAD><TITLE>Test Document</TITLE></HEAD>
<BODY>
This page was last modified on:
<SCRIPT>
document.write(document.lastModified);
</SCRIPT>
<BR>
</HTML>
```

This can be a useful indication to the user of when the page was last changed, and if you use JavaScript, you don't have to remember to update the date each time you modify the page.

CAUTION: The lastModified property doesn't work correctly and may cause crashes in certain platforms and Netscape versions. In addition, some Web servers don't send modification dates properly. See Chapter 14, "Debugging JavaScript Programs," for further information.

Link and Form Information

The next set of properties of the document object concern the links, forms, anchors, and images in the HTML document:

❏ The form objects include information about each <FORM> in the current document.

❏ The anchors array identifies each of the anchors (places that can be jumped to) in the current document.

❏ The links array includes information for each of the links in the current document.

❏ The images array contains information about each of the images in the document.

The forms, anchors, and links objects are each discussed in their own sections later in this chapter. The images array is explained in Chapter 12.

Controlling Document Appearance

You can sometimes change a document's background color "on the fly;" see Chapter 12.

The final set of document object properties are used to store information about color settings for the document. Again, you can't change these directly; they are specified as attributes to the document's <BODY> tag. Here are the available color properties:

❏ bgColor is the background color, specified with the BGCOLOR attribute.

❏ fgColor is the foreground (text) color, specified with the TEXT attribute.

❏ linkColor is the color used for nonvisited links, specified with the LINK attribute.

❏ vlinkColor is the color for visited links, specified with the VLINK attribute.

document Object Methods

In addition to these properties, the document object has a few handy methods. These can be used to control the opening and closing of documents and to output HTML as part of the document.

Writing HTML Text

The simplest document object methods are also the ones you will use most often. In fact, you've used one of them already. The document.write() method prints text as part of the HTML page in a document window. This statement is used whenever you need to include output in a Web page.

An alternative statement, document.writeln(), also prints text, but it also includes a newline (\n) character at the end. This is handy when you want your text to be the last thing on the line.

Bear in mind that the newline character is ignored by HTML, except inside the <PRE> container. You will need to use the <BR> tag if you want an actual line break.

You can only use these methods within the body of the Web page, so they will be executed when the page loads; you can't add to a page that has already loaded. You can write new content for a document, however, as the next section explains.

Opening and Closing Streams

The document object includes open() and close() methods. Unlike the window object methods of the same name, these methods don't actually open and close new documents or windows. Instead, the open() method opens a *stream*; this clears the document and enables you to create a new one with the write() or writeln() methods.

The data you send to a stream isn't actually displayed until the close() method is used. You can use this to ensure that blocks of write commands execute at the same time. Chapter 9 includes an example of using these methods to write new content to a frame.

You can optionally specify a MIME document type in the document.open command. This enables you to create a document of any type, including images and documents used by plug-in applications. You'll learn about plug-ins in detail in Chapter 13, "Working with Multimedia and Plug-ins."

NOTE: When you use the document.open() method, the current document is cleared. Any data already displayed in the document is erased.

Clearing the Document Window

The final document method is the clear() method. It simply clears the document's contents. For example, the following statement clears the main window:

```
document.clear();
```

WARNING: The clear() method doesn't work reliably in most versions of Netscape. The best solution for clearing and updating documents is to use the open() method to clear the document window, use the write() method to write the new contents (or no contents), and then use the `close()` method to close the stream.

The `history` Object

The `history` object is another child (property) of the `window` object. This object holds information about the URLs that have been visited before and after the current one, and it includes methods to go to previous or next locations.

The `history` object has one property: `length`. This keeps track of the length of the history list—in other words, the number of different locations that the user has visited.

You might notice one thing missing from the `history` object's properties: the URLs themselves. These used to be available as a property, but Netscape removed them due to privacy concerns. When they worked, Web pages could grab your history list and use it for statistics, marketing, or even blackmail.

> **NOTE:** The saying "You can't change history" also applies to JavaScript. You can't modify a window's history list or delete items from the list.

The `history` object's methods enable you to send the user to other locations:

- ❏ `history.back()` goes back to the previous location. This is equivalent to the browser's back-arrow button.
- ❏ `history.forward()` goes forward to the next location. This is equivalent to the browser's forward-arrow button.
- ❏ `history.go()` goes to a specified location in the history list. You can specify a positive number to go forward, a negative number to go back, or a string to be searched for in the history list.

Implementing BACK and FORWARD Buttons

As an example of the `history` object's methods, Listing 5.6 shows an HTML page that includes BACK and FORWARD buttons, implemented with JavaScript event handlers. These work in the same way as the browser's back- and forward-arrow buttons. The output of this example is shown in Figure 5.9.

Sidebar: Each window or frame has its own independent history list.

Figure 5.9.
The BACK and FORWARD example's output in Netscape.

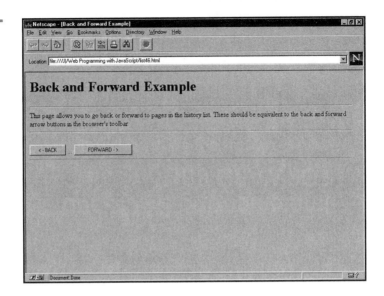

Listing 5.6. A Web page that uses JavaScript to include BACK and FORWARD buttons.

```
<HTML>
<HEAD><TITLE>Back and Forward Example</TITLE>
</HEAD>
<BODY>
<H1>Back and Forward Example</H1>
<HR>
This page allows you to go back or forward to pages in the history list.
These should be equivalent to the back and forward arrow buttons in the
browser's toolbar.
<HR>
<FORM NAME="form1">
<INPUT TYPE="button" VALUE="< - BACK" onClick="history.back();">
...
<INPUT TYPE="button" VALUE="FORWARD - >" onClick="history.forward();">
<HR>
</BODY>
</HTML>
```

The link Object

Another child of the document object is the link object. Actually, there can be multiple link objects in a document. Each one includes information about a link to another location or anchor.

Each link object has a name and an index in the links array.

You can access link objects with the links array. Each member of the array is one of the link objects in the current page. A property of the array, document.links.length, indicates the number of links in the page.

Each link object (or member of the links array) has a list of properties defining the URL. These are the same properties as the location object, defined earlier in this chapter. You can refer to a property by indicating the link number and property name. For example, this statement assigns the variable link1 to the entire URL of the first link (index 0):

```
link1 = links[0].href;
```

TIP: The links array also includes area objects, which are used with client-side image maps. These are explained in Chapter 12.

The link object includes two event handlers:

❑ The onMouseOver event happens when the mouse pointer moves over the link's text.

❑ The onClick event happens when the user clicks on the link.

You'll use the onMouseOver event to create friendly status-line descriptions for links in Chapter 8. As for the onClick event handler, it's very handy for executing a JavaScript function when the user clicks on a link. For example, this defines a link that displays an alert:

```
<a href="#" onClick="window.alert('This is a test.');">
```

Notice that I used a simple # sign as the URL in this example, to avoid sending the user to another page when the link is clicked. Another use for the onClick event handler is to prevent a link from being followed; your event handler can do this by returning false. For example, this link asks for confirmation:

```
<a href="sound.wav" onClick="return window.confirm('play sound?');">
```

If the user clicks the OK button, the link is followed because true is returned; otherwise, false is returned and the link is ignored. This might be handy for files that will take a while to download, or any situation where you want to control links with JavaScript.

The anchor Object

anchor objects are also children of the document object. Each anchor object represents an anchor in the current document—a particular location that can be jumped to directly.

Like links, anchors can be accessed through an array: anchors. Each element of this array is an anchor object. The document.anchors.length property gives you the number of elements in the anchors array.

At least for now, the number of anchors is all you can know. The `anchor` objects don't include the name or locations of the anchors. The exact reason for this is a mystery, but it will hopefully be remedied in a future version of Netscape (or another browser).

`form` Objects

Each `form` object can contain a wide variety of form elements.

Another child of the `document` object is the `form` object, which represents an HTML form. Like anchors and links, there can be several `form` objects within a document. You can access a form by name (specified with the NAME attribute to the `<FORM>` tag) or by using the `forms` array, which includes an element for each form.

The form has many properties that are objects themselves: the *elements*, or components, of the form. These are the text fields, buttons, and other objects that make up a form. You can access these by using their individual names, or once again with an array; the `elements` array indexes each element of the form.

Forms have been used in a few of the examples in this chapter. Because forms are one of the greatest strengths of JavaScript, there's a lot of information to cover. Chapter 6 covers forms and `form` objects in detail.

Workshop Wrap-Up

In this chapter, you took a guided tour of the JavaScript object hierarchy, which contains objects to represent parts of the current window and document:

- ❏ The `window` object represents the browser window or each window in a framed document.
- ❏ The `document` object represents the currently loaded document in a window.
- ❏ The `location` object stores the current location or URL for each window.
- ❏ The `history` object stores the history of documents for a window or frame.
- ❏ The `link` and `anchor` objects store information about links and link targets in a document.
- ❏ The `forms` array, or `form` objects, store information about each form in a document.

Next Steps

You should now know the JavaScript object hierarchy inside and out. Continue with one of these:

- ❏ To learn about built-in objects outside the hierarchy, such as `Math`, `Date`, `Array`, and `String`, see Chapter 4, "Using Built-In Objects and Custom Objects."

❑ To learn to use the objects to work with HTML forms, see Chapter 6, "Using Interactive Forms."

❑ To learn more about using frames and other features of the latest generation of Web browsers, see Chapter 9, "Using Frames, Cookies, and Other Advanced Features."

❑ To see some of the techniques in this chapter in action, see Chapter 7, "Real-Life Examples I."

❑ To learn techniques for perfecting and debugging your JavaScript programs, see Chapter 14, "Debugging JavaScript Programs."

Q&A

Q: Why do I have to specify the `document` object, but not the `window` object, when using its properties and methods?

A: Good question! The reason is that the `window` object contains the current script, so it's treated as a default object. Also, be warned that there are situations in which you shouldn't omit the `window` object's name—when frames or multiple windows are involved, for example, or in an event handler.

Q: When I try to close the current window with `window.close()`, I get an error or no result. Is there a solution?

A: This is another capability that was removed from JavaScript due to a security concern. (The last thing Netscape wants is for people to click on a button and exit Navigator immediately.) You can officially use the `close()` method only on windows that you opened yourself. Some versions of Netscape crash when you attempt to close the main window; the most recent version asks the user for confirmation before closing it.

Q: Why is the text `"JavaScript Alert:"` displayed at the top of all my alert messages? Is there no way to stop this?

A: No, and it's another security feature. Without it, I could make my script display an alert with a message like `"Netscape error: please enter your password"` and get a few unwary users to send me their passwords. (Not that I would do that, of course.)

Q: I want to make a control panel window for my Web page. Is there a way to keep this window on top at all times?

A: No, no easy way; JavaScript doesn't have an "always on top" feature. You could use the `focus()` method in an `onBlur` event handler to make it return to the top, but this doesn't always work.

SIX

Using Interactive Forms

In this chapter you'll explore one of the most powerful uses for JavaScript: working with HTML forms. You can use JavaScript to make a form more interactive, to validate data the user enters, and to enter data based on other data.

Let's begin with a basic order form for an imaginary company and use JavaScript to add features to the form. Along the way you'll learn about the various form elements, how they relate to JavaScript, and just what you can do with each one.

Building a JavaScript-Compatible HTML Form

HTML started out as a read-only language; you could present information to readers and allow them to follow links to sites with different information, but there was no way to accept input from the user.

In this chapter, you

❑ Review the syntax for HTML forms and their elements, and learn to make JavaScript-compatible forms

❑ Learn about the form objects and form elements, and their properties, methods, and event handlers

❑ Use JavaScript to add automatic totals and other automation to a form

❑ Use JavaScript to validate the form's fields before it is submitted

Tasks in this chapter:

❑ Creating an HTML Form
❑ Adding Automatic Totals
❑ Automating the Shipping Address
❑ Creating Functions for Validation
❑ Adding an Event Handler for Validation

One of the most common and most powerful uses of JavaScript is working with forms.

With HTML forms, the Web has become an interactive medium.

The advent of HTML forms changed things considerably. Forms added new HTML tags that could take input from the user. This enables you easily to create a fill-out form to register users or take orders, or for any other purpose.

Before you build a sample form, let's start with a quick overview of the elements you can use in a form. Each of these will relate to a JavaScript object, which is discussed later in this chapter.

Understanding Form Actions and Methods

By itself, an HTML form can only hold information; it can't send it to the server. This part of the job is accomplished by Common Gateway Interface (CGI), a standard for server-side applications. When you press the SUBMIT button on a form, the data in the fields is sent to the CGI program, which can act on the data—mail you a response, send a result back to the user, or add an item to a database.

When you submit the form data, it is sent to the server using one of two methods:

❑ The GET method places the data in the URL itself.

❑ The POST method sends the data as a block of input.

Not all forms send data to the server, but it's the only way to receive data from the user.

You'll learn about the technical aspects of these methods and which you should use in Chapter 17, "Combining JavaScript, CGI, and SSI." Basically, it will depend on the data and on what the CGI script you are using supports. For the moment, you can use either one.

LiveWire is a server-side version of JavaScript, which really can be an alternative to CGI. Learn about it in Chapter 20, "The Future of JavaScript."

Because JavaScript can't communicate with the server, it doesn't eliminate the need for CGI; instead, it enables you to control the data as it is entered and check it for accuracy before the CGI program receives it. This saves you work creating the CGI program. In fact, you can easily use the same CGI program for many different forms. One such script is presented in Chapter 17.

TIP: It is possible to have a JavaScript-only form. You used simple forms in Chapter 5, "Accessing Window Elements as Objects," to interact with the user. You'll find many more examples throughout this book.

After the CGI script receives the data, it sends a response back to the user. This can send the user to a different Web page or can generate a page "on the fly" and display it.

Overview of Form Elements

An HTML form begins with the <FORM> tag. This tag indicates that a form is beginning, and it enables form elements to be used. The <FORM> tag includes three parameters:

- ❑ NAME is simply a name for the form. You can use forms without giving them names, but you'll need to assign a name in order to use the form with JavaScript.
- ❑ METHOD is either GET or POST; these are the two ways the data can be sent to the server.
- ❑ ACTION is the CGI script that the form data will be sent to when submitted. You'll look at an actual script in Chapter 17. You can also use the mailto: action to send the form's results to an e-mail address.

For example, here is a <FORM> tag for a form named Order. This form uses the GET method and sends its data to a CGI script called order.cgi in the same directory as the Web page itself:

```
<FORM NAME="Order" METHOD="GET" ACTION="order.cgi">
```

For a form that will be processed entirely by JavaScript (such as a calculator or interactive game), the METHOD and ACTION attributes are not needed. You can use a simple <FORM> tag that names the form:

```
<FORM NAME="calcform">
```

All form elements must be enclosed within <FORM> tags.

The <FORM> tag is followed by one or more form elements. These are the data fields in the form, such as text fields and checkboxes. You will look at each type of element in the following sections. After all the elements comes the form ending tag, </FORM>. After this tag, you can't use form elements without starting another form.

NOTE: You can also include any normal HTML elements within the <FORM> tags. This is useful for labeling each of the elements.

Text Fields and Text Areas

Many of the form elements use the <INPUT> tag. This tag is followed by a TYPE parameter to determine which type of input is expected. The first such field is the TEXT field. This is the simplest of the form elements; it enables the user to enter text in a one-line area. The following is an example of a simple TEXT field:

```
<INPUT TYPE="TEXT" NAME="text1" VALUE="hello" SIZE="30">
```

This defines a text field called `text1`. The field is given a default value of `"hello"` and allows up to 30 characters to be entered.

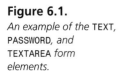

Text fields are typically used for names, addresses, or other single-line items.

An alternate form of text field is the PASSWORD field. This is a specialized text field that displays the text as asterisks on the screen. This type of input is often used for passwords so that observers don't see which password is being entered. The password field is defined like TEXT:

```
<INPUT TYPE="PASSWORD" NAME="pass1" SIZE=30>
```

A third option is the text area, which allows multiple lines of text to be entered. Rather than using the `<INPUT>` tag, text areas are defined with a special tag, `<TEXTAREA>`. Here is a typical `<TEXTAREA>` definition:

```
<TEXTAREA NAME="text1" ROWS="2" COLS="70">
This is the content of the TEXTAREA tag.
</TEXTAREA>
```

A text area can be used to hold a comment area, e-mail message, or entire document.

The text between the opening and closing `<TEXTAREA>` tags is used as the initial value for the text area. This type of tag is ideal when you need a larger amount of information, such as a complete address or a paragraph of text. You can include line breaks within the default value.

Figure 6.1 shows examples of TEXT, PASSWORD, and TEXTAREA tags on an HTML page, as displayed by Netscape.

Figure 6.1.

An example of the TEXT, PASSWORD, *and* TEXTAREA *form elements.*

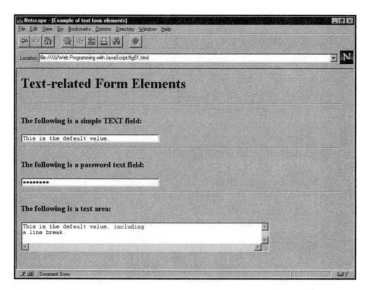

Checkboxes, Radio Buttons, and Selection Lists

For some parts of your form, you may want to ask simple questions: yes/no questions, multiple-choice questions, and so on. Three form elements make it easy to do this.

Checkboxes are perfect for yes/no questions.

The first element is the checkbox; this simply displays a box that can be checked or unchecked. The CHECKBOX type to the INPUT tag is used to create a checkbox, as follows:

```
<INPUT TYPE="CHECKBOX" NAME="check1" VALUE="Yes" CHECKED>
```

Again, this gives a name to the form element. The VALUE attribute assigns a meaning to the checkbox; this is a value that is returned if the box is checked. The default value is "on." Finally, the CHECKED attribute can be included to make the box checked by default.

Another element for decisions is the radio button, using the <INPUT> tag's RADIO type. These buttons are similar to checkboxes, but they exist in groups, and only one button can be checked in each group. These are used for a multiple-choice or "one of many" input. Here's an example of a group of radio buttons:

```
<INPUT TYPE="RADIO" NAME="radio1" VALUE="Option1" CHECKED> Option 1
<INPUT TYPE="RADIO" NAME="radio1" VALUE="Option2"> Option 2
<INPUT TYPE="RADIO" NAME="radio1" VALUE="Option3"> Option 3
```

For multiple-choice questions, you can use radio buttons or selection lists.

Once again, the NAME attribute is used; in this case, it names the entire group of radio buttons. All the buttons with the same name are considered to be in a group. The VALUE attribute gives each button a name; this is essential so that you can tell which one is pressed.

A final form element is also useful for multiple-choice selections: the <SELECT> HTML tag is used to define a *selection list*, or a multiple-choice list of text items. This is an example of a selection list:

```
<SELECT NAME="select1" SIZE=40>
<OPTION VALUE="choice1" SELECTED>This is the first choice.
<OPTION VALUE="choice2">This is the second choice.
<OPTION VALUE="choice3">This is the third choice.
</SELECT>
```

Each of the OPTION tags defines one of the possible choices. The VALUE attribute is the name that is returned to the program, and the text outside the OPTION tag is displayed as the text of the option.

An optional attribute to the SELECT tag, MULTIPLE, can be specified to allow multiple items to be selected. Browsers usually display a single-selection SELECT as a drop-down list and a multiple-selection list as a scrollable list.

Figure 6.2 is an example of an HTML page in Netscape that shows examples of checkboxes, radio buttons, and single- and multiple-selection lists.

Hidden Fields

HTML form elements include a special type of field: the hidden field. This includes a name and a value, similar to a text field; however, you can't edit it, and it is not displayed on the Web page. Hidden fields are useful for passing information to the CGI script or between multiple scripts.

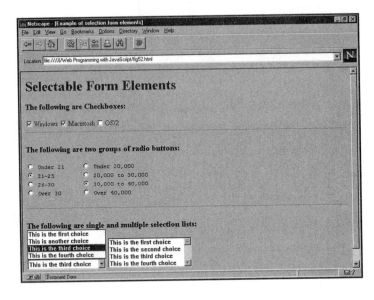

A hidden field uses the <INPUT> tag and simply has a name and a value. For example, this command defines a hidden field called score with a value of 40200:

```
<INPUT TYPE="HIDDEN" NAME="score" VALUE="40200">
```

SUBMIT and RESET Buttons

The final type of form element is a button. Buttons use the <INPUT> tag and can use one of three different types:

❑ type=SUBMIT is a submit button. This button causes the data in the form fields to be sent to the CGI script.

❑ type=RESET is a reset button. This button sets all the form fields back to their default value, or blank.

❑ type=BUTTON is a generic button. This button performs no action on its own, but you can assign it one using JavaScript.

Buttons of type BUTTON are useful for JavaScript, but should not be used with CGI.

All three types of buttons include a NAME to identify the button, and a VALUE that indicates the text to display on the button's face. A few buttons were used in the examples in Chapter 5. As an example, the following defines a SUBMIT button with the name sub1 and the value "Click Here":

```
<INPUT TYPE="SUBMIT" NAME="sub1" VALUE="Click Here">
```

Creating an HTML Form

Using the form elements discussed, let's create an order form for a fictional software company called, coincidentally enough, Fictional Software Company (FSC). This company sells four products: a word processor, a spreadsheet, a database, and an instruction booklet. You will use the following elements:

- ❏ Text fields for the buyer's name, phone number, and e-mail address, and text areas for the billing and shipping address.

- ❏ Because the company has only four products, there's room to list them all on the form. Each has its own text fields for quantity and cost.

- ❏ A total cost text field is used to store the total cost. The user then selects the method of payment from the selection list and enters a credit card number or check number if needed.

- ❏ Finally, a SUBMIT button enables users to send the order, and a RESET button enables them to start over with the defaults.

Listing 6.1 shows the complete HTML form, and Figure 6.3 shows Netscape's display of the form.

Listing 6.1. The HTML document for the order form.

```
<HTML>
<HEAD><TITLE>Order Form</TITLE></HEAD>
<BODY>
<H1>Order Form</H1>
<FORM NAME="order">
<B>Name:</B> <INPUT TYPE="text" NAME="name1" SIZE=20>
<B>Phone: </B><INPUT TYPE="text" NAME="phone" SIZE=15>
<B>E-mail address:</B><INPUT TYPE="text" NAME="email" SIZE=20><BR>
<B>Billing and Shipping Addresses:</B><BR>
<TEXTAREA NAME="billto" COLS=40 ROWS=4>
Enter your billing address here.
</TEXTAREA>
<TEXTAREA NAME="shipto" COLS=40 ROWS=4>
Enter your shipping address here.
</TEXTAREA>
<B>Products to Order:</B><BR>
Qty: <INPUT TYPE="TEXT" NAME="qty1" VALUE="0" SIZE=4>
Cost: <INPUT TYPE="TEXT" NAME="cost1" SIZE=6>
($40.00 ea) Fictional Spreadsheet 7.0 <BR>
Qty: <INPUT TYPE="TEXT" NAME="qty2" VALUE="0" SIZE=4>
Cost: <INPUT TYPE="TEXT" NAME="cost2" SIZE=6>
($69.95 ea) Fictional Word Processor 6.0<BR>
Qty: <INPUT TYPE="TEXT" NAME="qty3" VALUE="0" SIZE=4>
Cost: <INPUT TYPE="TEXT" NAME="cost3" SIZE=6>
($99.95 ea) Fictional Database 7.0 <BR>
Qty: <INPUT TYPE="TEXT" NAME="qty4" VALUE="0" SIZE=4>
Cost: <INPUT TYPE="TEXT" NAME="cost4" SIZE=6>
```

continues

Listing 6.1. continued

```
($4.95 ea) Instruction Booklet for the above <HR>
<B>Total Cost:</B>
<INPUT TYPE="TEXT" NAME="totalcost" SIZE=8><HR>
<B>Method of Payment</B>:
<SELECT NAME="payby">
<OPTION VALUE="check" SELECTED>Check or Money Order
<OPTION VALUE="cash">Cash or Cashier's Check
<OPTION VALUE="credit">Credit Card (specify number)
</SELECT><BR>
<B>Credit Card or Check Number:</B>:
<INPUT TYPE="TEXT" NAME="creditno" SIZE="20"><BR>
<INPUT TYPE="SUBMIT" NAME="submit" VALUE="Send Your Order">
<INPUT TYPE="RESET" VALUE="Start Over">
</FORM>
</BODY>
</HTML>
```

Figure 6.3.
The first draft of the FSC order form.

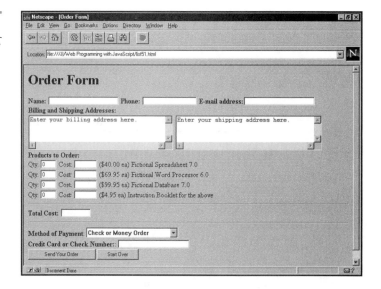

Forms like this one are used all over the Web. As you can see, this form isn't very user-friendly; the user has to calculate the cost for each item and the total cost. You will use JavaScript to add automatic calculation and other interactive features later in this chapter.

Using `form` Objects in JavaScript

Remember, each `form` object is part of the `forms` array and a child of the `document` object.

Before you continue working with the order form, let's look at the way JavaScript handles form data. Each form in your HTML page is represented in JavaScript by a `form` object. The `form` object has the same name as the `NAME` attribute in the `<FORM>` tag you used to define it.

Alternately, you can use the `forms` array to refer to forms. This array includes an item for each form element, indexed starting with zero. For example, if the first form in a document has the name `form1`, you can refer to it in one of two ways:

```
document.form1
document.forms[0]
```

form Object Properties

The most important property of the `form` object is the `elements` array, which contains an object for each of the form elements. You can refer to an element by its own name or by its index in the array. For example, these expressions both refer to the first element in the `order` form, the `name1` text field:

```
document.order.elements[0]
document.order.name1
```

NOTE:
Both forms and elements can be referred to with their own names, or as indices in the `forms` and `elements` arrays. For clarity, this chapter will use individual form and element names rather than array references.

If you do refer to forms and elements as arrays, you can use the `length` property to determine the number of objects in the array: `document.forms.length` is the number of forms in a document, and `document.form1.elements.length` is the number of elements in the `form1` form.

Some form attributes are read-only and cannot be set by JavaScript.

Along with the elements, each `form` object also has a list of properties, most of which are defined by the corresponding `<FORM>` tag. You can also set these from within JavaScript. They include the following:

- ❏ `action` is the form's `ACTION` attribute, or the program to which the form data will be submitted.
- ❏ `encoding` is the `MIME` type of the form, specified with the `ENCTYPE` attribute. In most cases, this is not needed.
- ❏ `length` is the number of elements in the form.
- ❏ `method` is the method used to submit the form, either `GET` or `POST`.
- ❏ `target` specifies the window in which the result of the form (from the CGI script) will be displayed. Normally, this is done in the main window, replacing the form itself.

`form` Object Methods and Events

The `form` object has two event handlers, `onSubmit` and `onReset`. You can specify a group of JavaScript statements or a function call for these events within the `<FORM>` tag that defines the form.

If you specify a statement or function for the `onSubmit` event, the statement is called before the data is submitted to the CGI script. You can prevent the submission from happening by returning a value of `false` from the `onSubmit` event handler. If the statement returns `true`, the data will be submitted. In the same fashion, you can prevent a RESET button from working with an `onReset` event handler.

The `form` object has two methods, `submit()` and `reset()`. You can use these methods to submit the data or reset the form yourself, without requiring the user to press a button. The `submit()` method should be used only in special cases; it's generally bad manners to send data to the server without the user's permission.

NOTE: You can use a `mailto` URL in the ACTION attribute of a form and have the data mailed to you instead of submitted to a CGI script. Using the `submit()` method with such an action enabled scripts to obtain information about your computer or to send mail from your address without your knowledge. Because of this potential security and privacy concern, Netscape disabled the submit method for mailto URLs.

The JavaScript `form` Object Hierarchy

The elements of a form each have their own object classes, and each of these has certain properties, methods, and events. In the next sections, you will look at each type of JavaScript object used for form elements in detail.

The rest of the object hierarchy is explained in Chapter 5.

One property applies to all form elements: the `type` property is a string that describes the type of element. For most of the elements, this is the value you specified in the TYPE attribute of the `<INPUT>` tag. The exceptions are the following:

- ❏ For text areas (defined with `<TEXTAREA>`), the type is `"textarea"`.
- ❏ For single selection lists (defined with `<SELECT>`), the type is `"select-one"`.
- ❏ For selection lists that include the MULTIPLE attribute, the type is `"select-multiple"`.

Another property that applies to all `form` elements is the `form property`, which indicates an element's parent `form object`.

Text Fields and Password Fields

Text fields are the simplest field to work with in JavaScript. Password fields are nearly identical; the main difference is that the text is not displayed. The text and password objects have the following properties:

- name is the name given to the field. This is also used as the object name.
- defaultValue is the default value; this corresponds to the VALUE attribute. This is a read-only property.
- value is the current value. This starts out the same as the default value, but can be changed—either by the user or by JavaScript functions.

Most of the time when you work with text fields, you will use the value attribute to read the value the user has entered, or to change the value. For example, this statement changes the value of a text field called username in the order form to "John Q. User":

```
document.order.username.value = "John Q. User"
```

NOTE: For security reasons, you cannot normally access the value property of a password object in JavaScript. You can access it if you enable data tainting, as explained in Chapter 10, "Working with Multiple Pages and Data."

Text Field Methods

The text and password objects also have a few methods you can use:

- focus() sets the focus to the field. This positions the cursor in the field and makes it the "current" field.
- blur() is the opposite; it removes the focus from the field.
- select() selects the text in the field, just as a user can do with the mouse. You cannot currently select only part of a field.

TIP: These aren't the only methods you can use with text fields; don't forget that because the value property is a string object, you can use any of the string methods on the value. The string object is explained in Chapter 4, "Using Built-In Objects and Custom Objects."

Text Field Events

The `text` and `password` objects support the following event handlers:

- ❏ The `onFocus` event happens when the text field gains focus.
- ❏ The `onBlur` event happens when the text field loses focus.
- ❏ The `onChange` event happens when the user changes the text in the field, then moves out of it.
- ❏ The `onSelect` event happens when the user selects some or all of the text in the field. Unfortunately, there's no way to tell exactly which part of the text was selected.

If used, these event handlers should be included in the `<INPUT>` tag declaration. For example, the following is a text field including an `onChange` event that displays an alert:

```
<INPUT TYPE="TEXT" NAME="text1" onChange="window.alert('Changed.');">
```

Text Areas

Text areas are defined with their own tag, `<TEXTAREA>`, and are represented by the `textarea` object. This object includes the same properties, methods, and event handlers as the `text` and `password` objects. For example, this `<TEXTAREA>` tag includes an `onFocus` event handler to change the status line:

```
<TEXTAREA NAME="text2" onFocus = "window.status = 'got focus.';">Default
Value</TEXTAREA>
```

There is one difference about a text area's value: it can include more than one line, with end-of-line characters between. This can be complicated by the fact that the end-of-line character is different on the three platforms (`\r\n` in Windows; `\n` in UNIX and Macintosh). Be sure to check for both types when needed.

If you are placing your own values into a text field, the latest version of JavaScript automatically converts any end-of-line characters to match the user's platform, so you can use either type.

NOTE: This is an example of a platform-specific issue within JavaScript; although JavaScript is intended as a platform-independent language, there are still a few stubborn features. See Chapter 14, "Debugging JavaScript Programs," for additional information.

Checkboxes

A checkbox is simple: it has only two states. Nevertheless, the checkbox object has four different properties:

- ❏ name is the name of the checkbox, and also the object name.
- ❏ value is the "true" value for the checkbox—usually on. This value is used by the server to indicate that the checkbox was checked. In JavaScript, you should use the checked property instead.
- ❏ defaultChecked is the default status of the checkbox, assigned by the CHECKED attribute.
- ❏ checked is the current value (true for checked, and false for unchecked).

To manipulate the checkbox or use its value, you use the checked attribute. For example, this statement turns on a checkbox called same in the order form:

```
document.order.same.checked = true;
```

The checkbox has a single method, click(). This method simulates a click on the box. It also has a single event, onClick, which occurs whenever the checkbox is clicked. This happens whether the box was turned on or off, so you'll need to check the checked property.

CAUTION: The click() method does not work properly in some versions of Netscape. You should avoid it when possible.

Radio Buttons

Radio buttons are similar to checkboxes, but an entire group of them shares a single name and a single object. You can refer to the following properties of the radio object:

- ❏ name is the name common to the radio buttons.
- ❏ length is the number of radio buttons in the group.

To access individual buttons, you treat the radio object as an array. The buttons are indexed, starting with 0. Each individual button has the following properties:

- ❏ value is the value assigned to the button. (This is used by the server.)
- ❏ defaultChecked indicates the value of the CHECKED attribute and the default state of the button.
- ❏ checked is the current state.

For example, you can check the first radio button in the radio1 group on the form1 form with this statement:

```
document.form1.radio1[0].checked = true;
```

However, if you do this, be sure you set the other values to false as needed. This is not done automatically. You can use the click method to do both of these in one step.

Like a checkbox, radio buttons have a click() method and an onClick event handler. Each radio button can have a separate statement for this event.

NOTE: A bug in Netscape Navigator 2.0 causes radio buttons to be indexed backward; index 0 will actually be the last button on the page. This is fixed in version 3.0 and later, but watch out for strange behavior when users use an old version.

Selection Lists

Selection lists enable either a single choice or multiple choices.

A selection list is similar to radio buttons, because the entire group of options shares a name. In this case, the data for each element is stored in the options array, which indexes the different options starting with 0.

The object for selection lists is the select object. The object itself has the following properties:

- ❏ name is the name of the selection list.
- ❏ length is the number of options in the list.
- ❏ options is the array of options (explained later).
- ❏ selectedIndex returns the index value of the currently selected item. You can use this to check the value easily. In a multiple-selection list, this indicates the first selected item.

The options array has a single property of its own, length, which indicates the number of selections. In addition, each item in the options array has the following properties:

- ❏ index is the index into the array.
- ❏ defaultSelected indicates the state of the SELECTED attribute.
- ❏ selected is the current state of the option. Setting this property to true selects the option. You can select multiple options if the MULTIPLE attribute is included in the <SELECT> tag.
- ❏ name is the value of the NAME attribute. This is used by the server.

❑ text is the text that is displayed in the option. In Netscape 3.0 or later, you can change this value.

The select object has two methods, blur() and focus(). These perform the same purpose as the corresponding methods for text objects. The event handlers are onBlur, onFocus, and onChange, also similar to other objects.

You can change selection lists dynamically—for example, choosing a product in one list could control which options are available in another list. You can also add and delete options from the list. You will look at these capabilities in Chapter 11, "Real-Life Examples II."

NOTE:
The onChange event doesn't work for select lists in some versions of Netscape . It does work properly in version 3.0 and later.

Hidden Fields

Hidden fields are stored in hidden objects. This object has two properties, name and value. These function similarly to a text field. There are no methods or event handlers for the hidden object—it can't be changed, so the user can't really mess with a hidden field.

Buttons

Buttons can be defined as SUBMIT buttons, RESET buttons, or generic BUTTON buttons. All of these types have the same properties, methods, and events.

Buttons support the name property, used to identify the button, and the value property, which defines the button's text. You cannot change either of these values. Buttons support a single method, click(), and an event handler, onClick.

The onClick action is performed with any button. In the case of a generic button, nothing else happens. In a SUBMIT or RESET button, you can prevent the submission or resetting by returning a false value.

NOTE:
As with radio buttons and checkboxes, the click method may not work with some older versions of Netscape. Check your version before attempting to use it, and expect trouble from users of older versions.

File Upload Fields

A relatively new feature of Netscape enables you to define a *file upload* field on a form. This enables the user to upload a file to the server. You can define a file upload field with an `<INPUT>` tag:

```
<INPUT TYPE="file" NAME="fname">
```

Because this field is mainly for interacting with the server, JavaScript has little control over it. A `FileUpload` object represents the field, and you can access two properties:

- ❏ `name` is the name of the field, as defined in the `<INPUT>` tag.
- ❏ `value` is the name of the file (if any) the user is uploading.

Automating the Form with JavaScript

JavaScript can help the user avoid redundant typing in a form.

You now have quite a bit of information about the many form-related objects and how they can be used in JavaScript. Let's bring this information into the real world by demonstrating how you can add friendly, interactive features to the FSC order form created earlier in this chapter.

Adding Automatic Totals

At present, the order form isn't any more convenient than a paper one—the user still has to calculate the total for each item and the grand total manually. Let's use JavaScript to make those functions automatic. You will do this with the onChange event handler, so each time a quantity is changed, the associated totals will be updated.

To start with, you will make each item's cost field update when its quantity field is changed. To do this, you'll use the onChange event handler for each of the quantity text fields. For example, here's what the first one will look like:

```
Qty: <INPUT TYPE="TEXT" NAME="qty1" VALUE="0" SIZE=4
onChange = "UpdateCost(1, 40.00);">
```

This calls a function called UpdateCost(), which takes two parameters: the item number to update (1 through 4) and the associated unit cost. You then need to define the UpdateCost() function in the HTML header. Here's the function:

```
// function to update cost when quantity is changed
function UpdateCost(number, unitcost) {
   costname = "cost" + number;
   qtyname = "qty" + number;
   var q = document.order[qtyname].value;
   document.order[costname].value = q * unitcost;
   Total();
}
```

This function stores the item number and unit cost in the `number` and `unitcost` variables. It then constructs names for the cost and quantity elements; because they have been named consistently (such as `qty1` through `qty4`), this is simple.

A temporary variable, `q`, is used to hold the quantity field's current value. Notice that you have to use brackets around `qtyname`, because you want to use the value of this variable, not its actual name. The quantity in `q` is then multiplied by the unit cost and stored in the appropriate cost text field.

Finally, you include a function call for the `Total()` function, which will calculate the total cost each time a field is changed. Here is the definition for this function:

```
// function to calculate the total cost field
function Total() {
   var tot = 0;
   tot += (40.00 * document.order.qty1.value);
   tot += (69.95 * document.order.qty2.value);
   tot += (99.95 * document.order.qty3.value);
   tot += (4.95 * document.order.qty4.value);
   document.order.totalcost.value = tot;
}
```

This function simply uses a temporary variable called `tot` to add up each of the costs, which it gets by multiplying the appropriate prices by the quantities. It then stores the value of `tot` in the total cost text field.

Listing 6.2 shows the revised HTML order form including the new functions. You now have an order form that updates automatically—each time you enter or change a quantity, the cost for that item and the total cost are updated. Figure 6.4 shows the order form after several quantities have been entered.

Figure 6.4.

The order form with automatically updated numeric totals.

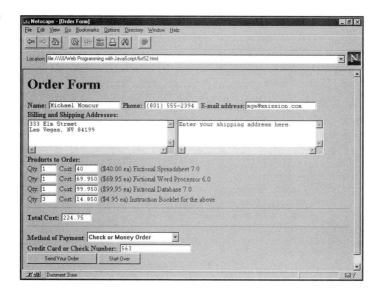

Listing 6.2. The revised HTML order form, including automatic update functions.

```
<HTML>
<HEAD><TITLE>Order Form</TITLE>
<SCRIPT>
// function to calculate the total cost field
function Total() {
   var tot = 0;
   tot += (40.00 * document.order.qty1.value);
   tot += (69.95 * document.order.qty2.value);
   tot += (99.95 * document.order.qty3.value);
   tot += (4.95 * document.order.qty4.value);
   document.order.totalcost.value = tot;
}

// function to update cost when quantity is changed
function UpdateCost(number, unitcost) {
   costname = "cost" + number;
   qtyname = "qty" + number;
   var q = document.order[qtyname].value;
   document.order[costname].value = q * unitcost;
   Total();
}
</SCRIPT>
</HEAD>
<BODY>
<H1>Order Form</H1>
<FORM NAME="order">
<B>Name:</B> <INPUT TYPE="text" NAME="name1" SIZE=20>
<B>Phone: </B><INPUT TYPE="text" NAME="phone" SIZE=15>
<B>E-mail address:</B><INPUT TYPE="text" NAME="email" SIZE=20><BR>
<B>Billing and Shipping Addresses:</B><BR>
<TEXTAREA NAME="billto" COLS=40 ROWS=4>
Enter your billing address here.
</TEXTAREA>
<TEXTAREA NAME="shipto" COLS=40 ROWS=4>
Enter your shipping address here.
</TEXTAREA>
<B>Products to Order:</B><BR>
Qty: <INPUT TYPE="TEXT" NAME="qty1" VALUE="0" SIZE=4
onChange = "UpdateCost(1, 40.00);">
Cost: <INPUT TYPE="TEXT" NAME="cost1" SIZE=6>
($40.00 ea) Fictional Spreadsheet 7.0 <BR>
Qty: <INPUT TYPE="TEXT" NAME="qty2" VALUE="0" SIZE=4
onChange = "UpdateCost(2, 69.95);">
Cost: <INPUT TYPE="TEXT" NAME="cost2" SIZE=6>
($69.95 ea) Fictional Word Processor 6.0<BR>
Qty: <INPUT TYPE="TEXT" NAME="qty3" VALUE="0" SIZE=4
onChange = "UpdateCost(3, 99.95);">
Cost: <INPUT TYPE="TEXT" NAME="cost3" SIZE=6>
($99.95 ea) Fictional Database 7.0 <BR>
Qty: <INPUT TYPE="TEXT" NAME="qty4" VALUE="0" SIZE=4
onChange = "UpdateCost(4, 4.95);">
Cost: <INPUT TYPE="TEXT" NAME="cost4" SIZE=6>
($4.95 ea) Instruction Booklet for the above <HR>
<B>Total Cost:</B>
<INPUT TYPE="TEXT" NAME="totalcost" SIZE=8><HR>
```

```
<B>Method of Payment</B>:
<SELECT NAME="payby">
<OPTION VALUE="check" SELECTED>Check or Money Order
<OPTION VALUE="cash">Cash or Cashier's Check
<OPTION VALUE="credit">Credit Card (specify number)
</SELECT><BR>
<B>Credit Card or Check Number:</B>:
<INPUT TYPE="TEXT" NAME="creditno" SIZE="20"><BR>
<INPUT TYPE="SUBMIT" NAME="submit" VALUE="Send Your Order">
<INPUT TYPE="RESET" VALUE="Start Over">
</FORM>
</BODY>
</HTML>
```

 # Automating the Shipping Address

Because the order form includes spaces for separate billing and shipping addresses, it's a good idea to give the user an option to use the same address for both. Using JavaScript, you can add such an option easily—and it makes for a neat bit of automation.

To accomplish this, you'll add a checkbox above the addresses and label it:

```
<INPUT TYPE="CHECKBOX" NAME="same" onClick="CopyAddress();">
Ship to Billing Address
```

You'll use the onClick event handler for the checkbox to handle the copying. Here is the CopyAddress function for copying the address:

```
// function to copy billing address to shipping address
function CopyAddress() {
   if (document.order.same.checked) {
      document.order.shipto.value = document.order.billto.value;
   }
}
```

This function checks the checked property of the checkbox, and if it's currently checked, it copies the billing address to the shipping address.

This works when the checkbox is checked, but what about when the user changes the billing address after checking the box? You will use the onChange event handler to do the copy again whenever the billing address changes:

```
<TEXTAREA NAME="billto" COLS=40 ROWS=4 onChange="CopyAddress();">
Enter your billing address here.
</TEXTAREA>
```

Be sure to account for anything the user might do when automating a form.

There's one possibility left: after checking the box, the user might mistakenly change the shipping address. Because you want the addresses to be the same, you use the same event handler on the shipping address. Therefore, when the user changes the shipping address with the box checked, it will immediately be changed back to the billing address.

Listing 6.3 is the latest version of the HTML form, including the automatic address-copying function you just added. Figure 6.5 shows how the new form looks in Netscape.

Figure 6.5.

The order form with address-copying feature.

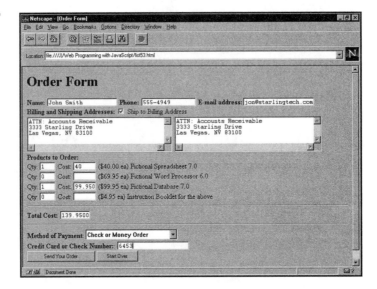

Listing 6.3. The revised HTML order form with the address-copying features.

```
<HTML>
<HEAD><TITLE>Order Form</TITLE>
<SCRIPT>
// function to calculate the total cost field
function Total() {
   var tot = 0;
   tot += (40.00 * document.order.qty1.value);
   tot += (69.95 * document.order.qty2.value);
   tot += (99.95 * document.order.qty3.value);
   tot += (4.95 * document.order.qty4.value);
   document.order.totalcost.value = tot;
}

// function to update cost when quantity is changed
function UpdateCost(number, unitcost) {
   costname = "cost" + number;
   qtyname = "qty" + number;
   var q = document.order[qtyname].value;
   document.order[costname].value = q * unitcost;
   Total();
}

// function to copy billing address to shipping address
function CopyAddress() {
```

```
        if (document.order.same.checked) {
            document.order.shipto.value = document.order.billto.value;
        }
    }

</SCRIPT>
</HEAD>
<BODY>
<H1>Order Form</H1>
<FORM NAME="order">
<B>Name:</B> <INPUT TYPE="text" NAME="name1" SIZE=20>
<B>Phone: </B><INPUT TYPE="text" NAME="phone" SIZE=15>
<B>E-mail address:</B><INPUT TYPE="text" NAME="email" SIZE=20><BR>
<B>Billing and Shipping Addresses:</B>
<INPUT TYPE="CHECKBOX" NAME="same" onClick="CopyAddress();">
Ship to Billing Address
<BR>
<TEXTAREA NAME="billto" COLS=40 ROWS=4 onChange="CopyAddress();">
Enter your billing address here.
</TEXTAREA>
<TEXTAREA NAME="shipto" COLS=40 ROWS=4 onChange="CopyAddress();">
Enter your shipping address here.
</TEXTAREA>
<B>Products to Order:</B><BR>
Qty: <INPUT TYPE="TEXT" NAME="qty1" VALUE="0" SIZE=4
onChange = "UpdateCost(1, 40.00);">
Cost: <INPUT TYPE="TEXT" NAME="cost1" SIZE=6>
($40.00 ea) Fictional Spreadsheet 7.0 <BR>
Qty: <INPUT TYPE="TEXT" NAME="qty2" VALUE="0" SIZE=4
onChange = "UpdateCost(2, 69.95);">
Cost: <INPUT TYPE="TEXT" NAME="cost2" SIZE=6>
($69.95 ea) Fictional Word Processor 6.0<BR>
Qty: <INPUT TYPE="TEXT" NAME="qty3" VALUE="0" SIZE=4
onChange = "UpdateCost(3, 99.95);">
Cost: <INPUT TYPE="TEXT" NAME="cost3" SIZE=6>
($99.95 ea) Fictional Database 7.0 <BR>
Qty: <INPUT TYPE="TEXT" NAME="qty4" VALUE="0" SIZE=4
onChange = "UpdateCost(4, 4.95);">
Cost: <INPUT TYPE="TEXT" NAME="cost4" SIZE=6>
($4.95 ea) Instruction Booklet for the above <HR>
<B>Total Cost:</B>
<INPUT TYPE="TEXT" NAME="totalcost" SIZE=8><HR>
<B>Method of Payment</B>:
<SELECT NAME="payby">
<OPTION VALUE="check" SELECTED>Check or Money Order
<OPTION VALUE="cash">Cash or Cashier's Check
<OPTION VALUE="credit">Credit Card (specify number)
</SELECT><BR>
<B>Credit Card or Check Number:</B>:
<INPUT TYPE="TEXT" NAME="creditno" SIZE="20"><BR>
<INPUT TYPE="SUBMIT" NAME="submit" VALUE="Send Your Order">
<INPUT TYPE="RESET" VALUE="Start Over">
</FORM>
</BODY>
</HTML>
```

Validating the Form Data with Event Handlers

Form validation is one of the most important uses for JavaScript.

The final feature you can add to a form with JavaScript is perhaps the most important: validation. This means checking each field to ensure that it contains a proper value and advising the user if it is incorrect.

Obviously, validating can only do so much. For example, you can't tell whether a phone number is valid or whether a name is an alias. You can tell whether it exists, though, and whether it's in the right format.

Validation saves you some trouble when you receive a response. More importantly, it saves you the trouble of performing the validation in the CGI script. This enables you to use a generic CGI script, and enables the user to receive immediate feedback without waiting on the server.

Where to Validate?

You could use the onChange event handler on each of the fields to validate it. For example, as soon as users enter their names and move to the next field, you could alert them if the names are invalid.

This method is worth considering in some cases, but for most forms it's best to validate all the fields at once, using the form's onSubmit event handler. This enables users to correct any fields necessary, then press submit when they're really ready.

For the FSC order form, you will use a single onSubmit event handler to perform the validation for all the fields.

TIP: If you choose to validate fields as they change, you might find it useful to use the this keyword. Within an event handler, this represents the object that triggered the event. This technique enables you to use a single validation routine for several fields.

Which Fields to Validate?

Validation can't be perfect, but it can eliminate most simple errors.

When choosing how to handle validation for a form, the first step is to decide which fields you need to validate and what to check for. For some items, such as a name, the most you can do is see whether anything is entered.

For other items you can be more specific; for example, if your form asked for the user's age, you can check for numbers over 100 or so. (I would suggest a lower limit, but the Internet audience is getting younger every day.)

For the FSC order form, let's use the following validation criteria:

❑ The name must be at least 6 characters, and the billing address and shipping address must be at least 30 characters. The phone number must be at least 10 characters. (You want them to include the area code.)

❑ The e-mail address must be at least 5 characters and include the @ symbol.

❑ Because the cost fields are calculated automatically, you won't bother validating them. However, you'll check the total cost; if it's 0 or blank, they haven't ordered anything.

❑ If the payment method is anything but cash, the credit card number/check number field must be at least 2 characters.

Obviously, you could make some of these more specific, but they'll do to illustrate the concept. You'll need to choose the appropriate values for each form with which you work.

 # Creating Functions for Validation

Based on the decisions made previously, you now need to create a function to handle each of the fields. In some cases, you can use the same function for multiple fields. Let's start with the simplest function: checking for the proper length. This function will work with the name, billing address, and phone number fields.

```
function ValidLength(item, len) {
   return (item.length >= len);
}
```

This function expects the name of an item and the required length. It simply checks whether the item is greater than or equal to that length, and it returns true or false appropriately.

Next, let's create a function for the e-mail address. This will simply call the ValidLength function to check the length, then use the indexOf string method to check for the @ sign:

```
//function to validate an email address
function ValidEmail(item) {
   if (!ValidLength(item, 5)) return false;
   if (item.indexOf ('@', 0) == -1) return false;
   return true;
}
```

Finally, let's create a main validation routine. This routine validates all the fields one at a time, then returns true or false:

```
function Validate() {
   errfound = false;
   if (!ValidLength(document.order.name1.value,6))
      error(document.order.name1,"Invalid Name");
   if (!ValidLength(document.order.phone.value,10))
      error(document.order.phone,"Invalid Phone");
   if (!ValidLength(document.order.billto.value,30))
      error(document.order.billto,"Invalid Billing Address");
   if (!ValidLength(document.order.shipto.value,30))
      error(document.order.shipto,"Invalid Shipping Address");
   if (!ValidEmail(document.order.email.value))
      error(document.order.email, "Invalid Email Address");
   if (document.order.totalcost.value == "")
      error(document.order.qty1, "Please Order at least one item.");
   if (document.order.payby.selectedIndex != 1) {
      if (!ValidLength(document.order.creditno.value,2))
         error(document.order.creditno,"Invalid Credit/Check number");
   }
   return !errfound; /* true if there are no errors */
}
```

As you can see, this function includes tests for the length-related functions and the e-mail address; in addition, I have added checks for the credit card number and the total cost. If any of these checks fails, an error routine is called:

```
function error(elem, text) {
// abort if we already found an error
   if (errfound) return;
   window.alert(text);
   elem.select();
   elem.focus();
   errfound = true;
}
```

This function displays a dialog explaining the error, then sets the focus to the element with the error; this positions the cursor in that field so the user can easily change it. In addition, the `select` method is used to select the item's text.

NOTE: Because the user doesn't normally enter data in the total cost field, the validate routine points the cursor to the first quantity field, so the user can add an item to the order.

One more thing: the `error` function sets a variable, `errfound`, to indicate that an error has happened. It returns immediately if an error was already found; this prevents multiple dialogs from showing if more than one field is invalid.

Adding an Event Handler for Validation

Finally, you can link the validation routine to the form itself. You will add an `onSubmit` event handler to the FORM declaration:

```
<FORM NAME="order" onSubmit="return Validate();">
```

This calls the `Validate` function and uses its return value as the return value of the event. This means that if `Validate` returns false—in other words, if something is invalid—the data will not be submitted.

This basically completes the order form. Listing 6.4 is the complete HTML listing, including all the validation scripting. The complete form is shown in Figure 6.6, including a dialog indicating that the e-mail address is invalid.

Listing 6.4. The revised HTML order form with validation.

```
<HTML>
<HEAD><TITLE>Order Form</TITLE>
<SCRIPT>
// function to calculate the total cost field
function Total() {
    var tot = 0;
    tot += (40.00 * document.order.qty1.value);
    tot += (69.95 * document.order.qty2.value);
    tot += (99.95 * document.order.qty3.value);
    tot += (4.95 * document.order.qty4.value);
    document.order.totalcost.value = tot;
}
// function to update cost when quantity is changed
function UpdateCost(number, unitcost) {
    costname = "cost" + number;
    qtyname = "qty" + number;
    var q = document.order[qtyname].value;
    document.order[costname].value = q * unitcost;
    Total();
}
// function to copy billing address to shipping address
function CopyAddress() {
    if (document.order.same.checked) {
        document.order.shipto.value = document.order.billto.value;
    }
}
//global variable for error flag
var errfound = false;
//function to validate by length
function ValidLength(item, len) {
    return (item.length >= len);
}
//function to validate an email address
function ValidEmail(item) {
    if (!ValidLength(item, 5)) return false;
```

continues

Listing 6.4. continued

```
    if (item.indexOf ('@', 0) == -1) return false;
    return true;
}
// display an error alert
function error(elem, text) {
// abort if we already found an error
    if (errfound) return;
    window.alert(text);
    elem.select();
    elem.focus();
    errfound = true;
}
// main validation function
function Validate() {
    errfound = false;
    if (!ValidLength(document.order.name1.value,6))
        error(document.order.name1,"Invalid Name");
    if (!ValidLength(document.order.phone.value,10))
        error(document.order.phone,"Invalid Phone");
    if (!ValidLength(document.order.billto.value,30))
        error(document.order.billto,"Invalid Billing Address");
    if (!ValidLength(document.order.shipto.value,30))
        error(document.order.shipto,"Invalid Shipping Address");
    if (!ValidEmail(document.order.email.value))
        error(document.order.email, "Invalid Email Address");
    if (document.order.totalcost.value == "")
        error(document.order.qty1, "Please Order at least one item.");
    if (document.order.payby.selectedIndex != 1) {
        if (!ValidLength(document.order.creditno.value,2))
            error(document.order.creditno,"Invalid Credit/Check number");
    }
    return !errfound; /* true if there are no errors */
}
</SCRIPT>
</HEAD>
<BODY>
<H1>Order Form</H1>
<FORM NAME="order" onSubmit="return Validate();">
<B>Name:</B> <INPUT TYPE="text" NAME="name1" SIZE=20>
<B>Phone: </B><INPUT TYPE="text" NAME="phone" SIZE=15>
<B>E-mail address:</B><INPUT TYPE="text" NAME="email" SIZE=20><BR>
<B>Billing and Shipping Addresses:</B>
<INPUT TYPE="CHECKBOX" NAME="same" onClick="CopyAddress();">
Ship to Billing Address
<BR>
<TEXTAREA NAME="billto" COLS=40 ROWS=4 onChange="CopyAddress();">
Enter your billing address here.
</TEXTAREA>
<TEXTAREA NAME="shipto" COLS=40 ROWS=4 onChange="CopyAddress();">
Enter your shipping address here.
</TEXTAREA>
<B>Products to Order:</B><BR>
Qty: <INPUT TYPE="TEXT" NAME="qty1" VALUE="0" SIZE=4
onChange = "UpdateCost(1, 40.00);">
Cost: <INPUT TYPE="TEXT" NAME="cost1" SIZE=6>
($40.00 ea) Fictional Spreadsheet 7.0 <BR>
```

```
Qty: <INPUT TYPE="TEXT" NAME="qty2" VALUE="0" SIZE=4
onChange = "UpdateCost(2, 69.95);">
Cost: <INPUT TYPE="TEXT" NAME="cost2" SIZE=6>
($69.95 ea) Fictional Word Processor 6.0<BR>
Qty: <INPUT TYPE="TEXT" NAME="qty3" VALUE="0" SIZE=4
onChange = "UpdateCost(3, 99.95);">
Cost: <INPUT TYPE="TEXT" NAME="cost3" SIZE=6>
($99.95 ea) Fictional Database 7.0 <BR>
Qty: <INPUT TYPE="TEXT" NAME="qty4" VALUE="0" SIZE=4
onChange = "UpdateCost(4, 4.95);">
Cost: <INPUT TYPE="TEXT" NAME="cost4" SIZE=6>
($4.95 ea) Instruction Booklet for the above <HR>
<B>Total Cost:</B>
<INPUT TYPE="TEXT" NAME="totalcost" SIZE=8><HR>
<B>Method of Payment</B>:
<SELECT NAME="payby">
<OPTION VALUE="check" SELECTED>Check or Money Order
<OPTION VALUE="cash">Cash or Cashier's Check
<OPTION VALUE="credit">Credit Card (specify number)
</SELECT><BR>
<B>Credit Card or Check Number:</B>:
<INPUT TYPE="TEXT" NAME="creditno" SIZE="20"><BR>
<INPUT TYPE="SUBMIT" NAME="submit" VALUE="Send Your Order">
<INPUT TYPE="RESET" VALUE="Start Over">
</FORM>
</BODY>
</HTML>
```

Figure 6.6.

The complete HTML order form, including validation for all fields.

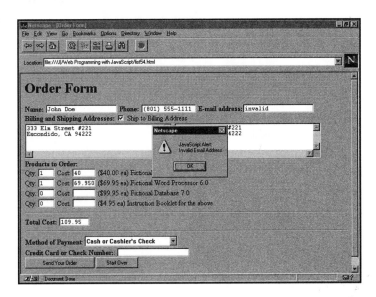

TIP: At this point, submitting the form won't do anything; however, you can still test the submission. Submitting will reload the current page and add the various data to the URL.

Workshop Wrap-Up

In this chapter, you built a fully functional ordering system for an imaginary company, which could easily be modified for use by a real company. In the process, you learned the following:

- ❏ How to use HTML forms and their many elements in a Web page
- ❏ How to use JavaScript to add validation to the form
- ❏ How to use JavaScript to add automation to a form
- ❏ About the <FORM> object and form elements, and how to manipulate and read each of their values in JavaScript

Next Steps

You should now know how to use JavaScript with forms. To move on, turn to one of the following chapters:

- ❏ To learn about the object hierarchy that underlies forms, see Chapter 5, "Accessing Window Elements as Objects."
- ❏ To see another example of form validation, turn to Chapter 7, "Real-Life Examples I."
- ❏ To learn to add functionality to a Web page, such as navigation bars and the status line, see Chapter 8, "Improving a Web Page with JavaScript."
- ❏ To learn about advanced browser features such as frames, see Chapter 9, "Using Frames, Cookies, and Other Advanced Features."
- ❏ To learn more about CGI and interactive forms, see Chapter 17, "Combining JavaScript, CGI and SSI."

Q&A

Q: Is there any way to force a form to be submitted automatically, without the user pressing a button?

A: Yes. You can do this with the `form.submit()` method. However, this is bad manners; it's usually best to let the user know what's going on. Also note that due to security concerns, you can't do this with a form that uses the `mailto` action.

Q: I am having problems trying to force a checkbox to be selected using the `click` method. Is there a way to solve this?

A: Unfortunately, at least for many versions of Netscape, the only solution is not to use the `click` method. Fortunately, it's easy to do most things without it. For a checkbox, you can manipulate the `checked` property; for a button, you can call the same function as its `onClick` event handler.

Q: If I use JavaScript to add validation and other features to my form, can users with non-JavaScript browsers still use the form?

A: Yes, if you're careful. Be sure to use a SUBMIT button rather than the `submit` action. Also, because the CGI script may receive nonvalidated data, be sure to include validation in the CGI script. Non-JavaScript users will be able to use the form but won't receive instant feedback about their errors.

Q: Can I add new form elements "on the fly," or change them—for example, change a text box into a password field?

A: No. The form elements are set by the HTML code. There are ways to work around this, such as updating the form in a separate frame.

Q: Is there any way to create a large number of text fields without dealing with different names for all of them?

A: Yes. If you use the same name for several elements in the form, their objects will form an array. For example, if you defined 20 text fields with the name `member`, you could refer to them as `member[0]` through `member[19]`. Chapter 15, "Real-Life Examples III," uses this technique for score values in a game.

Q: When validating an e-mail address, is there any way to be sure the address is valid, or that it is the user's address?

A: No. This is a classic question about CGI; neither JavaScript nor CGI has a good solution. The only way to be sure an e-mail address is valid is to send information, such as a password, to the address; even then, you can't be sure users are entering their own addresses.

Q: Why doesn't JavaScript recognize my form elements when I use a table to lay them out?

A: JavaScript does not deal well with forms within tables when `<TABLE>` tags are nested. For now, the only solution is to avoid using nested tables.

Q: Is there a way to place the cursor on a particular field when the form is loaded?

A: Yes. You can use the field's `focus()` method to send the cursor there. The best way to do this is to use an `onLoad` event handler and add a slight delay with the `setTimeout()` method to allow the page to finish loading.

SEVEN

Real-Life Examples I

This chapter includes several example JavaScript applications that apply the techniques you learned in Part II, "Using JavaScript Objects and Forms." These include the following:

- ❏ **Example 1: Displaying a Pop-Up Message:** A page that includes an "instructions" link, which opens a small window to display the instructions.
- ❏ **Example 2: Displaying Random Quotations:** An example of a method of displaying a different quotation each time the user loads the page.
- ❏ **Example 3: A Validated Registration Form:** An example of a registration form for a commercial Web site, including validation for key fields.

Example 1: Displaying a Pop-Up Message

One thing lacking in HTML is a method of including pop-up messages. These messages appear in a small window and go away when you click on them or perform another action. This could be useful for a disclaimer, brief instructions, or anything you want to display to the user quickly without leaving the current page.

The following techniques are used in this example:

❑ Defining and using a function (Chapter 3)

❑ Using an event handler to trigger an action (Chapter 3)

❑ Creating a new window and controlling its appearance (Chapter 5)

❑ Using the window object's close() method (Chapters 3 and 5)

For this example, let's create a link to the word instructions on a Web page. Clicking this link will pop up a window with some brief instructions; you can then click a button in that window or move the focus to the main window, and the window will disappear.

You could create a simple pop-up message using a JavaScript alert, but this isn't perfect—for starters, it includes the nonfriendly message "JavaScript Alert:" at the top. It also uses plain text; your pop-up instructions can include boldface, italics, and anything else supported by HTML.

The main HTML document for the pop-up window example is Listing 7.1. This is the main page, and it includes a link to the word instructions to display the pop-up instructions.

Listing 7.1. (POPUP.HTM) The main HTML document for the pop-up window example.

```
<HTML>
<HEAD><TITLE>Pop-up Messages</TITLE>
<SCRIPT LANGUAGE="JavaScript">
function instruct()  {
   iwin = window.open("instruct.htm","IWIN",
   "status=no,toolbar=no,location=no,menu=no,width=400,height=300");
}
</SCRIPT>
</HEAD>
<BODY>
<H1>Pop-up Message Test</H1>
<HR>
This page demonstrates the use of a pop-up window. The window is
created when the link below is clicked, and disappears when the OK
button is pressed.
<HR>
Before you continue with this page, please take a quick
look at the
<A HREF="#" onClick="instruct();">
instructions</A>.
<HR>
The page continues...
</BODY>
</HTML>
```

The word `instructions` is a link. To avoid sending the user to an actual destination, this listing uses # as the link destination. The actual work for this link is done by the event handler, which calls the `instruct()` function.

The `instruct()` function is defined in the header. It includes the command to create the new window, specifying `INSTRUCT.HTML` as the document to be loaded into the new window. The window attributes are set to turn off the status line, menu bar, toolbar, and other features, and set the window size.

The second HTML document, shown in Listing 7.2, is the document containing the actual instructions. This document also includes a bit of JavaScript—the OK button is defined with an event handler to close the window.

Listing 7.2. (INSTRUCT.HTM) The second HTML document for the pop-up window example.

```
<HTML>
<HEAD><TITLE>Instructions</TITLE>
</HEAD>
<BODY>
<H1>Instructions</H1>
These are the instructions. This is actually a separate HTML
document, INSTRUCT.HTM. This can include <b>bold</b>,
<i>italic</i>, and other HTML features, since it's an ordinary
HTML document. Click the button below to return.
<FORM NAME="form1">
<INPUT TYPE="button" VALUE="OK"
onClick="window.close();">
</FORM>
</BODY>
</HTML>
```

Figure 7.1 shows this example in action, with the instructions window displayed. Here are a few interesting observations about this example:

❑ One potential problem could be caused if the user doesn't click on the OK button in the instructions window. The window will remain open. One solution is to use the `onUnload` event handler to close the instructions window when the main window closes.

❑ Notice that although the new window you created is called `iwin`, it is referred to in INSTRUCT.HTML as simply `window`. This is because for this document, the instructions window is the current window.

❑ You have control over the appearance of the new window, but not complete control—for example, the title bar cannot be turned off. This is partially due to cross-platform issues; not all GUIs support a window with no title.

Figure 7.1.
The pop-up window example in action.

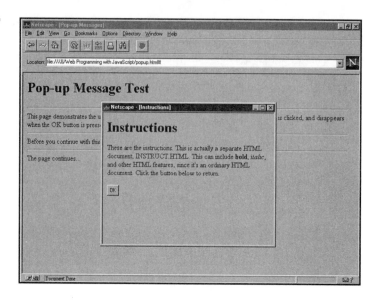

Example 2: Displaying Random Quotations

One of the things that keeps users coming back to a good Web page is variety—something different every time they visit. Using JavaScript, you can add a random quotation, a random link, or a random tip to the page.

For this example, let's display a random quotation at the top of a Web page. This example illustrates the following techniques:

❏ Using the `Math` object's methods (Chapter 4)

❏ Creating arrays and storing data (Chapter 4)

❏ Creating HTML "on the fly" with the `document.write` method (Chapter 5)

You will embed the script to generate random quotations in the body of the Web page with the `<SCRIPT>` tag. Listing 7.3 is the HTML document, including the JavaScript program.

NOTE: This script uses the `Math.random()` method, which wasn't supported for all platforms until Netscape 3.0b3. Be sure you try it with the most recent version.

Listing 7.3. (RANDQUOT.HTM) The HTML document for the random quotations example.

```
<HTML>
<HEAD><TITLE>Random Quotations</TITLE>
</HEAD>
<BODY>
<H1>Random Quotations</H1>
<HR>
<SCRIPT LANGUAGE="JavaScript">
//store the quotations in arrays
quotes = new Array(6);
authors = new Array(6);
quotes[0] = "I have a new philosophy. I'm only going to dread one day at a
➥time.";
authors[0] = "Charles Schulz";
quotes[1] = "Reality is the leading cause of stress for those in touch with
➥it.";
authors[1] = "Jack Wagner";
quotes[2] = "Few things are harder to put up with than the annoyance of a good
➥example.";
authors[2] = "Mark Twain";
quotes[3] = "The pure and simple truth is rarely pure and never simple.";
authors[3] = "Oscar Wilde";
quotes[4] = "There's no business like show business, but there are several
➥businesses like accounting.";
authors[4] = "David Letterman";
quotes[5] = "Man invented language to satisfy his deep need to complain.";
authors[5] = "Lily Tomlin";

//calculate a random index
index = Math.floor(Math.random() * quotes.length);

//display the quotation
document.write("<DL>\n");
document.write("<DT>" + "\"" + quotes[index] + "\"\n");
document.write("<DD>" + "— " + authors[index] + "\n");
document.write("</DL>\n");

//done
</SCRIPT>
<HR>
The quotation above was generated randomly when you loaded this page.
Reload for another one, or cheat—view the source code and see them all.
<HR>
</BODY>
</HTML>
```

This example uses two arrays, quotes and authors, to store the quotations. Notice that an array can hold more than just numbers—in this case, each array element is a string.

To select a random quotation, you use Math.random() to produce a random number between 0 and 1. You then multiply it by the number of quotations, provided by the length property of the array, to produce a number in the right range. All this is enclosed in the Math.floor function, which removes the fractional part of the result.

Figure 7.2 shows the output of this example. Here are a few observations and notes about this program:

❏ I've used this example to display a random humorous quotation. You could substitute tips about the current page, short advertisements about the company, or even random links—you can include HTML within the array elements without causing a problem.

❏ There are only six quotations in this example—to keep things short. You could easily add more; just continue with `quotes[6]` and so on. Be aware that this is within the HTML source, though, so the more available quotes, the slower the user's access to the page. Just for fun, I've included a version of this program with over 100 quotations on the CD-ROM.

❏ Notice that there are two arrays, one for quotations and one for authors. An object-oriented alternative is to create a new object with two string properties, then store an object in each array element. For example, you could create a `Quotation` object with `author` and `quote` properties. You might find this useful if you have more than two parts for each of your random items.

Figure 7.2.
The output of the random quotations example.

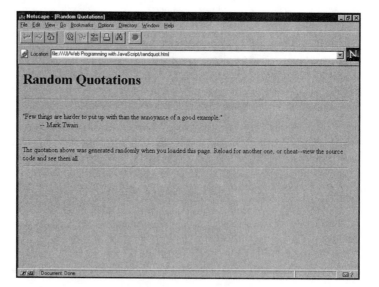

Example 3: A Validated Registration Form

Many Web pages—especially commercial ones, or services you pay for—include some sort of registration form so that users can submit information about themselves. For this example, let's create a registration form, including validation with JavaScript.

This example illustrates the following techniques:

- ❏ Using string objects (Chapter 4)
- ❏ Building and validating forms (Chapter 6)
- ❏ Using the `mailto:` method to get results from a form without using CGI (Chapter 6)

As with the examples in Chapter 6, "Using Interactive Forms," you need to include the functions to validate the form in the header of the HTML document. The HTML source for the validated registration form is shown in Listing 7.4.

Listing 7.4. The HTML source code for the validated registration form.

```
<HTML>
<HEAD><TITLE>Registration Form</TITLE>
<SCRIPT>
//global variable for error flag
var errfound = false;
//function to validate by length
function ValidLength(item, len) {
   return (item.length >= len);
}
//function to validate an email address
function ValidEmail(item) {
   if (!ValidLength(item, 5)) return false;
   if (item.indexOf ('@', 0) == -1) return false;
   return true;
}
// display an error alert
function error(elem, text) {
// abort if we already found an error
   if (errfound) return;
   window.alert(text);
   elem.select();
   elem.focus();
   errfound = true;
}
// main validation function
function Validate() {
   errfound = false;
   if (!ValidLength(document.regform.username.value,6))
      error(document.regform.username,"Invalid Name");
   if (!ValidLength(document.regform.phone.value,10))
      error(document.regform.phone,"Invalid phone number");
   if (!ValidEmail(document.regform.email.value))
      error(document.regform.email, "Invalid Email Address");
   if (!ValidLength(document.regform.address.value,10))
      error(document.regform.address, "Invalid Mailing Address");
   if (!ValidLength(document.regform.city.value,15))
      error(document.regform.city, "Invalid City/State/Zip");
   return !errfound; /* true if there are no errors */
}
</SCRIPT>
</HEAD>
```

continues

Listing 7.4. continued

```
<BODY>
<H1>Registration Form</H1>
<HR>
Please fill out the fields below to register for our web page. Press the
Submit button at the end of the form when done.
<HR>
<FORM NAME="regform" onSubmit="return Validate();"
ACTION="mailto:username@host" METHOD="post">
<B>Your Name:</B>
<INPUT TYPE="text" NAME="username" SIZE=20><BR>
<B>Your Phone Number: </B>
<INPUT TYPE="text" NAME="phone" SIZE=15><BR>
<B>E-mail address:</B>
<INPUT TYPE="text" NAME="email" SIZE=20><BR>
<B>Mailing address:</B>
<INPUT TYPE="text" NAME="address" SIZE=30><BR>
<B>City, State, Zip:</B>
<INPUT TYPE="text" NAME="city" SIZE=30>
<HR>
<INPUT TYPE="SUBMIT" NAME="submit" VALUE="Submit Registration">
<INPUT TYPE="RESET" VALUE="Start Over">
</FORM>
</BODY>
</HTML>
```

This application includes several functions:

❏ `Validate()` validates the fields of the form and returns true or false depending on whether any errors were found. The user's name, phone number, e-mail address, and mailing address are all validated.

❏ `error()` displays an appropriate error message when a field is invalid.

❏ `ValidLength()` is used to verify that the text the user entered into a field is greater than a certain length. This is used for most of the fields.

❏ `ValidEmail()` validates an e-mail address. It checks for a total length greater than five characters and makes sure an "at" sign (@) appears somewhere in the text.

Netscape's view of this form is shown in Figure 7.3. In the figure, an invalid e-mail address has been entered, and an alert is being displayed with the error message.

The `mailto:` action is used to submit the data. (Be sure to replace `user@host` with your e-mail address.) If the user submits the form and validation is successful, a simple e-mail message is sent with the information from each of the fields. An example of such a message is shown in Listing 7.5.

Figure 7.3.
The validated registration form in action.

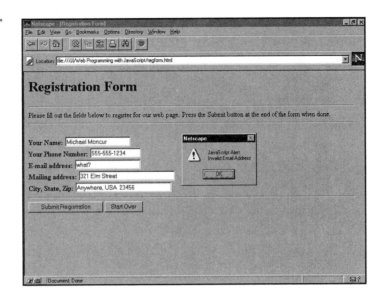

Listing 7.5. The e-mail message sent as a result of the registration form.

```
username=Michael+Moncur&phone=555-555-2314
&email=books@starlingtech.com
&address=234+Elm+Street
&city=Anywhere%2C+USA+44444
&submit=Submit+Registration
```

As you can see, this doesn't exactly come back in English. It's even worse than you think—I added the line breaks in the listing. Nevertheless, you can read the results. Software is also available to read it automatically.

The encoding in Listing 7.5 is called URL encoding and is used when data is sent to a CGI script. You'll look at this process in detail in Chapter 17, "Combining JavaScript, CGI, and SSI."

PART

II

Creating Smart Web Pages

EIGHT

Improving a Web Page with JavaScript

Although JavaScript is useful for forms, it can also be useful for an ordinary Web page. It can add user-friendliness, convenience, and eye-catching gadgets to liven up a page.

In this chapter, you will look at some of the ways JavaScript can improve a Web page. You'll start with a simple Web page, then add interactive features with JavaScript.

In this chapter, you

- ❏ Add a navigation bar to make it easy to navigate between pages
- ❏ Use the status line to display descriptions of links rather than their URLs
- ❏ Learn to use the status line or a text field to scroll a message

Tasks in this chapter:

- ❏ Creating the Data Structures and HTML for the Navigation Bar
- ❏ Creating the Function for the Navigation Bar
- ❏ Integrating the Navigation Bar with the HTML Page
- ❏ Creating Friendly Links
- ❏ Adding a Scrolling Message
- ❏ Using a Text Field to Scroll a Message

The Beginning: A Simple Web Page

JavaScript can make it easy to navigate through menu structures.

Let's begin with an example of a typical Web page. Once again let's use FSC (the Fictional Software Company) as an example. FSC has a simple set of Web pages that introduce the company and include detailed information about each of the products.

Although the FSC pages are functional and include good information about the company and its products, they're not about to win any awards. In this chapter and the next, you'll learn how JavaScript can make the page more friendly and exciting.

The Main Page

The main FSC Web page is shown in Figure 8.1. It includes a logo at the top, three paragraphs of information, and a simple bulleted list of links to the various subpages. This page is defined using the HTML in Listing 8.1.

Figure 8.1.

A simple Web page using only HTML.

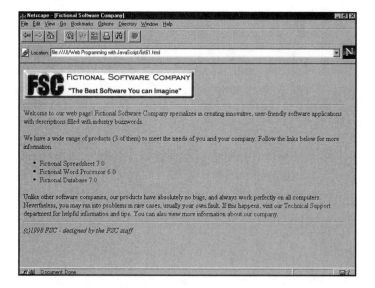

Listing 8.1. (FSCHOME.HTM) The HTML document for the initial FSC Web page.

```
<HTML>
<HEAD><TITLE>Fictional Software Company</TITLE></HEAD>
<BODY>
<IMG SRC="fsclogo.gif" alt="Fictional Software Company">
<HR>
Welcome to our web page! Fictional Software Company
specializes in creating innovative, user-friendly software
applications with descriptions filled with industry
buzzwords.
```

```
<P>We have a wide range of products (3 of them) to meet
the needs of you and your company. Follow the links
below for more information.
<P>
<UL>
<LI><A HREF="spread.html">Fictional Spreadsheet 7.0</A>
<LI><A HREF="word.html">Fictional Word Processor 6.0</A>
<LI><A HREF="data.html">Fictional Database 7.0</A>
</UL>
<P>
Unlike other software companies, our products have
absolutely no bugs, and always work perfectly on all
computers. Nevertheless, you may run into problems in
rare cases, usually your own fault. If this happens,
visit our <A HREF="support.html">Technical Support</A>
department for helpful information and tips. You can
also view more information <A HREF="company.html">about
our company</A> or order products with our friendly
<a href="order.html">Order Form</A>.
<HR>
<I>(c)1998 FSC - designed by the FSC staff</I>
</BODY>
</HTML>
```

The various links on the page send you to the company's other pages. One describes each of the company's products, another contains information about the company, and another gives technical support information. A link is also provided to the order form, which was created in Chapter 6, "Using Interactive Forms."

Creating a Navigation Bar

More recently, FSC decided to add more detailed information to its pages. The main page remains the same, but each product's page is now a menu of links to subpages with various categories of information.

As it is, the pages can be difficult to navigate. For example, if you want to view the system requirements for the Fictional Word Processor product, you must select the product name from the main page, wait for the page to load, then select the `"System Requirements"` link.

You'll find an expanded version of this example using frames in Chapter 9, "Using Frames, Cookies, and Other Advanced Features."

With JavaScript, you can create a friendly interface to all the pages on the main page— without taking much space. Let's use one selection list to choose the product and another selection list to choose the type of information about the product to view.

NOTE: In this example, the two selection lists stay the same because each product has the same categories of information available. You will learn a technique for changing the contents of a selection list in Chapter 11, "Real-Life Examples II."

Naming the Pages

Doing a bit of thinking and planning can save you time programming.

In writing a program, the programming isn't always the hardest part. You should define the task the program will perform and the data it will use in advance; this will make the actual task of writing the program simple.

In order to make the navigation bar programming task easier, let's choose simple, meaningful names for each of the subpages. This will make it easy to construct their names based on the value of the selection lists.

Assign a one-letter code to each product: w for the word processor, s for the spreadsheet, and d for the database. Then follow that with an underscore and a word indicating the type of information. Here are the categories of information and their corresponding codes:

- ❏ tech: Technical support for the product
- ❏ sales: Sales and availability information
- ❏ feat: A list of features
- ❏ price: Pricing information for the product
- ❏ tips: Tips for getting the most of the product

For example, s_feat.html is the features list for the spreadsheet program. Meaningful names like this are a good idea in any HTML task, because they make it easier to maintain the pages. When you're automating with JavaScript, they can make a big difference.

NOTE: To try this example yourself, you'll need all the individual HTML files. This chapter does not present them, because they're simple HTML; however, the complete set of files is on the CD-ROM included with this book.

Creating the Data Structures and HTML for the Navigation Bar

Before you write the function to navigate the pages, you need to store the needed data. In this case, you need to store the three codes for the software products and the five codes for types of pages. You could create an array for each list, but that isn't necessary in this case.

Rather than creating an array, you can simply place the information in the HTML page itself, and it will be stored in the properties of the form object by the JavaScript interpreter. You will use the codes as the VALUE attribute of each option.

Although you didn't need to here, you could also define an object to store the data. This is explained in Chapter 4, "Using Built-In Objects and Custom Objects."

You will need to define an HTML selection list for each of the lists of information. In addition, the user needs a way to visit the page after selecting it; you will accomplish this with a "go" button next to the drop-down lists.

Listing 8.2 shows the HTML to add to the main page. It's included toward the end of the page, but it's generally self-contained and could be placed anywhere. Chapter 9 includes an example of using this same navigation bar within a separate frame.

Listing 8.2. The HTML to define the table of contents.

```
<FORM name="navform">
<SELECT name="program">
<OPTION VALUE="x" SELECTED>Select a Product
<OPTION VALUE="w">Fictional Word Processor
<OPTION VALUE="s">Fictional Spreadsheet
<OPTION VALUE="d">Fictional Database
</SELECT>
<SELECT name="category">
<OPTION VALUE="x" SELECTED>Select a Category
<OPTION VALUE="tech">Technical Support
<OPTION VALUE="sales">Sales and Availability
<OPTION VALUE="feat">List of Features
<OPTION VALUE="price">Pricing Information
<OPTION VALUE="tips">Tips and Techniques
</SELECT>
<INPUT TYPE="button" NAME="go" VALUE="Go to Page"
onClick="Navigate();">
</FORM>
```

In addition to the categories discussed, I have included an additional option with the value x in each selection list. These options will display an instructional message to the user. Clicking on them will do nothing but will provide the user with a hint about using the selection lists. These are marked as the default selections, so the instructions will be displayed until the user makes a selection.

TIP: When adding features with JavaScript, don't forget to explain their use, especially if you are using a technique used in few other pages. The user shouldn't have to spend any time figuring out how to use your page.

Creating the Function for the Navigation Bar

You defined an onClick event handler for the "go" button, which calls the Navigate() function. Next, you need to create this function. This function will read the current value of both selection lists and construct a filename, then load that file in the browser.

Listing 8.3 shows the Navigate() function. You will look at the features of this function in detail next.

Listing 8.3. The function for navigating based on the selection lists.

```
function Navigate() {
    prod = document.navform.program.selectedIndex;
    cat = document.navform.category.selectedIndex;
    prodval = document.navform.program.options[prod].value;
    catval = document.navform.category.options[cat].value;
    if (prodval == "x" ¦¦ catval == "x") return;
    window.location = prodval + "_" + catval + ".html";
}
```

To begin, this function sets two variables, prod and cat, to hold the currently selected index for each selection list. Next, prodval and catval are assigned to the corresponding value properties.

The if statement checks for the x value, meaning that the user hasn't yet selected an item, in both lists; if no value has been selected in either list, it returns without doing anything.

String manipulation is explained in detail in Chapter 4.

Finally, the new document filename is constructed by concatenating the two codes, the underscore (_), and the html suffix. This value is assigned to the window.location property, which causes the new page to be loaded.

NOTE: Because changing the location property loads the new document, you can't do anything more in the current JavaScript program. In fact, the Navigate() function never returns. However, you could include JavaScript functions on the new page.

Integrating the Navigation Bar with the HTML Page

Your final task is to combine the new navigation form and the `Navigate()` function with the Web page HTML. Listing 8.4 shows the revised Web page with the new features, and Figure 8.2 shows how the page looks in Netscape.

Figure 8.2.

The revised Web page with interactive table of contents.

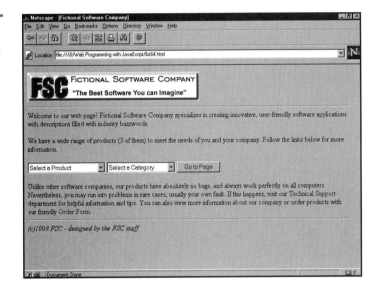

Listing 8.4. (NAVBAR.HTM) The complete HTML page with table of contents feature.

```
<HTML>
<HEAD>
<TITLE>Fictional Software Company</TITLE>
<SCRIPT>
function Navigate() {
    prod = document.navform.program.selectedIndex;
    cat = document.navform.category.selectedIndex;
    prodval = document.navform.program.options[prod].value;
    catval = document.navform.category.options[cat].value;
    if (prodval == "x" ¦¦ catval == "x") return;
    window.location = prodval + "_" + catval + ".html";
}
</SCRIPT>
</HEAD>
<BODY>
<IMG SRC="fsclogo.gif" alt="Fictional Software Company">
<HR>
Welcome to our web page! Fictional Software Company
specializes in creating innovative, user-friendly software
```

continues

Listing 8.4. continued

```
applications with descriptions filled with industry
buzzwords.
<P>
We have a wide range of products (3 of them) to meet
the needs of you and your company. Follow the links
below for more information.
<P>
<FORM name="navform">
<SELECT name="program">
<OPTION VALUE="x" SELECTED>Select a Product
<OPTION VALUE="w">Fictional Word Processor
<OPTION VALUE="s">Fictional Spreadsheet
<OPTION VALUE="d">Fictional Database
</SELECT>
<SELECT name="category">
<OPTION VALUE="x" SELECTED>Select a Category
<OPTION VALUE="tech">Technical Support
<OPTION VALUE="sales">Sales and Availability
<OPTION VALUE="feat">List of Features
<OPTION VALUE="price">Pricing Information
<OPTION VALUE="tips">Tips and Techniques
</SELECT>
<INPUT TYPE="button" NAME="go" VALUE="Go to Page"
onClick="Navigate();">
</FORM>
<P>
Unlike other software companies, our products have
absolutely no bugs, and always work perfectly on all
computers. Nevertheless, you may run into problems in
rare cases, usually your own fault. If this happens,
visit our <A HREF="support.html">Technical Support</A>
department for helpful information and tips. You can
also view more information <A HREF="company.html">about
our company</A> or order products with our friendly
<a href="order.html">Order Form</A>.
<HR>
<I>(c)1998 FSC - designed by the FSC staff</I>
</BODY>
</HTML>
```

NOTE: The one thing missing in this Web page is a way to navigate the pages for non-JavaScript browsers. This could easily be done with normal links; in addition, the form you create could be used to call a CGI script to perform the same function (but a bit slower). You'll learn more about combining JavaScript and CGI in Chapter 17, "Combining JavaScript, CGI, and SSI."

Using the Status Line

As discussed in Chapter 5, "Accessing Window Elements as Objects," you can change the value of the window.status property to display a message on the status line. You can use this feature to add features to a Web page, displaying helpful information about links or about the company.

TASK

Creating Friendly Links

Netscape also uses the status line to display status while receiving an HTML page and graphics.

Normally, as you move the mouse over each link in a Web page, the status line displays the URL of the link. You can improve on this with JavaScript by displaying a description of the link's destination instead.

You can accomplish this easily using onMouseOver event handlers. When the user moves the mouse over a link, this event will call a function to display the appropriate message on the status line. For example, the following HTML defines a link with a friendly status line:

```
<A HREF="order.html"
onMouseOver="window.status='Allows you to order products';return true;">
Order form</A>
```

You can do this with graphic links, as well as text links. See Chapter 12, "Working with Graphics in JavaScript," for examples using graphics.

This simply sets the value of window.status to display the message. In addition, the true value is returned; this is necessary to override the normal action (displaying the URL) for the status line.

Listing 8.5 shows the result of adding onMouseOver functions to each of the links in the original version of the FSC Software page. The page is shown in action in Figure 8.3.

Figure 8.3.
Using event handlers to display link information in the status line.

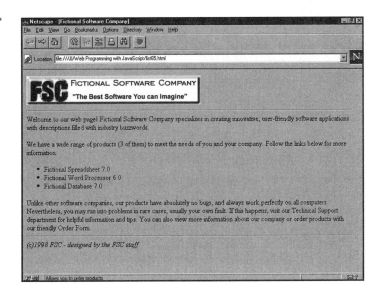

Listing 8.5. (LINKDESC.HTM) The FSC page with the addition of friendly links.

```
<HTML>
<HEAD>
<TITLE>Fictional Software Company</TITLE>
<SCRIPT>
function message(text) {
   window.status = text;
   return true;
}
</SCRIPT>
</HEAD>
<BODY>
<IMG SRC="fsclogo.gif" alt="Fictional Software Company">
<HR>
Welcome to our web page! Fictional Software Company
specializes in creating innovative, user-friendly software
applications with descriptions filled with industry
buzzwords.
<P>
We have a wide range of products (3 of them) to meet
the needs of you and your company. Follow the links
below for more information.
<P>
<UL>
<LI><A HREF="spread.html"
onMouseOver="window.status='Information about the spreadsheet';return true;">
Fictional Spreadsheet 7.0</A>
<LI><A HREF="word.html"
onMouseOver="window.status='Information about the word processor';return
➥true;">
Fictional Word Processor 6.0</A>
<LI><A HREF="data.html"
onMouseOver="window.status='Information about the database';return true;">
Fictional Database 7.0</A>
</UL>
<P>
Unlike other software companies, our products have
absolutely no bugs, and always work perfectly on all
computers. Nevertheless, you may run into problems in
rare cases, usually your own fault. If this happens,
visit our <A HREF="support.html"
onMouseOver="window.status='Technical Support for our products';return true;">
Technical Support</A>
department for helpful information and tips. You can
also view more information <A HREF="company.html"
onMouseOver="window.status='Information about FSC Software Co.';return true;">
about our company</A> or order products with our friendly
<a href="order.html"
onMouseOver="window.status='Allows you to order products';return true;">
Order Form</A>.
<HR>
<I>(c)1998 FSC - designed by the FSC staff</I>
</BODY>
</HTML>
```

NOTE: You might be tempted to make a function to avoid using such long statements as event handlers. Unfortunately, because the `return true` statement must be in the event handler itself, it wouldn't save much typing at all. You can still do it with a command such as `return function()` in the event handler.

TASK

Adding a Scrolling Message

Be warned: Not all users like seeing messages in their status bar. Be sure to listen if users complain.

Currently, one of the most common uses of JavaScript is to display a scrolling message on the status line. This might be useful to point out features of the page or to let the user know about a current offer.

Scrolling a message is simple in JavaScript. First, you define a variable with the message to be scrolled, and another with a "spacer" that will be used between copies of the message. A third variable, pos, will be used to store the current position of the string on the status line:

```
var msg = "Welcome to Fictional Software Company. Watch for a new product
➥coming next month!";
var spacer = "...          ...";
pos = 0;
```

Next, you define a function that will be called periodically to scroll the message. Here is the `ScrollMessage()` function:

```
function ScrollMessage() {
   window.status = msg.substring(pos, msg.length) + spacer + msg.substring(0,
➥pos);
   pos++;
   if (pos > msg.length) pos = 0;
// set timeout for next update
   window.setTimeout("ScrollMessage()",200);
}
```

This function creates the value of the status line by adding three values:

❑ The substring of the message, starting at the current position and ending at the end of the string

❑ The spacer value

❑ The rest of the message, starting at the beginning and ending at the current position

It then increments the position indicator pos. If it has reached the end of the string, it resets pos to zero. Finally, the `window.setTimeout()` method is used to cause the `ScrollMessage()` function to execute again, using a timeout of one-fifth of a second.

This message-scrolling routine works fine, but it suffers from a failing common to most such routines: it obliterates anything else in the status line. This makes it hard to tell where the links go—in fact, it defeats the purpose of the friendly link messages created in the previous section.

To fix this, you'll define a new variable, `showmsg`. This variable will hold a Boolean value, initially true. When it is set to false, the `ShowMessage()` function will refrain from showing the message. Instead, it will set a timeout to show the message later. Here is the revised `ShowMessage()` function:

```
//flag to control message
var showmsg = true;
function ScrollMessage() {
   if (!showmsg) {
      window.setTimeout("ScrollMessage()",1500);
      showmsg = true;
      return;
   }
   window.status = msg.substring(pos, msg.length) + spacer + msg.substring(0,
➡pos);
   pos++;
   if (pos > msg.length) pos = 0;
// set timeout for next update
   window.setTimeout("ScrollMessage()",200);
}
```

The additional code checks for a false value of the `showmsg` variable. If it is false, it uses the `window.setTimeout()` method to set a timeout for 1.5 seconds—plenty of time to read the description in the status bar.

To use this function, you will need to set `showmsg` to false in each one of the event handlers. To make this simpler, you use a function for the event handlers:

```
// Display a link help message
function LinkMessage(text) {
   showmsg = false;
   window.status = text;
}
```

This function sets the `showmsg` variable to false, then displays the message in the status line. To call the function, you use an event handler like this:

```
onMouseOver="LinkMessage('This is the message');return true;"
```

You will need to change each of the links to use the new event handler syntax. Listing 8.6 shows the revised version of the FSC page, complete with both a scrolling message and helpful link messages. Figure 8.4 shows this page in Netscape with the message scrolling.

TIP: As an alternative to scrolling messages, Chapter 11 includes a routine that displays random, nonscrolling tips, messages, or advertisements in the status line.

Figure 8.4.
The scrolling message example in Netscape.

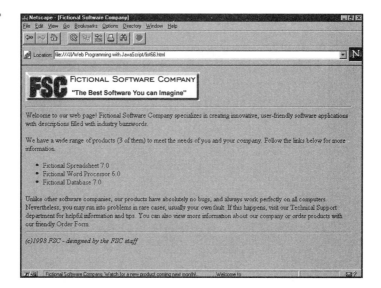

Listing 8.6. (SCROLMSG.HTM) The FSC page with the scrolling message routine.

```
<HTML>
<HEAD>
<TITLE>Fictional Software Company</TITLE>
<SCRIPT>
// message to scroll in scrollbar
var msg = "Welcome to Fictional Software Company. Watch for a new product
➥coming next month!";
var spacer = "...          ...";
// current message position
var pos = 0;
//flag to control message
var showmsg = true;
function ScrollMessage() {
   if (!showmsg) {
      window.setTimeout("ScrollMessage()",1500);
      showmsg = true;
      return;
   }
```

continues

Listing 8.6. continued

```
    window.status = msg.substring(pos, msg.length) + spacer + msg.substring(0,
➥pos);
    pos++;
    if (pos > msg.length) pos = 0;
// set timeout for next update
    window.setTimeout("ScrollMessage()",200);
}
// Start the scrolling message
ScrollMessage();
// Display a link help message
function LinkMessage(text) {
    showmsg = false;
    window.status = text;
}
</SCRIPT>
</HEAD>
<BODY>
<IMG SRC="fsclogo.gif" alt="Fictional Software Company">
<HR>
Welcome to our web page! Fictional Software Company
specializes in creating innovative, user-friendly software
applications with descriptions filled with industry
buzzwords.
<P>
We have a wide range of products (3 of them) to meet
the needs of you and your company. Follow the links
below for more information.
<P>
<UL>
<LI><A HREF="spread.html"
onMouseOver="LinkMessage('Information about the spreadsheet');return true;">
Fictional Spreadsheet 7.0</A>
<LI><A HREF="word.html"
onMouseOver="LinkMessage('Information about the word processor');return true;">
Fictional Word Processor 6.0</A>
<LI><A HREF="data.html"
onMouseOver="LinkMessage('Information about the database');return true;">
Fictional Database 7.0</A>
</UL>
<P>
Unlike other software companies, our products have
absolutely no bugs, and always work perfectly on all
computers. Nevertheless, you may run into problems in
rare cases, usually your own fault. If this happens,
visit our <A HREF="support.html"
onMouseOver="LinkMessage('Technical Support for our products');return true;">
Technical Support</A>
department for helpful information and tips. You can
also view more information <A HREF="company.html"
onMouseOver="LinkMessage('Information about FSC Software Co.');return true;">
about our company</A> or order products with our friendly
<a href="order.html"
onMouseOver="LinkMessage('Allows you to order products');return true;">
Order Form</A>.
<HR>
<I>(c)1998 FSC - designed by the FSC staff</I>
</BODY>
</HTML>
```

Using a Text Field to Scroll a Message

The status line isn't always the best place to display a message.

There are some disadvantages to using the status line to display scrolling messages. For one thing, the user may want to view URLs rather than your descriptions. Also, the browser uses it to display status when loading documents.

Finally, the status line is at the bottom of the page—hardly the place for an important announcement. Some users habitually ignore the status line, and may not even see your message.

To solve these problems, you can use a text field as an alternative to the status line. You can display help for links in such a field or use it to scroll a message.

Changing the ScrollMessage() function to use a text field instead of the status line requires only a minor change. Here is the revised function:

```
function ScrollMessage() {
    document.form1.text1.value = msg.substring(pos, msg.length) + spacer +
➥msg.substring(0, pos);
    pos++;
    if (pos > msg.length) pos = 0;
// set timeout for next update
    window.setTimeout("ScrollMessage()",200);
}
```

You are now placing the current message value in the value property of the text1 form element. Notice that the check for the showmsg variable is no longer necessary, because the scrolling message will not conflict with the link descriptions (which are still in the status line).

You define the text field (in its own little form) with the HTML:

```
<FORM name="form1">
<INPUT TYPE="text" name="text1" SIZE="60">
</FORM>
```

One more change is necessary. Because the form1 element doesn't actually exist until it is defined in the Web page, you can no longer start the scrolling in the <HEAD> section of the document. It must start after the page is loaded.

An easy way to accomplish this is with the document's onLoad event handler. You use the following <BODY> tag to start the document and define the event handler:

```
<BODY onLoad = "ScrollMessage();">
```

NOTE: One disadvantage of using a text field in this way is that the user can modify the value. However, because you're updating the field every fifth of a second, the user can't affect it much.

Listing 8.7 integrates the new function and the text field into the FSC home page. The status line is still used to display help about each of the links. Figure 8.5 shows Netscape's output of this page.

Figure 8.5.

Netscape shows the FSC home page with the scrolling text field.

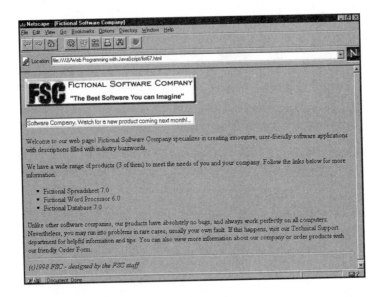

Listing 8.7. (SCROLTXT.HTM) The FSC page with the scrolling text field routine.

```
<HTML>
<HEAD>
<TITLE>Fictional Software Company</TITLE>
<SCRIPT>
// message to scroll in text field
var msg = "Welcome to Fictional Software Company. Watch for a new product
➥coming next month!";
var spacer = "...           ...";
// current message position
var pos = 0;
//flag to control message
function ScrollMessage() {
    document.form1.text1.value = msg.substring(pos, msg.length) + spacer +
➥msg.substring(0, pos);
    pos++;
    if (pos > msg.length) pos = 0;
// set timeout for next update
    window.setTimeout("ScrollMessage()",200);
}
// Display a link help message
function LinkMessage(text) {
    window.status = text;
}
</SCRIPT>
</HEAD>
<BODY onLoad = "ScrollMessage();">
<IMG SRC="fsclogo.gif" alt="Fictional Software Company">
```

```
<FORM name="form1">
<INPUT TYPE="text" name="text1" SIZE="55">
</FORM>
Welcome to our web page! Fictional Software Company
specializes in creating innovative, user-friendly software
applications with descriptions filled with industry
buzzwords.
<P>
We have a wide range of products (3 of them) to meet
the needs of you and your company. Follow the links
below for more information.
<P>
<UL>
<LI><A HREF="spread.html"
onMouseOver="LinkMessage('Information about the spreadsheet');return true;">
Fictional Spreadsheet 7.0</A>
<LI><A HREF="word.html"
onMouseOver="LinkMessage('Information about the word processor');return true;">
Fictional Word Processor 6.0</A>
<LI><A HREF="data.html"
onMouseOver="LinkMessage('Information about the database');return true;">
Fictional Database 7.0</A>
</UL>
<P>
Unlike other software companies, our products have
absolutely no bugs, and always work perfectly on all
computers. Nevertheless, you may run into problems in
rare cases, usually your own fault. If this happens,
visit our <A HREF="support.html"
onMouseOver="LinkMessage('Technical Support for our products');return true;">
Technical Support</A>
department for helpful information and tips. You can
also view more information <A HREF="company.html"
onMouseOver="LinkMessage('Information about FSC Software Co.');return true;">
about our company</A> or order products with our friendly
<a href="order.html"
onMouseOver="LinkMessage('Allows you to order products');return true;">
Order Form</A>.
<HR>
<I>(c)1998 FSC - designed by the FSC staff</I>
</BODY>
</HTML>
```

Workshop Wrap-Up

In this chapter, you learned some of the ways a Web page can be improved by using JavaScript, including the following:

- ❏ Using selection lists to create a table of contents to make the page easy to navigate

- ❏ Using the status line to display information about links rather than the URLs

- ❏ Using the status line to display a scrolling message, and using a text field as an alternative for the purpose

Next Steps

To continue your studies of JavaScript, move on to one of the following chapters:

❏ To learn the specifics about the objects and window elements used in this chapter, see Chapter 5, "Accessing Window Elements as Objects."

❏ To continue improving a Web page, this time using advanced features such as frames, see Chapter 9, "Using Frames, Cookies, and Other Advanced Features."

❏ To learn some techniques for organizing a larger and more complicated Web site, see Chapter 10, "Working with Multiple Pages and Data."

❏ To see some more real-world examples of the techniques in this chapter, see Chapter 11, "Real-Life Examples II."

Q&A

Q: What's wrong with the many popular scrolling message routines available on the Web?

A: Most of them are victims of the memory leak bug in Netscape, because they reassign a string every time the text in the status bar moves. The example in this chapter avoids this problem. See Chapter 14, "Debugging JavaScript Programs," for details.

Q: Is there any way to use some kind of "floating hints" or "balloon help" with links instead of using the status bar?

A: Not currently. This may be added in some fashion in a future implementation of JavaScript.

Q: Can the navigation bar in this chapter be used with browsers that don't support JavaScript?

A: Yes. You could easily modify it to send the selections to a CGI script, which could send the user to the correct page. You'll take a closer look at CGI in Chapter 18.

CHAPTER

NINE

Using Frames, Cookies, and Other Advanced Features

In this chapter, you'll continue to revise the FSC Web pages created in Chapter 8, moving on to features found in the latest browsers—specifically, the latest version of Netscape. Features such as frames and cookies enable you to add unique capabilities to a JavaScript-enhanced page.

Although Netscape version 3.0 is the current version at this writing, most of the features discussed in this chapter were introduced in version 2.0, which also introduced JavaScript.

You'll use some of the documents created in Chapter 8, "Improving a Web Page with JavaScript," in this chapter.

NOTE: At this writing, Microsoft has released a beta version of version 3.0 of its Internet Explorer (MSIE) Web browser. This release supports frames and cookies, along with much of JavaScript.

Advanced Browser Features

Before you get into the use of the new features with JavaScript, let's take a quick look at how you use them in a simple HTML page. This will enable you to make them work easily with JavaScript later in this chapter.

Frames

Frames divide the browser window into panes, or segments.

Netscape introduced frames in version 2.0. Recall that frames, also called framesets, are used to divide a Web page's display into multiple sections, each of which can display a different document or portion of a document. Frames are becoming a popular feature in Web pages and are already supported by some non-Netscape browsers.

An example of a document that uses frames is Netscape's JavaScript Authoring Guide, shown in Figure 9.1. The window is divided into three frames: a frame on the left with the table of contents, one on the right with the actual text, and a small strip on the bottom with two buttons used for JavaScript functions.

Figure 9.1.

Netscape's JavaScript Authoring Guide is an example of a document that uses frames.

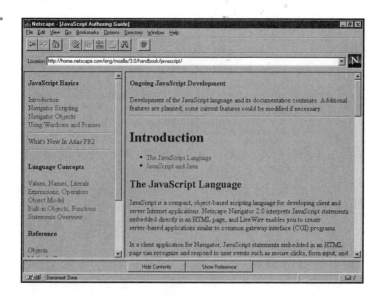

As far as JavaScript is concerned, each frame is represented by a separate window object.

Each frame acts as a separate window; it has its own URL. Each frame can also have horizontal and vertical scrollbars. The user can move the dividing lines to resize the different frames. You can enable and disable scrollbars and resizing through HTML attributes.

Defining a Frameset

You use the <FRAMESET> tag to define a framed document. This tag is used instead of the <BODY> tag. The page with the <FRAMESET> declaration defines the layout of the different frames and which documents are loaded into them, but contains no actual data—the contents of each frame are at their own URLs.

The frame definition begins with the <FRAMESET> tag and ends with the closing </FRAMESET> tag. Within these tags you can't use any ordinary HTML; you can use only tags and attributes that define frames. You can also nest a frameset within another frameset.

The <FRAMESET> tag has two attributes: ROWS and COLS. These define how the window is divided. You can use either of these attributes or both. Both of these attributes have the same value, which is a list of dimensions for each row or column. You can define the rows or columns in the following ways:

- ❏ Specify a numeric value to define the size of a row or column in pixels. For example, "40,40,40" defines three frames, each 40 pixels in size. Note that Netscape will expand the frames to fill the browser window, though.
- ❏ Specify a percentage value to allocate a percentage of the window. For example, "20%,40%,40%" allocates 20 percent of the window to the first frame and 40 percent to the other two.
- ❏ Specify a relative value with the asterisk (*) character. For example, "*,*,*,*" divides a page evenly into four frames. You can specify a number to give a frame more than one share; for example, "1*,2*" creates two frames, one with 1/3 of the space and the other with 2/3.

NOTE: It is considered bad style to specify an exact number of pixels for a frame except in certain cases. Users may have different window sizes and different fonts, and you will end up annoying some users. One exception is when you are using a frame to display an image, such as a logo or navigation icons. You can then set the frame size to fit the image exactly.

Try not to use frames unnecessarily; they can be inconvenient to the user, especially on low-resolution screens.

You can combine the different methods any way you like; in fact, this is almost always the best way to define a frameset. The following examples will give you some ideas of how these can be combined:

❏ `<FRAMESET ROWS="30,*">` devotes 30 rows of pixels to the first frame (for a navigation bar image, perhaps) and the remaining space to the second frame.

❏ `<FRAMESET COLS="50%,25%,*">` splits the screen vertically into three frames. The first uses 50 percent of the available space, the second uses 25 percent, and the third uses the remaining space (25 percent).

❏ `<FRAMESET ROWS="*,*,50">` splits the screen horizontally. The bottom frame is exactly 50 pixels high, and the top two frames divide the remaining space equally.

❏ `<FRAMESET ROWS="*,*" COLS="*,*">` splits the screen into four equally spaced frames.

NOTE: Notice that you are not required to define a value for the number of frames in the frameset. This value is calculated based on the number of values in the ROWS and COLS lists.

Defining Individual Frames

Within the frameset, you use the `<FRAME>` tag to define each of the frames and the document it will contain. You should include one `<FRAME>` tag for each of the frames you defined in the ROWS and COLS attributes. The `<FRAME>` tag includes the following attributes:

❏ SRC specifies the URL of the document to place in this frame. If this attribute is left out, the frame will be empty.

❏ NAME enables you to specify a name for the frame. You will use this in targeted links, described later in this chapter; you can also use this name in JavaScript. If a frame will contain a single document and will not be changed, you can omit the NAME attribute.

❏ MARGINWIDTH defines the left and right margins of the frame, in pixels. This number of pixels will be left blank on either side of the frame's contents. This attribute must be at least 1, the default, and can be any size—provided room is left for the document between the margins.

❏ MARGINHEIGHT defines the top and bottom margins of the frame. This works in the same way as the MARGINWIDTH tag.

❏ SCROLLING defines whether the frame includes horizontal and vertical scrollbars. This can have three values: YES forces the scrollbars to be included; NO prevents them from being included; and AUTO, the default value, displays scrollbars only if the document is larger than the frame's size.

❏ NORESIZE has no value. If it is included, it indicates that the frame cannot be resized by the user. By default, the user is allowed to resize all frames.

As an example of the <FRAMESET> and <FRAME> tags, Listing 9.1 shows a complete definition for a frameset containing three documents, each displayed in a horizontal frame.

Listing 9.1. (FRAME1.HTM) A simple frameset definition with three horizontal frames.

```
<FRAMESET ROWS="10%,*,*">
<FRAME SRC="doc1.htm">
<FRAME SRC="doc2.htm">
<FRAME SRC="doc3.htm" MARGINWIDTH="50">
</FRAMESET>
```

The first frame takes 10 percent of the available space, and the second and third divide the remaining space equally, giving them 45 percent each. The third frame includes a left and right margin of 50 pixels. Figure 9.2 shows how this set of documents looks in Netscape.

Figure 9.2.

An example of a framed document with three horizontal frames.

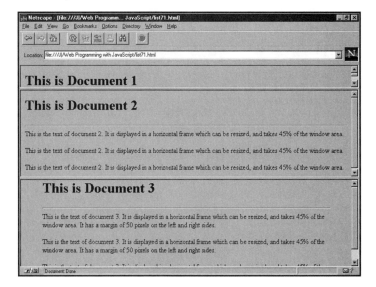

Using Nested Framesets

Nested framesets enable you to create more complicated arrangements of frames.

Although you can combine ROWS and COLS to divide a page both ways, you might wonder how you create unevenly divided frames. This is done by nesting the <FRAMESET> tags. You can use a <FRAMESET> tag instead of a <FRAME> tag to further subdivide that frame.

To use nested frames, try to start with the largest divisions of the page and end with the smallest. As an example, Listing 9.2 shows a frameset document that defines a set of nested frames.

Listing 9.2. (FRAME2.HTM) A document with four frames, using nested framesets.

```
<FRAMESET ROWS="*,*">
    <FRAMESET COLS="*,*">
        <FRAME SRC="doc1.htm">
        <FRAME SRC="doc2.htm">
    </FRAMESET>
    <FRAMESET COLS="30%,*">
        <FRAME SRC="doc3.htm">
        <FRAME SRC="doc4.htm">
    </FRAMESET>
</FRAMESET>
```

This first divides the window into two rows, each with half of the area. The first row is divided into two columns of equal size; the second row is divided into a narrow column and a wide column. The output of this example is shown in Figure 9.3.

Figure 9.3.

A window with nested framesets showing four documents.

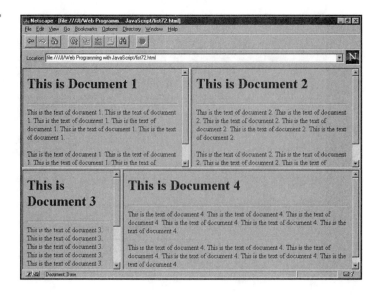

The `<NOFRAMES>` Tag: Providing an Alternative

Along with the `<FRAME>` tag and nested framesets, one other tag can be used within a frameset document: `<NOFRAMES>`. This is a container that you can use to display information to users with non-frame browsers.

The way it works is this: Netscape and other browsers that support frames ignore everything within the `<NOFRAMES>` tags. Other browsers don't know what to do with the tag, so they ignore it and display the information between the tags.

This enables you to do things like this:

```
<FRAMESET ROWS="*,*">
<FRAME SRC="doc1.htm">
<FRAME SRC="doc2.htm">
<NOFRAMES>
<h1>Hello</h1>
You are using a non-frame browser. Please go away
and don't come back until you support frames.
</NOFRAMES>
</FRAMESET>
```

`<NOFRAMES>` enables you to display a message to browsers that don't support frames.

This simply displays a rather rude message to users of non-frame browsers, although frame browsers display the framed documents normally. Unfortunately, `<NOFRAMES>` is often used to display messages like this; there are many users with non-frames browsers, though, and they often don't have the option of upgrading.

A much better approach is to use the `<NOFRAMES>` section to enclose a non-frame version of the same document set or an index of links to the documents. You could also include a simple link to send the user to the non-frame version.

NOTE: One common mistake is to assume that browsers that support frames also support JavaScript. Some Web authors have used `<NOFRAMES>` to weed out non-JavaScript browsers. There are now several browsers that support frames but not JavaScript, so this is not reliable. The `<NOSCRIPT>` tag, introduced in Netscape 3.0b4, provides a solution.

Common Uses for Frames

You might wonder why you would want to display several documents on the screen at once with frames. In fact, many users of the Web complain about just that. Nonetheless, there are several valid uses for frames. Here are a few ideas:

❏ You can display a table of contents in one frame and the document in the other. This enables the table of contents to remain visible.

❏ Frames are often used for status messages, or for navigation aids, or to display a logo on all pages in a static frame.

❏ Web-based games and utilities can use frames to control their layouts.

You will look at some of these uses later in this chapter; you will also use frames in many of the applications created in the upcoming chapters.

Targeted Links

Because you can display multiple documents in a window with frames and multiple windows, you need a way to specify which window or frame to use. The TARGET property enables you to do this.

Targeted links are essential for linking to separate frames.

The TARGET property is used in links, and it indicates the window or frame in which the document will be displayed. This is the name you assigned using the NAME attribute of the <FRAME> tag. For windows you create in JavaScript, this is the window reference you specified when creating the window.

For example, this link will open the order.htm document in the win1 frame or window:

```
<A HREF="order.htm" TARGET="win1">Order form</A>
```

If the window doesn't already exist, a new window will be created with the document loaded. For example, this link creates a new window called win2 and loads the support.htm document into it:

```
<A HREF="support.htm" TARGET="win2">Technical Support</A>
```

Another tag, <BASE>, enables you to define a default target window for a document. This target will be used for all links in the document except those with a differing TARGET property of their own. This statement sets the default target to win2:

```
<BASE TARGET="win2">
```

This is particularly useful for a frame that will be used as a navigation bar or table of contents, because you will want every link in the document to load in a different frame.

NOTE: As mentioned in Chapter 6, "Using Interactive Forms," the <FORM> tag can also have a TARGET property. In this case, it defines which window or frame will be used to display the results after the form is submitted.

Cookies

In CGI programming, one of the most vexing problems is storing state information. When users go from one page to the next, it's hard to keep track of what they were doing, or even if they are the same users.

Netscape created *cookies* as one solution to this problem. A cookie is a chunk of information sent by the server, which can be stored on the client. Cookies are stored with a date they expire and the name of the host from which they came. When the user communicates with the same host later, the data is sent back.

Here are some examples where cookies can be useful:

❏ They can store a user's "preferences" for a Web page. When users return to the page, they can view it in their desired fashion. For example, Netscape's home page uses this technique to turn frames on or off based on the user's preference.

❏ They can maintain state between CGI scripts or JavaScript programs. For example, a quiz might ask you one question, then load a new page for the next question, storing your score in a cookie.

❏ They can remember information so that users can avoid entering it every time they access a page. For example, a page that requires a user's name can remember it with a cookie.

Cookies can also be used in JavaScript. You can use them to store information between pages, or even to store information on users' computers to remember their preferences next time they load your page.

Each cookie stores a named piece of information and includes an expiration date. With few exceptions, this date is usually one of the following:

❏ When used to store preferences, a faraway date is usually used—in essence, it never expires.

❏ When used to maintain state, a date in the near future—typically the next day—is used. In the previous quiz example, a user that came back the next day would have to start the quiz over.

The cookies are stored in a "cookie jar" on the user's computer. Specifically, each cookie is a line in a file called `cookies.txt`, usually in the same directory as Netscape itself.

Plug-Ins

Microsoft Internet Explorer and other browsers have promised plug-in support.

One feature added by Netscape surpasses even frames: the plug-in specification. This is an Application Program Interface (API) that enables programmers to create add-ons for Netscape. These are typically used to enable the browser to view non-HTML data.

Plug-ins are available for a wide variety of formats, and more are coming out every day. You can use plug-ins to display new kinds of images, animations, video, and 3D graphics directly in the browser window.

Because plug-ins are all about multimedia and bring many new media formats to the Web, you'll explore them in detail in Chapter 13, "Working with Multimedia and Plug-Ins."

NOTE: You can't write plug-ins with JavaScript, but there are features to enable you to control and interact with them using JavaScript.

Using Frames with JavaScript

By combining JavaScript and frames, you can create multiwindow documents that interact with each other in new ways. Frames and JavaScript are used together frequently, and you'll use them many times in the rest of this book.

This section begins with an introduction to the objects and terminology you'll need to know to work with frames in JavaScript. Next, you'll apply what you've learned to add frames capability to the FSC Web page created in Chapter 8.

Objects for Frames

When a window contains multiple frames, each frame is represented in JavaScript by a `frame` object. This object is equivalent to a `window` object, but it is used for dealing with that frame. The `frame` object's name is the same as the NAME attribute you gave it in the `<FRAME>` tag.

The `window` and `self` keywords are introduced in Chapter 5, "Accessing Window Elements as Objects."

Remember the `window` and `self` keywords, which refer to the current window? When you are using frames, these keywords refer to the current frame instead. Another keyword, `parent`, enables you to refer to the main window.

Each frame object in a window is a child of the `parent` window object. Suppose you define a set of frames using the HTML in Listing 9.3.

Listing 9.3. (FRAME3.HTM) A framed document that divides the page into quarters.

```
<FRAMESET ROWS="*,*" COLS="*,*">
<FRAME NAME="topleft" SRC="topleft.htm">
<FRAME NAME="topright" SRC="topright.htm">
<FRAME NAME="bottomleft" SRC="botleft.htm">
<FRAME NAME="bottomright" SRC="botright.htm">
</FRAMESET>
```

This simply divides the window into quarters. If you have a JavaScript program in the `topleft.htm` file, it would refer to the other windows as `parent.topright`, `parent.bottomleft`, and so on. The keywords `window` and `self` would refer to the `topleft` frame.

NOTE: If you use nested framesets, things are a bit more complicated. `window` still represents the current frame, `parent` represents the frameset containing the current frame, and `top` represents the main frameset that contains all the others.

The `frames` Array

Rather than referring to frames in a document by name, you can use the `frames` array. This array stores information about each of the frames in the document. The frames are indexed starting with zero and beginning with the first `<FRAME>` tag in the frameset document.

As an example, you could refer to the frames defined in Listing 9.3 using array references:

- ❏ `parent.frames[0]` is equivalent to the `topleft` frame.
- ❏ `parent.frames[1]` is equivalent to the `topright` frame.
- ❏ `parent.frames[2]` is equivalent to the `bottomleft` frame.
- ❏ `parent.frames[3]` is equivalent to the `bottomright` frame.

You can refer to a frame using either method interchangeably, and depending on your application, you should use the most convenient method. For example, a document with 10 frames would probably be easier to use by number, but a simple two-frame document is easier to use if the frames have meaningful names.

Frame Object Properties, Events, and Methods

Each frame object (or each member of the `frames` array) has two properties:

- ❑ `name` is the value of the NAME attribute in the `<FRAME>` tag.
- ❑ `length` is the number of child frames within the frame.

Because frames have their own window objects, each has a separate history list.

In addition, you can use all the properties of the `window` object, which you looked at in Chapter 5, in a frame. You can also use the methods `setTimeout()`, `clearTimeout()`, `blur()`, and `focus()`.

You can define the `onLoad` and `onUnload` event handlers for the parent window object within the `<FRAMESET>` tag. The individual frames in a document do not have their own event handlers for loading and unloading; the parent window's `onLoad` event indicates that all frames have been loaded.

Using JavaScript in Multiframe Windows

At this point, you should have an idea of how to access the various frames in a window from JavaScript. Now let's apply this knowledge by making improvements to the FSC Software page created in Chapter 8.

You'll use a simple two-frame structure for the revised FSC page. You will move the navigation bar (the selection lists and "go" button) to the top frame, along with the logo. This will enable the logo and table of contents to remain at the top while the user visits the various pages in the bottom frame.

Creating a Framed Document

To begin, you'll need a frameset document. This will be the document the user loads first, and it will define the frame layout and the contents of each frame. This is the easiest part; the frame definition document is shown in Listing 9.4.

Listing 9.4. (FRAMEFSC.HTM) The frame definition document for the revised FSC page.

```
<HTML>
<FRAMESET ROWS="30%,*">
<FRAME NAME="contents" SRC="contents.htm">
<FRAME NAME="main" SRC="fscmain.htm">
</FRAMESET>
</HTML>
```

This simply defines two rows of frames. The first will be used for the navigation bar, which you will store in the file `contents.htm`. The second frame will be used for whichever document the user is looking at; it will start with the introductory page, `fscmain.htm`.

Modifying the Navigation Bar

Next, you need to create the `contents.htm` file. This will include the `Navigate()` function created in Chapter 8, the navigation form, and the company logo. Listing 9.5 shows the contents document.

Listing 9.5. (CONTENTS.HTM) The contents of the top frame.

```
<HTML>
<HEAD>
<TITLE>Fictional Software Company</TITLE>
<SCRIPT>
function Navigate() {
   prod = document.navform.program.selectedIndex;
   cat = document.navform.category.selectedIndex;
   prodval = document.navform.program.options[prod].value;
   catval = document.navform.category.options[cat].value;
   if (prodval == "x" ¦¦ catval == "x") return;
   parent.frames[1].location.href = prodval + "_" + catval + ".htm";
}
</SCRIPT>
</HEAD>
<BODY>
<IMG SRC="fsclogo.gif" alt="Fictional Software Company">
<FORM name="navform">
<SELECT name="program">
<OPTION VALUE="x" SELECTED>Select a Product
<OPTION VALUE="w">Fictional Word Processor
<OPTION VALUE="s">Fictional Spreadsheet
<OPTION VALUE="d">Fictional Database
</SELECT>
<SELECT name="category">
<OPTION VALUE="x" SELECTED>Select a Category
<OPTION VALUE="tech">Technical Support
<OPTION VALUE="sales">Sales and Availability
<OPTION VALUE="feat">List of Features
<OPTION VALUE="price">Pricing Information
<OPTION VALUE="tips">Tips and Techniques
</SELECT>
<INPUT TYPE="button" NAME="go" VALUE="Go to Page"
onClick="Navigate();">
</FORM>
</BODY>
</HTML>
```

The form definition is the same one used in Chapter 8. Only one change was needed in the `Navigate()` function. The last line was changed to this:

```
parent.frames[1].location.href = prodval + "_" + catval + ".htm";
```

This sets the location of the second frame to the new URL, rather than the current frame. Thus, the documents the user selects load in the second frame, and the navigation bar stays in the first frame.

Testing the Multiframe Document

To test this multiframe FSC page, you will need the introductory page, fscmain.htm, to display in the second frame. This file is shown in Listing 9.6. This is simply a modified version of the version in Chapter 8 after adding onMouseOver status line help.

Listing 9.6. (FSCMAIN.HTM) The document for the second frame.

```
<HTML>
<HEAD>
<TITLE>Fictional Software Company</TITLE>
</HEAD>
<BODY>
Welcome to our web page! Fictional Software Company
specializes in creating innovative, user-friendly software
applications with descriptions filled with industry
buzzwords.
<P>
We have a wide range of products (3 of them) to meet
the needs of you and your company. Follow the links
below for more information.
<P>
<UL>
<LI><A HREF="spread.htm"
onMouseOver="window.status='Information about the spreadsheet';return true;">
Fictional Spreadsheet 7.0</A>
<LI><A HREF="word.htm"
onMouseOver="window.status='Information about the word processor';return
true;">
Fictional Word Processor 6.0</A>
<LI><A HREF="data.htm"
onMouseOver="window.status='Information about the database';return true;">
Fictional Database 7.0</A>
</UL>
<P>
Unlike other software companies, our products have
absolutely no bugs, and always work perfectly on all
computers. Nevertheless, you may run into problems in
rare cases, usually your own fault. If this happens,
visit our <A HREF="support.htm"
onMouseOver="window.status='Technical Support for our products';return true;">
Technical Support</A>
department for helpful information and tips. You can
also view more information <A HREF="company.htm"
onMouseOver="window.status='Information about FSC Software Co.';return true;">
about our company</A> or order products with our friendly
<a href="order.htm"
onMouseOver="window.status='Allows you to order products';return true;">
Order Form</A>.
<HR>
<I>(c)1998 FSC - designed by the FSC staff</I>
</BODY>
</HTML>
```

You are now ready to test the multiframe document. All you need to do now is load the frameset document (Listing 9.4) into the browser. The complete document in Netscape is shown in Figure 9.4.

Figure 9.4.
*The complete
multiframe document.*

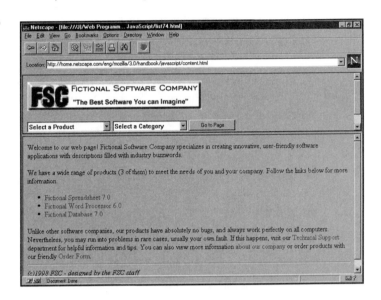

You can include a
separate JavaScript
program or event
handlers in each frame.

Notice that you are now using two HTML documents and two JavaScript applications. The application in the top frame is used to manage the navigation. The second frame includes the onMouseOver functions to display useful information in the status line. JavaScript works in both at the same time.

You should now understand how frames can be used and the benefits they offer. You will use frames throughout the rest of this book in many more complicated applications.

 # Updating a Frame with JavaScript

As a final example of frames, let's create a document that uses the open() and close() methods to rewrite a frame's contents from a script in another frame. As a simple application of this technique, you will create a clock that displays the time in a frame in a large font.

As usual, the frameset document is the simplest part. The frameset document for this example is shown in Listing 9.7.

Listing 9.7. (FRAMEUP1.HTM) The frameset document for the frame update example.

```
<FRAMESET ROWS="50%,50%"
 onLoad="window.setTimeout('parent.CodeFrame.Update();',5000);">
  <FRAME NAME="TimeFrame" SRC="Doc1.htm">
  <FRAME NAME="CodeFrame" SRC="frameup2.htm">
</FRAMESET>
```

The top frame, called TimeFrame, is initially loaded with a generic file; if you don't specify the SRC property, frames don't always work correctly with JavaScript. This document will be erased by the clock five seconds after the page loads, as defined in the frameset's onLoad event handler.

The real work for the clock is done by the document in the second frame, called CodeFrame. Listing 9.8 shows this document.

Listing 9.8. (FRAMEUP2.HTM) The main document for the frame update example.

```
<HTML>
<HEAD>
<TITLE>A Silly JavaScript Clock</TITLE>
<SCRIPT LANGUAGE="JavaScript">
var now;
//function to update time in frame
function Update() {
// get the time
   now = new Date();
   hh = now.getHours();
   mm = now.getMinutes();
   ss = now.getSeconds();
// clear and rewrite the "time" frame
   parent.TimeFrame.document.open();
   parent.TimeFrame.document.write("<HTML><BODY><CENTER><FONT SIZE='+35'>");
   parent.TimeFrame.document.write(hh + ":" + mm + ":" + ss);
   parent.TimeFrame.document.writeln("</H1></BODY></FONT>");
   parent.TimeFrame.document.close();
// set the next timeout
   window.setTimeout("Update();",5000);
}
</SCRIPT>
</HEAD>
<BODY>
The above frame displays the time, which is updated once every 5 seconds
after you load this page. The frame is updated with the <b>document.open()</b>
and <b>close()</b> methods in JavaScript.
</BODY>
</HTML>
```

This document includes the Update() function, which updates the clock by rewriting the TimeFrame frame's contents. The document.open() and document.close() methods used to accomplish this are explained in Chapter 5. Figure 9.5 shows this example in action.

Figure 9.5.
The output of the frame update example.

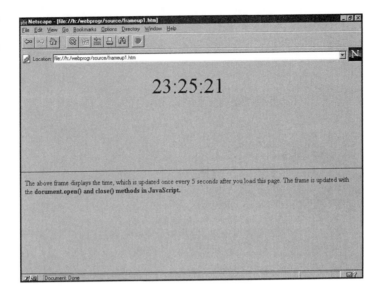

<image: Netscape window showing>

23:25:21

The above frame displays the time, which is updated once every 5 seconds after you load this page. The frame is updated with the document.open() and close() methods in JavaScript.

TASK

Remembering User Preferences with Cookies

Chapter 11, "Real-Life Examples II," includes a more complicated example of this technique.

Let's take a look at using cookies with JavaScript. You can use cookies to store a preference for the user, or to remember the user when they come back to your page. (No, you can't eat them.)

Cookies are stored for the current document, and they are accessed with the `document.cookie` property. This property is a text value which can contain the following components:

- ❏ `name=value`: A name and value, separated by the equal sign. This is the actual data stored in the cookie.
- ❏ `expires=date`: An expiration date. If this date is not included, the cookie is erased when the user exits the browser. (For the format of the date, see the example later.)
- ❏ `domain=machine:` The domain name for which the cookie is valid. By default, this is the domain of the current page.
- ❏ `path=path`: The URL path for which the cookie is valid. By default, this is the current URL.

As an example, Listing 9.9 shows a document that remembers the name of each user who accesses it. Each section of the document is explained later.

Listing 9.9. (COOKIE.HTM) An example of cookies in JavaScript.

```
<HTML>
<HEAD>
<TITLE>The page that remembers your name</TITLE>
<SCRIPT>
if (document.cookie.substring(0,2) != "n=") {
   nam = window.prompt("Enter your name");
   document.cookie = "n=" + nam + ";";
   document.cookie += "expires=Tuesday, 31-Dec-99 23:59:00 GMT"
}
</SCRIPT>
</HEAD>
<BODY>
<H1>Here is Your name</H1>
<HR>
<SCRIPT>
indx = document.cookie.indexOf(";");
nam = document.cookie.substring(2,indx+1);
document.write("Hello there, ", nam);
</SCRIPT>
<P>
next paragraph
</BODY>
</HTML>
```

The script in the document header simply checks the name portion of the cookie string for the n= characters. If they are not found, it prompts for the user's name, and stores the value in the "n=" cookie. A faraway expiration date is used to save the information indefinitely.

The script in the body of the document is then able to greet the user by displaying a name, if one has been defined. The output of this page is shown in Figure 9.6. Obviously, there are more uses for cookies than just names. You will explore another use in Chapter 11.

Figure 9.6.

The output of the JavaScript cookie example.

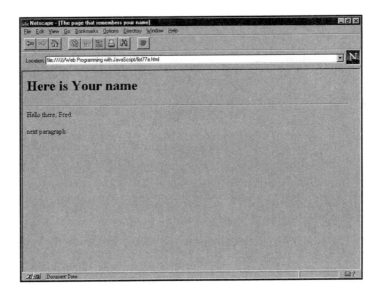

Workshop Wrap-Up

In this chapter, you continued the process of adding interactive features to a company Web page with JavaScript, taking advantage of the latest browser features:

❑ The most important feature you can use with JavaScript is frames, which enable you to divide a window into multiple areas. You can use frames to create separate navigation bars, status areas, and many other useful divisions.

❑ You can use cookies to store information about the user or the current session. This can be useful for keeping state between different documents and for storing user preferences.

Next Steps

You have now expanded your knowledge of JavaScript to include frames and cookies, and you should have an idea of the possibilities they offer. Move on with one of the following:

❑ To review the JavaScript objects referred to in this chapter and their uses, see Chapter 5, "Accessing Window Elements as Objects."

❑ To learn various ways to liven up a page without frames, see Chapter 8, "Improving a Web Page with JavaScript."

❑ To learn how to use frames and cookies in more complicated ways, turn to Chapter 10, "Working with Multiple Pages and Data."

❏ To see more examples of the techniques in this chapter, see Chapter 11, "Real-Life Examples II."

❏ To learn more about Netscape plug-ins, see Chapter 13, "Working with Multimedia and Plug-Ins."

Q&A

Q: How do frames and cookies fit into the HTML standards, if at all?

A: Frames have been proposed as an extension to HTML, but have not been implemented in the latest version (HTML 3.2). You can bet they will become a standard, with both Netscape and Microsoft behind them. Cookies have not yet been discussed as an addition to HTML.

Q: Is there any way for a user to access information stored in a cookie by a previous user?

A: No. Cookies are stored on the user's machine, so each user has a separate database. There is no way to send this data to the server with JavaScript.

Q: Can I modify the frameset "on the fly"—for example, adding a new frame or eliminating an existing one?

A: Not without loading a different frameset. JavaScript has no capability of changing framesets, at least in the current version.

Q: Can I call a function I defined in a different frame's document?

A: Yes. JavaScript functions are properties of the `window` object, so you can specify the window and document when you call the function, such as `parent.frame2.Update()`. Listing 9.7 uses this technique.

Q: Nobody takes me seriously when I talk about cookies. Who at Netscape can I blame for creating a silly term like that?

A: Netscape is innocent in this case. The terms "cookie" and "cookie jar" have been used for years in the computer industry to represent named bits of information, usually stored in a computer's memory.

TEN

Working with Multiple Pages and Data

In this chapter, you'll look at some of the more complex capabilities of JavaScript. You learned the basics of using frames in Chapter 9, "Using Frames, Cookies, and Other Advanced Features;" you'll look at some more sophisticated examples here. You'll also explore techniques for storing data and learn about the data tainting feature, which enables you to overcome some of Netscape's security restrictions.

Working with a Complex Web Site

As you learned in Chapter 9, you can use nested framesets to create a complex framed document. When you combine nested framesets with JavaScript, you have to be careful about how you refer to fields in other frames.

Creating an Application in Nested Framesets

Chapter 9 explains the basics of frames.

For this section, let's return to the Fictional Software home page created in Chapter 9, turning it into a complex site using nested framesets. You'll find it looks much more like typical sites on the Web.

Let's start by creating the frameset document, shown in Listing 10.1.

Listing 10.1. (NESTED.HTM) The frameset document for the nested framesets example.

```
<HTML>
<FRAMESET ROWS="30%,*,52">
<FRAME NAME="contents" SRC="contents.htm">
<FRAME NAME="main" SRC="fscmain2.htm">
 <FRAMESET COLS="300,*">
   <FRAME NAME="imagemap" SRC="map.htm">
   <FRAME NAME="description" SRC="descrip.htm">
 </FRAMESET>
</FRAMESET>
</HTML>
```

This listing uses the following frames:

❏ The top frame is the navigation bar created in Chapter 8, "Improving a Web Page with JavaScript."

❏ The next frame covers most of the page, and it is the main description of the company and links.

❏ The third frame is on the lower left, and it includes a client-side image map for navigation.

❏ The fourth frame is on the lower right. It provides a text field that will be used to display descriptions as the user moves over a link.

Listing 10.2 shows the document for the second frame, which is adapted from the version used in Chapter 9.

Listing 10.2. (FSCMAIN2.HTM) The second frame for the nested frames example.

```
<HTML>
<HEAD>
<TITLE>Fictional Software Company</TITLE>
</HEAD>
<BODY>
Welcome to our web page! Fictional Software Company
specializes in creating innovative, user-friendly software
applications with descriptions filled with industry
buzzwords.
```

```
<P>
We have a wide range of products (3 of them) to meet
the needs of you and your company. Follow the links
below for more information.
<P>
<UL>
<LI><A HREF="spread.htm"
onMouseOver="parent.description.document.form1.text1.value='Information about
➥the spreadsheet';return true;">
Fictional Spreadsheet 7.0</A>
<LI><A HREF="word.htm"
onMouseOver="parent.description.document.form1.text1.value='Information about
➥the word processor';return true;">
Fictional Word Processor 6.0</A>
<LI><A HREF="data.htm"
onMouseOver="parent.description.document.form1.text1.value='Information about
➥the database';return true;">
Fictional Database 7.0</A>
</UL>
<HR>
<I>(c)1998 FSC - designed by the FSC staff</I>

</BODY>
</HTML>
```

Learn more about using image maps with JavaScript in Chapter 12, "Working with Graphics in JavaScript."

The third frame is an image map, which can be used for navigation. It uses event handlers to place informative messages in the text field in the fourth frame. Listing 10.3 shows the image map document.

Listing 10.3. (MAP.HTM) The image map document for the nested frames example.

```
<HTML>
<BODY>
<MAP NAME="map1">
<AREA SHAPE=RECT COORDS="6,7,61,43" HREF=support.htm
onMouseOver="parent.description.document.form1.text1.value='Support for our
➥products';return true;">
<AREA SHAPE=RECT COORDS="73,8,129,42" HREF=compinfo.htm
onMouseOver="parent.description.document.form1.text1.value='About our
➥Company';return true;">
<AREA SHAPE=RECT COORDS="140,7,200,42" HREF=order.htm
onMouseOver="parent.description.document.form1.text1.value='Order
➥Products';return true;">
<AREA SHAPE=RECT COORDS="211,6,276,43" HREF=customer.htm
onMouseOver="parent.description.document.form1.text1.value='Customer
➥Service';return true;">
<AREA SHAPE=default HREF=fscmain2.htm>
</MAP>
<IMG SRC="fscmap.gif" USEMAP="#map1">
</BODY>
</HTML>
```

Finally, the fourth frame contains a simple text field, which is used in place of the status bar to display descriptions as the user moves over links. Listing 10.4 shows this document.

Listing 10.4. (DESCRIP.HTM) The description text field document for the nested frames example.

```
<HTML>
<BODY>
<FORM NAME="form1">
<INPUT TYPE="TEXT" NAME="text1" SIZE="40" VALUE="Look Here for help.">
</BODY>
</HTML>
```

This is a good example of how complicated frames programming can get. Both the middle frame and the image map frame address the text field in the fourth frame to display descriptions. The final document, as displayed in Netscape, is shown in Figure 10.1.

Figure 10.1.
The nested frames example, as displayed by Netscape.

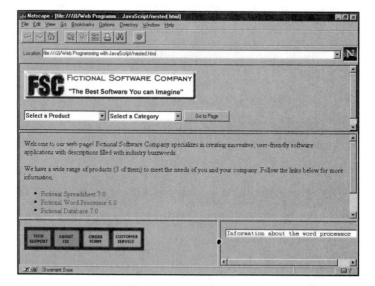

Working with Databases and Data

One of the most talked-about issues on the Web today is the integration of databases with Web content. JavaScript isn't a very powerful language for database applications, mainly because it's limited to client-side use. However, there are some tricks you can use to store data in a database-like format in JavaScript. You'll look at several such techniques in the following sections.

Using String Arrays

The basics of arrays and strings are explained in Chapter 4, "Using Built-In Objects and Custom Objects."

The first technique may seem simple, but it's often overlooked. Because a JavaScript variable can hold any type of data, it can be used as a string array. For example, the following code creates a three-element string array and assigns values to its elements:

```
strings = new Array(3);
strings[0] = "This is the first element.";
strings[1] = "This is the second element.";
strings[2] = "This is the third element.";
```

Each element of the array can be used as an ordinary string object. For example, this statement displays a substring from the third element of the array defined previously:

```
document.write(strings[2].substring(5,10));
```

Using Associative Arrays

If you've worked with Perl, a popular language for CGI programs, you've probably used associative arrays. An associative array is an array with names instead of indexes for each of its elements.

JavaScript doesn't officially include associative arrays, but you can easily simulate them using an object. The following statements define an object and assign values to three elements:

```
animals = new Object();
animals["frog"] = 2;
animals["bear"] = 3;
animals["chicken"] = 4;
```

This technique is useful if you are storing a number of named values, especially if the names are created during the course of your program.

Creating Custom Data Structures

One thing missing from JavaScript is two- or three-dimensional arrays. However, you can easily simulate them by creating an array of arrays. You can expand this technique to store any number of items—either numbered or named—in an array. This makes it easy to store just about anything.

TIP: The solitaire game in Chapter 15, "Real-Life Examples III," uses several of these techniques to store information about the cards in use.

Understanding Data Tainting

In the first versions of JavaScript (Netscape 2.0 and 2.01), properties of a document were always available to JavaScript code in other documents. For example, if you loaded a page in one frame, a JavaScript program in another frame could access properties of the page—its links, anchors, and form elements.

Although reading properties of a document doesn't sound like much of a security risk, some clever folks found ways to exploit it. If there's a security risk of any kind on a Web page, you can be sure someone out there will find it and take advantage. Here are a few of the tricks that were possible due to this feature:

> *You learn about this and other security problems with Netscape in detail in Chapter 14, "Debugging JavaScript Programs."*

❏ A document could open a file URL, such as `file://c:\dos\`, in a frame, which would display a list of files in the frame. A JavaScript program in another frame could then read the contents (available in the `links` array) and send them to a server.

❏ A Web page could open an invisible frame with a JavaScript program and leave it running while you visited other sites; after watching you for a while, it could send a list of the sites you visited to its server.

Although minor, these were risks to security and privacy. The public tends to worry about such things, particularly on the Internet (and Microsoft was encouraging them to). To deter these rumors and problems, Netscape quickly released a fixed version, Netscape 2.02.

The fix in Netscape 2.02 was to prevent a document from accessing properties of another document, unless it came from the same server. Thus, if your document loaded Netscape's home page in a frame, it couldn't access the links, anchors, or even the address of the Netscape page.

> *Other security fixes are listed in Chapter 14.*

Although the fixed version prevented these problems, it also removed a useful feature. If you could access properties of a document in another frame, for example, you could create a "link summary" frame with a quick reference to all the links on the page.

Luckily, Netscape found a solution to make everyone happy, beginning with Navigator 3.0b5, which introduced *data tainting*. This enables you to access properties of a document in another frame, but not without evidence.

As an analogy, consider the security devices used in a modern record or video store. The simple solution to prevent theft is to keep all the items in locked cabinets, but that would prevent customers from browsing them. Instead, magnetic strips are attached to each item, and can't be removed. Thus, you can take an item off the shelf and look it over—but come near the exit, and alarms go off all over the place.

Data tainting does the same thing for data from other servers. Data from another server is marked, or tainted. The data is still useful, but it is marked. No matter what you do with the data—assign it to variables, use it in calculations, and so on—it remains tainted.

When a JavaScript program attempts to send data to a server—either by submitting form data or by using an URL—it is checked for tainting. If any tainted data is present, the user is alerted and allowed to cancel the operation.

NOTE: To send data to a server using an URL, the application could use the data as a document name or as a parameter. In either case, a CGI script could receive the data on the server.

The actual tainting is done by using a special *taint code* in storing the value. The taint code is unique for each server. Thus, you can freely send data to the same server it was originally taken from, but the user is warned if you attempt to send it to a different server.

NOTE: When data tainting is enabled, you can also access the value of `password` objects in a form. Because their value is tainted, though, you can't send this information to a server.

Enabling Data Tainting

To use the data tainting feature, you need to enable it using an environmental variable. The following command can be used to set the variable to enable tainting:

```
SET NS_ENABLE_TAINT=1
```

If you are using Windows 3.1, you can exit to DOS, type this command, then return to Windows. In Windows 95, the easiest method is to add the command to your `C:\AUTOEXEC.BAT` file, then reboot the computer. For Macintosh systems, you need to create a resource called `NS_ENABLE_TAINT`.

You can check whether the user has enabled data tainting with the `navigator.taintEnabled ( )` method.

Data Tainting Commands

You can exercise some control over data tainting with two JavaScript functions to convert between tainted and nontainted values:

❏ `taint` adds taint to a value, using the current program's taint code.

❏ `untaint` removes the taint from a value.

These functions return a tainted or untainted result, but do not modify the original value. The main use for `untaint` is to make values available to other scripts without security restrictions.

NOTE: Although you can add taint to any value with `taint()`, you can only untaint values that have the current program's taint code. There is no way to remove taint from a value that originates from another window.

 # Working with Documents on Multiple Servers

As an example of a multiserver application that takes advantage of data tainting, let's create a framed document that displays a link summary for an existing document—at any URL. The simplest part of this task is the frameset document, shown in Listing 10.5.

Listing 10.5. (MULTSERV.HTM) The frameset document for the link summary application.

```
<HTML>
<FRAMESET COLS="20%,80%">
<FRAME name="summary" SRC="linksumm.htm">
<FRAME name="destination" SRC="doc1.htm">
</FRAMESET>
</HTML>
```

Next, let's create the link summary document for the first frame, which will use JavaScript to display a summary of the document in the second frame. This document is shown in Listing 10.6.

Listing 10.6. (LINKSUMM.HTM) The main HTML document for the link summary JavaScript application.

```
<HTML>
<HEAD>
<TITLE>Link Summary</TITLE>
<SCRIPT LANGUAGE="JavaScript">
function newloc() {
// send other frame to new URL
    parent.frames[1].location.href = document.form1.text1.value;
```

```
// update link summary
   self.location.reload();
}
</SCRIPT>
</HEAD>
<BODY>
</BODY>
<H3>Link Summary</H3>
<HR>
<FORM NAME="form1">
<INPUT TYPE="text" NAME="text1" VALUE="enter new URL">
<INPUT TYPE="button" VALUE="GO" onClick="newloc();">
</FORM>
<SCRIPT LANGUAGE="JavaScript">
// list links in other frame
len = parent.frames[1].document.links.length;
document.write("<B>Total links: " + len + "</B>");

// begin numbered list
document.write("<BR>\n<OL>");

// reproduce each link here
for (i=0; i < len; i++) {
   document.write("<LI><A HREF='");
   document.write(parent.frames[1].document.links[i].href);
   document.write("'>");
   document.write(parent.frames[1].document.links[i].pathname);
   document.write("</A>\n");
}
document.write("</OL>");
</SCRIPT>
<HR>
</HTML>
```

This is where the real action happens. The JavaScript functions in this document create a summary of the links in the second document. The links are listed in a numbered list, with each linked to its corresponding document name.

Of course, when you first load the document, there will be no document in the second frame. You can use the text field and form in the link summary frame to load a new document, and the link information will be displayed.

Thanks to data tainting, this should work with any Web document. It will not currently work with framed documents, because it hasn't provided for multiple frames. The output of this program, as displayed by Netscape, is shown in Figure 10.2. In the figure, I've loaded Netscape's page, and the links on the page are listed.

Figure 10.2.
The output of the link summary application.

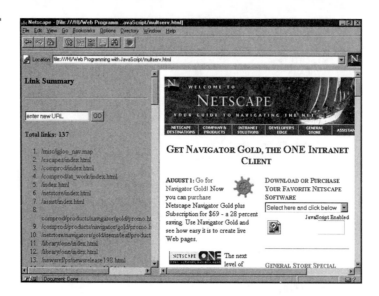

Maintaining State in JavaScript

Often, your program will need to maintain state information; you may display a series of pages and need to remember something between pages. Quizzes, questionnaires, and games often need to maintain state. There are two ways to do this:

❏ Using cookies, which you looked at in Chapter 9
❏ Keeping a frame open and using its variables and functions

If your application doesn't use frames, you can use cookies to keep track of information.

Both of these have their advantages and disadvantages. If your application also uses CGI, for example, you may find cookies more useful. The next task is an example of using a frame to maintain state information.

Creating a Questionnaire

As a complex example of using frames to keep track of state between pages, let's create a questionnaire. This program asks several questions; after you answer each question, it stores the answer in an array. The array is part of the script in the top frame; the bottom frame is used to show the questions. The frameset document for this example is shown in Listing 10.7.

Listing 10.7. (QUIZ.HTM) The frameset document for the questionnaire.

```
<HTML>
<FRAMESET ROWS="15%,*"
 onLoad="setTimeout('parent.MainFrame.NextQuestion();',1000);">
```

```
<FRAME NAME="MainFrame" SRC="quizmain.htm">
<FRAME NAME="QuizFrame" SRC="doc1.htm">
</FRAMESET>
```

Listing 10.8 shows the main program for the questionnaire. When you load the page, the questions are asked one at a time. After the last question, a summary of your answers is displayed. The final output of this program is shown in Figure 10.3.

Figure 10.3.
The questionnaire is complete, and the results are displayed.

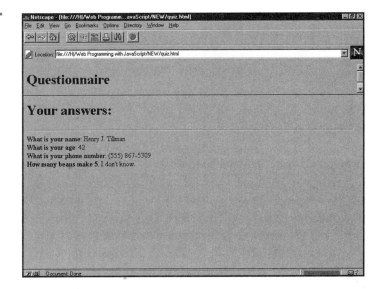

Listing 10.8. (QUIZMAIN.HTM) The main JavaScript program for the quiz example.

```
<HTML>
<HEAD><TITLE>Questionnaire Example</TITLE>
<SCRIPT LANGUAGE="JavaScript">
// global variables
var answers = new Array(5);
var questions = new Array(5);
questions[0] = "What is your name";
questions[1] = "What is your age";
questions[2] = "What is your phone number";
questions[3] = "How many beans make 5";
var current = 0;
var quest;
// function to ask a question in other frame
function NextQuestion() {
   if (current > 0) {
      ans = parent.QuizFrame.document.form1.question.value;
      answers[current-1] = ans;
   }
```

continues

Listing 10.8. continued

```
    if (current + 1 < questions.length) {
        text = questions[current];
        parent.QuizFrame.document.open();
        parent.QuizFrame.document.write("<HTML><BODY>\n");
        parent.QuizFrame.document.write("<h1>" + "Question #" + current + "</
        ➥h1>");
        parent.QuizFrame.document.write("<hr>");
        parent.QuizFrame.document.write("<b>" + text + "?</b><br>");
        parent.QuizFrame.document.write("<FORM NAME=\"form1\">\n");
        parent.QuizFrame.document.write("<INPUT TYPE=\"text\" NAME=\"question\">
        ➥");
        parent.QuizFrame.document.write("<BR><INPUT TYPE=\"BUTTON\"
        ➥VALUE=\"Submit Answer\" ");
    parent.QuizFrame.document.write("onClick=\"parent.MainFrame.NextQuestion();\"
        ➥>");
        parent.QuizFrame.document.write("</BODY></HTML>");
        parent.QuizFrame.document.close();
        current++;
    }
    else {
        parent.QuizFrame.document.open();
        parent.QuizFrame.document.write("<HTML><BODY>\n");
        parent.QuizFrame.document.write("<h1>Your answers:</h1><hr>");
        for (i=0; i<(questions.length-1); i++) {
            parent.QuizFrame.document.write("<B>" + questions[i] + "</B>: " +
            ➥answers[i] + "<BR>");
        }
        parent.QuizFrame.document.write("</BODY></HTML>");
        parent.QuizFrame.document.close();
    }
}

</SCRIPT>
</HEAD>
<BODY>
<H1>Questionnaire</H1>
</BODY>
</HTML>
```

This program uses the `questions` array to store the questions and the `answers` array to store the user's answers. When the page is loaded, the `NextQuestion()` function is called to display a question.

Each question is displayed in the bottom frame. The document you create in this frame also has a JavaScript event handler, which calls the `NextQuestion()` function (in the top frame) when the question is entered.

Workshop Wrap-Up

In this chapter, you learned some of the more complex aspects of JavaScript and how it can work with complicated pages and data:

❏ How to integrate documents in nested frames and refer between them

❏ How to store data with string arrays and associative arrays

❏ How to use the data tainting feature to access properties of pages from different servers

❏ How to use frames to store the current state of a JavaScript application and keep track of variables between pages

Next Steps

When you master the techniques in this chapter, you've come a long way toward becoming a JavaScript expert. Continue your studies with one of the following:

❏ For simpler examples of using frames in Web pages, turn to Chapter 9, "Using Frames, Cookies, and Other Advanced Features."

❏ For examples that illustrate the techniques you learned in this chapter, see Chapter 11, "Real-Life Examples II."

❏ To learn techniques for debugging JavaScript applications, see Chapter 14, "Debugging JavaScript Programs."

❏ To learn about using Java to further enhance your page, turn to Chapter 16, "Integrating JavaScript with Java."

Q&A

Q: Using data tainting, I can access properties of another document, such as links and anchors. Is there any way to read the HTML source of the document itself?

A: Currently, there is no way to do this. The properties made available in the object hierarchy (explained in Chapter 5, "Accessing Window Elements as Objects") are all you can access via JavaScript. This is not expected to change.

Q: Can a JavaScript program in one frame read variables (not properties) defined by a JavaScript program in another frame?

A: Yes. Just treat the variable name as a child of the frame's window object. For example, `parent.frame1.score` refers to the `score` variable in the `frame1` frame.

Q: What happens if the document I load into a frame is a framed document itself? Will this cause an error?

A: This will not cause an error—in fact, it works fine. The frames of the document are created within the frame in which it is loaded. Functionally, this is treated the same as a nested frameset.

ELEVEN

Real-Life Examples II

This chapter includes several example JavaScript applications that apply the techniques you learned in Part III, "Creating Smart Web Pages." These include the following:

❑ **Example 1: Nonscrolling Status Line Messages:** A different idea for displaying messages in the status line

❑ **Example 2: An Improved Navigation Bar:** Using dynamically changed selection lists to allow the user to select a specific page

❑ **Example 3: Storing User Preferences:** A page that remembers a user's preference and shows either the frames or no-frames version

Example 1: Nonscrolling Status Line Messages

Not everyone enjoys scrolling status line messages. Here's an alternative.

Chapter 8, "Improving a Web Page with JavaScript," introduced a program to scroll messages in the browser's status line. Such scrolling messages have become a bit of a cliché on the Web, and they do have their disadvantages—for one, few users want to watch for several minutes while a long message displays.

The following techniques are used in this example:

- ❏ Using timeouts to display messages (Chapter 8)
- ❏ Displaying instructions for links (Chapter 8)
- ❏ Storing data in string arrays (Chapter 10)

One alternative is to display messages that don't scroll in the status line. This enables you to have several different tips, advertisements, or other messages displayed, and enables the user to read them quickly.

Listing 11.1 shows the nonscrolling message program integrated into the FSC Software home page. You'll look at the program in detail later.

Listing 11.1. (NOSCROLL.HTM) Random, nonscrolling messages in the status line.

```
<HTML>
<HEAD>
<TITLE>Fictional Software Company</TITLE>
<SCRIPT>
// messages to display in scrollbar
msg = new Array(4);
msg[0]="This is the first message."
msg[1]="This is the second message."
msg[2]="This is the third message."
msg[3]="This is the fourth message."

//flag to control message
var showmsg = true;
function NextMessage() {
   if (!showmsg) {
      window.setTimeout("NextMessage()",5000);
      showmsg = true;
      return;
   }
   index = Math.floor(msg.length * Math.random());
   window.status = msg[index];
// set timeout for next update
   window.setTimeout("NextMessage()",5000);
}
// Display the first status line message
NextMessage();
// Display a link help message
```

```
function LinkMessage(text) {
   showmsg = false;
   window.status = text;
}
</SCRIPT>
</HEAD>
<BODY>
<IMG SRC="fsclogo.gif" alt="Fictional Software Company">
<HR>
Welcome to our web page! Fictional Software Company
specializes in creating innovative, user-friendly software
applications with descriptions filled with industry
buzzwords.
<P>
We have a wide range of products (3 of them) to meet
the needs of you and your company. Follow the links
below for more information.
<P>
<UL>
<LI><A HREF="spread.htm"
onMouseOver="LinkMessage('Information about the spreadsheet');return true;">
Fictional Spreadsheet 7.0</A>
<LI><A HREF="word.htm"
onMouseOver="LinkMessage('Information about the word processor');return true;">
Fictional Word Processor 6.0</A>
<LI><A HREF="data.htm"
onMouseOver="LinkMessage('Information about the database');return true;">
Fictional Database 7.0</A>
</UL>
<P>
Unlike other software companies, our products have
absolutely no bugs, and always work perfectly on all
computers. Nevertheless, you may run into problems in
rare cases, usually your own fault. If this happens,
visit our <A HREF="support.htm"
onMouseOver="LinkMessage('Technical Support for our products');return true;">
Technical Support</A>
department for helpful information and tips. You can
also view more information <A HREF="company.htm"
onMouseOver="LinkMessage('Information about FSC Software Co.');return true;">
about our company</A> or order products with our friendly
<a href="order.htm"
onMouseOver="LinkMessage('Allows you to order products');return true;">
Order Form</A>.
<HR>
<I>(c)1998 FSC - designed by the FSC staff</I>
</BODY>
</HTML>
```

Here's a summary of how key elements of this program work:

❏ An array, msg[], is created to hold the various messages that will be displayed.

❏ Each element of the msg array is assigned explicitly. This example has four messages, but there could easily be more.

❑ Every five seconds, a new random index into the msg array is created using the Math.random() method. The resulting string is stored in window.status to display it in the status line.

❑ This program also implements the "friendly links" technique used in Chapter 8. The showmessage flag is used to turn off the random messages when a link description is being displayed.

NOTE:
This program uses the Math.random() method, which was fully implemented in Netscape 3.0b3, although it worked in earlier UNIX versions. Be sure you're using the latest version to try this example.

This program is shown in action in Figure 11.1. I hope this not only gives you an alternative way of displaying messages, but the inspiration to come up with new and creative ways of your own.

Figure 11.1.
Netscape's display of the nonscrolling message example.

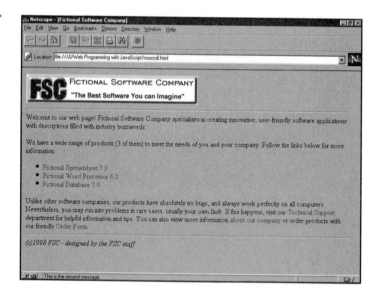

Example 2: An Improved Navigation Bar

You created a navigation bar for the FSC home page in Chapter 8. In that example, each product had the same list of categories available. What if there is a different list of pages for each product? In this example, you'll use dynamic selection lists to allow for different pages for each product.

This example uses the following techniques:

❑ Using selection lists for navigation (Chapter 8)

❑ Complex site organization and planning (Chapter 10)

Listing 11.2 shows the improved navigation bar in JavaScript and HTML.

Listing 11.2. (NAVBAR2.HTM) The HTML and JavaScript source for the improved navigation bar.

You could easily modify this example to place the navigation bar in a separate frame. See Chapter 9, "Using Frames, Cookies, and Other Advanced Features."

```
<HTML>
<HEAD>
<TITLE>Fictional Software Company</TITLE>
<SCRIPT>
function Navigate() {
   prod = document.navform.program.selectedIndex;
   cat = document.navform.category.selectedIndex;
   prodval = document.navform.program.options[prod].value;
   catval = document.navform.category.options[cat].value;
   if (prodval == "x" || catval == "x") return;
   window.location = prodval + "_" + catval + ".htm";
}
function update() {
// update available categories depending on product
   prod = document.navform.program.selectedIndex;
   prodval = document.navform.program.options[prod].value;
   if (prodval == "x")
      {document.navform.category.options[0].text = "Select a Category:";
       document.navform.category.options[0].value = "x";
       document.navform.category.options[1].text = "(please select ";
       document.navform.category.options[1].value = "x";
       document.navform.category.options[2].text = " a product";
       document.navform.category.options[2].value = "x";
       document.navform.category.options[3].text = " first)";
       document.navform.category.options[3].value = "x";
      }
   if (prodval == "w")
      {document.navform.category.options[0].text = "Word Processor:";
       document.navform.category.options[0].value = "x";
       document.navform.category.options[1].text = "Technical Support";
       document.navform.category.options[1].value = "tech";
       document.navform.category.options[2].text = "Pricing Information";
       document.navform.category.options[2].value = "price";
       document.navform.category.options[3].text = "Tips and Tricks";
       document.navform.category.options[3].value = "tips";
      }
   if (prodval == "s")
      {document.navform.category.options[0].text = "Spreadsheet:";
       document.navform.category.options[0].value = "x";
       document.navform.category.options[1].text = "Technical Support";
       document.navform.category.options[1].value = "tech";
       document.navform.category.options[2].text = "Distributors";
       document.navform.category.options[2].value = "dist";
       document.navform.category.options[3].text = "Sample Formulas";
       document.navform.category.options[3].value = "form";
      }
   if (prodval == "d")
```

continues

Listing 11.2. continued

```
        {document.navform.category.options[0].text = "Database:";
         document.navform.category.options[0].value = "x";
         document.navform.category.options[1].text = "Technical Support";
         document.navform.category.options[1].value = "tech";
         document.navform.category.options[2].text = "Pricing Information";
         document.navform.category.options[2].value = "price";
         document.navform.category.options[3].text = "Sample Programs";
         document.navform.category.options[3].value = "prog";
        }
}
</SCRIPT>
</HEAD>
<BODY>
<IMG SRC="fsclogo.gif" alt="Fictional Software Company">
<HR>
Welcome to our web page! Fictional Software Company
specializes in creating innovative, user-friendly software
applications with descriptions filled with industry
buzzwords.
<P>
We have a wide range of products (3 of them) to meet
the needs of you and your company. Follow the links
below for more information.
<P>
<FORM name="navform">
<SELECT name="program"
 onChange="update();">
<OPTION VALUE="x" SELECTED>Select a Product
<OPTION VALUE="w">Fictional Word Processor
<OPTION VALUE="s">Fictional Spreadsheet
<OPTION VALUE="d">Fictional Database
</SELECT>
<SELECT name="category">
<OPTION VALUE="x" SELECTED>Select a Category:
<OPTION VALUE="x"> (Please select
<OPTION VALUE="x"> a product
<OPTION VALUE="x"> first)
</SELECT>
<INPUT TYPE="button" NAME="go" VALUE="Go to Page"
onClick="Navigate();">
</FORM>
<P>
Unlike other software companies, our products have
absolutely no bugs, and always work perfectly on all
computers. Nevertheless, you may run into problems in
rare cases, usually your own fault. If this happens,
visit our <A HREF="support.htm">Technical Support</A>
department for helpful information and tips. You can
also view more information <A HREF="company.htm">about
our company</A> or order products with our friendly
<a href="order.htm">Order Form</A>.
<HR>
<I>(c)1998 FSC - designed by the FSC staff</I>
</BODY>
</HTML>
```

The program works as follows:

❏ The initial state of the selection lists provides instructions. The Go button doesn't work until the user selects an option.

❏ An onChange event handler is used to change the list of categories automatically when the user selects a product.

❏ The update() function handles the modification of the selection list. Both the text property, which defines the value displayed on the screen, and the value property, which defines the returned value, are changed.

As you can see, this is a much more interactive use of JavaScript—and a more practical one because you will rarely have exactly the same list of pages for each product. This could easily be adapted for a wide variety of uses.

Figure 11.2 shows this example in action. Here are a few observations about this program:

❏ The technique of changing selection lists was added in Netscape 3.0b4. This may not be available to all your users, and it will cause an error on earlier versions.

❏ Notice that although you change the list of categories, there are always four of them. I did this to keep things simple; you could also add and delete options. To add an option, use the Option() constructor to create a new object, assign its text property, and assign it to the last element of the options array. To delete items, assign their place in the array to null, starting at the end of the options array.

❏ Notice that you change the first option of the category when a product is selected, to prompt the user and indicate the selection. This makes it a bit more friendly than the original navigation bar.

❏ There may be problems if you try to assign a value to a selection list's text property that is longer than the value it replaces, because Netscape allocates space for the list when the page is first displayed. A solution is to be sure that one of the original options is longer than any others you will use, or explicitly refresh the page with the location.reload() method.

Figure 11.2.

The improved naviga-tion bar example, as displayed by Netscape.

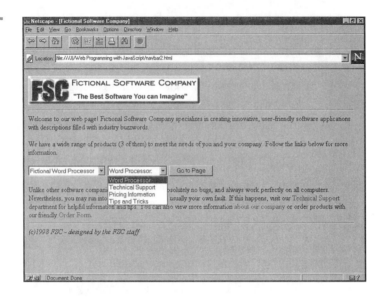

Example 3: Storing User Preference

This example is a useful application for cookies (Chapter 9). You will use a cookie to indicate the user's preference and either display a frames or no-frames version of the page.

This example illustrates the following techniques:

❏ Storing and retrieving cookies (Chapter 9)

❏ Controlling frames dynamically (Chapter 10)

This example is a bit more complicated. Let's begin with the page shown in Listing 11.3. This page is an introductory page that will send users to the appropriate page—probably before they even notice.

Listing 11.3. (SELFRAMES.HTM) Introductory page for the user prefer-ences example.

```
<HTML>
<HEAD>
<TITLE>Frames or No Frames?</TITLE>
<SCRIPT LANGUAGE="JavaScript">
function forward() {
// read cookie and send user to appropriate page
if (0 <= parseInt(document.cookie.indexOf('frames=yes', 0)))
   window.location.href="frames.htm";
else
   window.location.href="noframes.htm";
}
</SCRIPT>
```

```
</HEAD>
<BODY onLoad="window.setTimeout('forward();',1000);">
If you can read this, you're using a non-JavaScript browser. Please follow
one of the links below to access our page:
<UL>
<LI><a href="frames.htm">Frames version</a>
<LI><a href="noframes.htm">Non-Frames version</a>
</UL>
</BODY>
</HTML>
```

This program attempts to read the cookie for the current document with the
`document.cookie` property. If it contains the keyword `"frames=yes"`, the user will be
sent to the frames version; otherwise, the user is sent to the no-frames page. (Thus,
no frames is the default.)

Next, you will need the actual framed and non-framed pages. Listing 11.4 shows the
page for the frames version, which includes an option to switch to the no-frames
version.

Listing 11.4. (FRAMES.HTM) The frames version of the page.

```
<HTML>
<HEAD>
<TITLE>Our Home Page (Frames)</TITLE>
<SCRIPT LANGUAGE="JavaScript">
function goNoFrames() {
// switch preference to non-frames version, and send the user there.
document.cookie = "frames=no; expires=Monday, 31-Dec-99 23:59:59 GMT";
window.location = "noframes.htm";
}
</SCRIPT>
</HEAD>
<BODY>
<H1>This is the Frames Page</H1>
<FORM name="form1">
<INPUT TYPE="button" VALUE="Non-Frames Version" onClick="goNoFrames();">
</FORM>
Welcome to the frames page! If you would like to see the non-frames
version, press the button above.
<HR>
The actual content of the page would be here...
<HR>
</BODY>
</HTML>
```

To simplify the example, I didn't actually use frames in this page; that would require
using a FRAMESET document as the initial frames page and creating a second page with
the content.

The GoNoFrames() function, accessed with the button on the page, enables the user
to switch to the no-frames page. This sets a cookie indicating the preference, then
updates window.location to send the user there.

Similarly, Listing 11.5 shows the no-frames version. This page includes an option to switch to the frames version, including setting the cookie appropriately. Figure 11.3 shows the output of this page.

Figure 11.3.

The No Frames Page for the preferences example.

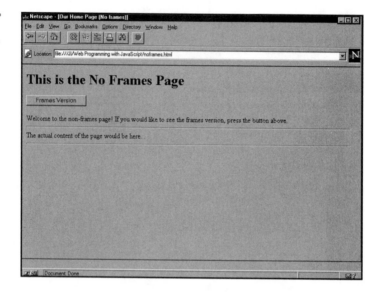

Listing 11.5. (NOFRAMES.HTM) The no-frames page for the preferences example.

```
<HTML>
<HEAD>
<TITLE>Our Home Page (No frames)</TITLE>
<SCRIPT LANGUAGE="JavaScript">
function goFrames() {
// switch preference to frames version, and send the user there.
document.cookie = "frames=yes; expires=Monday, 31-Dec-99 23:59:59 GMT";
window.location = "frames.htm";
}
</SCRIPT>
</HEAD>
<BODY>
<H1>This is the No Frames Page</H1>
<FORM name="form1">
<INPUT TYPE="button" VALUE="Frames Version" onClick="goFrames();">
</FORM>
Welcome to the non-frames page! If you would like to see the frames
version, press the button above.
<HR>
The actual content of the page would be here...
<HR>
</BODY>
</HTML>
```

Now comes the cool part—once users select one page or the other using the button, they go to that page from then on whenever they load SELFRAMES.htm. Users can change preferences at any time.

Here are a few observations about this example:

❏ A timeout is used to send the user to the new page by default in SELFRAMES.htm if no cookie has been set. This timeout is required so that the document is finished loading before the browser is redirected to the next page. The timeout could probably be smaller than the one I used.

❏ You could do this without using an initial page (SELFRAMES.htm) by displaying HTML tags from the script at the beginning of the page. These would include the <BODY> or <FRAMESET> tags. Needless to say, this would be a bit more complicated.

❏ The cookie set applies to the server that sent the document. If you are using many pages on the server, you should use a more specific name for the cookie to avoid conflicts. Alternatively, the same preference could be used for all pages.

PART

IV

Advanced JavaScript Concepts

TWELVE

Working with Graphics in JavaScript

One of the most challenging—and most rewarding—uses of a programming language is creating graphic applications and games. In this chapter you'll look at some techniques you can use for graphic pages—or to add excitement to any Web page.

Now don't get too excited—JavaScript is a young language, and a simple one, so it will be quite a while before someone writes a version of DOOM in JavaScript. However, you can create uniquely dynamic Web content. JavaScript includes several features, including dynamic images, that aren't even available in Java.

You will explore some simple examples of these techniques in this chapter. For an example of a large-scale graphic application—in this case, a poker solitaire game—see Chapter 15, "Real-Life Examples III."

In this chapter, you

❏ Learn how JavaScript works with graphics

❏ Use link event handlers to make clickable images

❏ Use dynamic images to create neat Web page effects

❏ Learn how client-side image maps work with JavaScript

Tasks in this chapter:

❏ Creating Graphical Back and Forward Buttons

❏ Replacing Images Dynamically

❏ Creating a Graphical Clock

❏ Rotating Between Advertisement Banners

❏ Using an Image Map with JavaScript

Creating Graphical Back and Forward Buttons

JavaScript's graphic functions are simple but powerful.

Let's start with an ultra-simple example of graphics in JavaScript. In Chapter 5, "Accessing Window Elements as Objects," you used a simple JavaScript event handler to create back and forward buttons, which enable the user to perform the same function as the browser's arrow buttons. To improve on this idea, let's make some spiffy-looking graphic buttons.

You can also use text links for back and forward with this technique.

Listing 12.1 demonstrates this technique. Notice that there are no script tags or event handlers—this is an example of calling JavaScript through a URL, which you'll see more of in Chapter 14, "Debugging JavaScript Programs."

Netscape's view of this page is shown in Figure 12.1. This could also be done with event handlers; as a matter of fact, the latest versions of JavaScript enable you to include an event handler directly within the <IMG> tag, without making the image a link.

Figure 12.1.
Graphical back and forward buttons on a Web page.

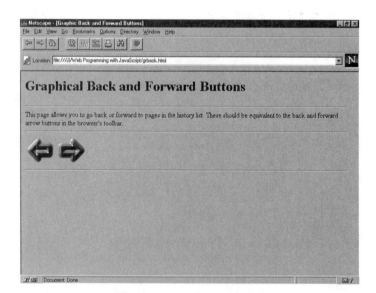

Listing 12.1. (GRBACK.HTM) A simple example of graphic back and forward buttons.

```
<HTML>
<HEAD><TITLE>Graphic Back and Forward Buttons</TITLE>
</HEAD>
<BODY>
<H1>Graphical Back and Forward Buttons</H1>
<HR>
This page allows you to go back or forward to pages in the history list.
```

```
These should be equivalent to the back and forward arrow buttons in the
browser's toolbar.
<HR>
<A HREF="javascript:history.back();">
  <IMG BORDER = 0 SRC="left.gif">
</A>
<A HREF="javascript:history.forward();">
  <IMG BORDER = 0 SRC="right.gif">
</A>
<HR>
</BODY>
</HTML>
```

Although this example works, it's nothing special. You can make back buttons, forward buttons, and other graphics more interactive by using dynamic images, described in the next section.

Using Dynamic Images in JavaScript

One of the most recent, and most exciting, features added to JavaScript is the capability of dynamically changing images. This means you can create images that "magically" change; this could be used for clocks, images that change when you click them, or even simple animations.

The images in a Web page are reflected in an array, just like form elements. By modifying the properties of the array items, you can replace the image with a different one. This enables you to create dynamically changing content on the page without even using frames.

This technique isn't perfect for all applications. Before you get started, note the following limitations:

- ❏ You can only change existing images in the page—you can't add new ones or remove an image entirely.
- ❏ You can replace an image with a larger or smaller image, but this may not look good, because the text won't be reformatted to match.
- ❏ Any image you use will have to be loaded from the server; this makes this technique impractical for complicated animations or large images.

The `images` Array

You can change images dynamically by using the `images` array. This array contains an item for each of the images defined in the page. Each image can also have a name. In the object hierarchy, each `image` object is a child of the `document` object.

Each `image` object has the following properties:

- ❏ `border` represents the BORDER attribute of the `<IMG>` tag; this defines whether a border is drawn around a linked image.
- ❏ `complete` is a flag that tells you whether the image has been completely loaded. This is a Boolean value (true or false).
- ❏ `height` and `width` reflect the corresponding image attributes. This is for information only; you can't change an image's size dynamically.
- ❏ `hspace` and `vspace` represent the corresponding image attributes, which define the image's placement on the page. Again, this is a read-only attribute.
- ❏ `name` is the image's name. You can define this with the NAME attribute in the image definition.
- ❏ `lowsrc` is the value of the LOWSRC attribute. This is a Netscape-specific attribute that enables you to specify a low-resolution image to be loaded before the "real" image.
- ❏ `src` is the image's source, or URL. This is the value you can change to change images dynamically.

For most purposes, the `src` attribute is the only one you'll use. However, you can also change the `lowsrc` attribute. This defines a low-resolution image to load first and will be used only when you change the `src` attribute.

The `image` object has no methods. It does have three event handlers you can use:

- ❏ The `onLoad` event occurs when the image finishes loading.
- ❏ The `onAbort` event occurs if the user aborts the page before the image is loaded.
- ❏ The `onError` event occurs if the image file is not found or is corrupt.

Preloading Images

You will use the image preload feature for the solitaire game in Chapter 15.

Although you can't add an image to the page dynamically, you can create an independent `image` object. This enables you to specify an image that will be loaded and placed in the cache, but not displayed on the page.

This may sound useless, but it's a great way to work with modem-speed connections. Once you've preloaded an image, you can replace any of the images on the page with the image—and because it's already cached, the change happens instantly.

You can cache an image by creating a new `image` object, using the `new` keyword. Here's an example:

```
Image2 = new Image();
Image2.src = "arrow1.gif";
```

NOTE: The new keyword, and its other uses for object-oriented programming, are described in Chapter 4, "Using Built-In Objects and Custom Objects."

Replacing Images Dynamically

Here's a quick example to show off JavaScript's dynamic image feature. The HTML document in Listing 12.2 includes five images; these are some fancy pictures of numbers from one to five. By using the selection lists and the GO button, you can place a different image in any position. Figure 12.2 shows how the page looks after a few changes.

Figure 12.2.

A page that enables you to change images dynamically.

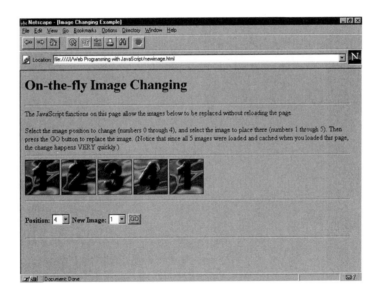

Listing 12.2. (NEWIMAGE.HTM) An example of dynamic images.

```html
<HTML>
<HEAD><TITLE>Image Changing Example</TITLE>
<SCRIPT>
//function to change an image's URL
//done "the long way" for clarity
function ChangeImg() {
// current position
   x = parseInt(document.form1.pos.selectedIndex);
   p = parseInt(document.form1.pos.options[x].value);
```

continues

Listing 12.2. continued

```
// new image value
   x = document.form1.newimg.selectedIndex;
   i = document.form1.newimg[x].value
// change the image URL
   document.images[p].src = i + ".gif";
}
</SCRIPT>
</HEAD>
<BODY>
<H1>On-the-fly Image Changing</H1>
<hr>
The JavaScript functions on this page allow the images below to be replaced
without reloading the page.
<P>
Select the image position to change (numbers 0 through 4), and select the image
to place there (numbers 1 through 5). Then press the GO button to
replace the image. (Notice that since all 5 images were loaded and cached
when you loaded this page, the change happens VERY quickly.)
<HR>
<IMG SRC="1.gif" HEIGHT="80" WIDTH="80">
<IMG SRC="2.gif" HEIGHT="80" WIDTH="80">
<IMG SRC="3.gif" HEIGHT="80" WIDTH="80">
<IMG SRC="4.gif" HEIGHT="80" WIDTH="80">
<IMG SRC="5.gif" HEIGHT="80" WIDTH="80">
<HR>
<FORM name="form1">
<b>Position:</b>
<SELECT NAME="pos">
<OPTION VALUE="0">0
<OPTION VALUE="1">1
<OPTION VALUE="2">2
<OPTION VALUE="3">3
<OPTION VALUE="4">4
</SELECT>
<b>New Image:</b>
<SELECT NAME="newimg">
<OPTION VALUE="1">1
<OPTION VALUE="2">2
<OPTION VALUE="3">3
<OPTION VALUE="4">4
<OPTION VALUE="5">5
</SELECT>
<INPUT TYPE="button" VALUE="GO" onClick="ChangeImg();">
</FORM>
<HR>
</BODY>
</HTML>
```

If an image is not cached, it will load slowly. Interlaced images will display while loading.

The work of this program is done in the `ChangeImg()` function. This function is called by the GO button. It reads the current value of the selection lists; the first specifies the image index to change, and the second specifies the new image to place there.

Notice that the images change very quickly—almost instantly. This is because all five of the images were already in the cache. If you wish to use images that are not displayed at first, you can preload them.

Creating a Graphical Clock

As a slightly more complex example, let's create a clock that uses JavaScript to display the current time. There are many JavaScript clocks out there on the Web, but this one is unique: using the dynamic image features, it updates the time without reloading the page or a frame.

The CD-ROM also includes several alternative sets of digits you can use.

The hardest part of this task is to create the images: the digits zero through nine, a colon to separate the time, and a slash to separate the date. You won't have to do this, because we've included some appropriate images on the CD-ROM accompanying this book.

Listing 12.3 shows the HTML and JavaScript source for the clock program, and Netscape's view of it is shown in Figure 12.3.

Figure 12.3.
Netscape's output of the clock example.

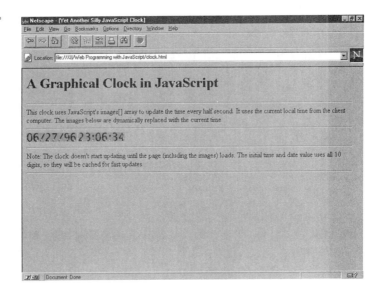

Listing 12.3. (CLOCK.HTM) A graphical clock with time and date.

```
<HTML>
<HEAD><TITLE>Yet Another Silly JavaScript Clock</TITLE>
<SCRIPT>
//javascript clock script
function Clock() {
    D = new Date();
    hh = D.getHours();
    mm = D.getMinutes();
    ss = D.getSeconds();
    yy = D.getYear();
    mt = D.getMonth() + 1;
    dd = D.getDate();
```

continues

Listing 12.3. continued

```
// change the digit images
   document.images[8].src = Url(hh/10);
   document.images[9].src = Url(hh%10);
   document.images[11].src = Url(mm/10);
   document.images[12].src = Url(mm%10);
   document.images[14].src = Url(ss/10);
   document.images[15].src = Url(ss%10);

// time above, date below
   document.images[0].src = Url(mt/10);
   document.images[1].src = Url(mt%10);
   document.images[3].src = Url(dd/10);
   document.images[4].src = Url(dd%10);
   document.images[6].src = Url(yy/10);
   document.images[7].src = Url(yy%10);

// set timeout for next time (half second)
   window.setTimeout("Clock()",500);
}


// converts 4 (numeric) to "c4.gif"
function Url(num) {
num = Math.floor(num);
return "c" + num + ".gif";

}
</SCRIPT>
</HEAD>
<BODY onLoad="window.setTimeout('Clock();',3000)">
<H1>A Graphical Clock in JavaScript</H1>
<hr>
This clock uses JavaScript's images[] array to update the time every half
second. It uses the current local time from the client computer. The images
below are dynamically replaced with the current time.
<HR>
<img src="c6.gif" HEIGHT=20 WIDTH=15><img src="c7.gif" HEIGHT=20 WIDTH=15><img
src="slash.gif" HEIGHT=20 WIDTH=13><img src="c8.gif" HEIGHT=20 WIDTH=15><img
src="c9.gif" HEIGHT=20 WIDTH=15><img src="slash.gif" HEIGHT=20 WIDTH=13><img
src="c0.gif" HEIGHT=20 WIDTH=15><img src="c0.gif" HEIGHT=20 WIDTH=15>
<img src="c0.gif" HEIGHT=20 WIDTH=15><img src="c1.gif" HEIGHT=20 WIDTH=15><img
src="colon.gif" HEIGHT=20 WIDTH=9><img src="c2.gif" HEIGHT=20 WIDTH=15><img
src="c3.gif" HEIGHT=20 WIDTH=15><img src="colon.gif" HEIGHT=20 WIDTH=9><img
src="c4.gif" HEIGHT=20 WIDTH=15><img src="c5.gif" HEIGHT=20 WIDTH=15>
<HR>
Note: The clock doesn't start updating until the page (including the images)
loads. The initial time and date value
uses all 10 digits, so they will be cached for fast updates.
<HR>
</BODY>
</HTML>
```

Let's take a look at how this program works:

❑ When the page first loads, the date and time are set to a bogus value that
   includes all the digits—as you may have guessed, this is so they'll all end up
   in the cache.

❏ An `onLoad()` event handler is used in the document body to begin updating the time three seconds after the page loads. This gives all the images time to load.

❏ The `Clock()` function does the actual work. This function is called by a timeout every half-second, because there's no way to call it each time the time changes. This function reads the current time and changes the images in the document for each digit.

❏ An extra function, `Url()`, converts numeric values to complete URLs for the image graphics.

Rotating Between Advertisement Banners

Web advertising has increased dramatically in the past year.

If you've browsed the Web at all in the last year, I'm sure you noticed the advertising banners at the top of many Web pages, encouraging you to visit another page. Opinions are mixed about Web advertising, but with the commercialization of the Web, it was bound to happen.

At risk of making Web advertisements even more annoying (or more exciting, depending on your attitude) here's another application for dynamic images. You'll include an advertisement banner on a page and use JavaScript to replace it every few seconds with a new banner.

This could be used to display different banners, in the hope of catching the user's eye. You could also use this technique to rotate between different sponsors. This example uses JavaScript to change the banners and also to link to the appropriate sponsor when a banner is clicked.

For the moment, it simply displays a dialog indicating the appropriate sponsor when the banner is clicked. The end result of this idea is shown in Listing 12.4, and the output is shown in Figure 12.4.

Listing 12.4. (ADVERTS.HTM) Using JavaScript to rotate advertisement banners.

```
<HTML>
<HEAD>
<TITLE>Rotating Advertisements</TITLE>
</HEAD>
<SCRIPT LANGUAGE="JavaScript">
// global variable for current sponsor
var sponsor = 1;

// function to link to appropriate sponsor
// (for demonstration, displays a dialog instead)
```

continues

Listing 12.4. continued

```
function GoSponsor() {
    window.alert("Sponsor number to link to:" + sponsor);
}

// function to rotate image (currently uses 3 images)
function rotate() {
    if (++sponsor > 3)  sponsor = 1;
    document.images[0].src = "banner" + sponsor + ".gif";
    window.setTimeout('rotate();',5000);
}
</SCRIPT>
<BODY onLoad="window.setTimeout('rotate();',5000);">
<h1>Rotating Advertisement Banners</h1>
<hr>
<A HREF="javascript:GoSponsor();">
<IMG NAME="banner" SRC="banner1.gif">
</A>
<hr>
The image above is being rotated between three different graphics. Clicking
on a banner will send you to the banner's corresponding sponsor. (For this
example, clicking will simply display a message in a dialog.)
<hr>

</BODY>
</HTML>
```

Figure 12.4.

Netscape's output of the advertising banner example.

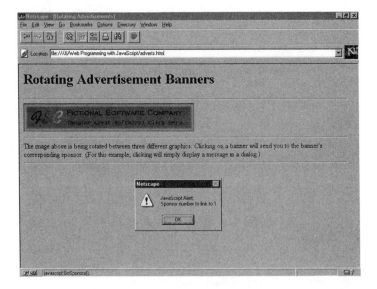

This program uses two functions:

❑ The rotate() function switches to a new banner every five seconds. The sponsor variable stores the current sponsor.

❏ The GoSponsor() function is called when the banner is clicked. Currently, it displays a dialog indicating the sponsor. In a real-world application, you could use a series of if statements to link to the appropriate sponsor by changing the window.location value.

TIP:
You might be tempted to speed up the timer in this example and use it for animation. This will work, but only if you preload each image first. In addition, JavaScript animations aren't very fast. You may want to look into GIF animations, which provide a good alternative. See Appendix C, "Online JavaScript Resources," for more information.

JavaScript and Client-Side Image Maps

A common use for graphics on the Web is in image maps—large images with clickable areas. Each area can link to a separate page. There are two types of image maps:

❏ *Server-side image maps* require a CGI script to interpret the user's actions.

❏ *Client-side image maps* are embedded in HTML, and require no interaction with the server. This is a newer standard and not officially part of HTML, but it is supported by most browsers.

You may have already guessed that JavaScript can't work with server-side image maps, because it has no link to the server. However, client-side image maps and JavaScript work well together.

You'll find an example of a client-side image map definition in the next task.

You can use client-side image maps with JavaScript in three ways:

❏ As with any link, you can link areas of the map to javascript: method URLs to execute functions.

❏ Each <AREA> tag, which defines a clickable area, can have event handlers: onMouseOver, onMouseOut, and onClick. These function in the same way as the corresponding link and image event handlers.

❏ Each <AREA> tag is reflected in an area object. These objects are part of the links array, and have the same properties.

Using an Image Map with JavaScript

As an example of using a client-side image map with JavaScript, let's create a simple image map menu for a fictional company. (The company's name isn't important, but it's obviously not a graphic design company.)

To create a client-side map, you need to do two things:

❏ Use your favorite graphics application to create the actual graphic as a GIF or JPEG image.

❏ Create a MAP definition that describes areas in the image.

❏ Include the image in the document, using the USEMAP attribute to point to the map definition.

NOTE: Several shareware programs enable you to create image maps without hassle. One of them, Map This!, is included on the CD-ROM accompanying this book.

Listing 12.5 shows the example client-side image map definition. This uses both `javascript:` links and event handlers to perform functions. Rather than link to an actual page, clicking on the areas will display a message in a text field (see Figure 12.5). In addition, the onMouseOver event handlers display a description in the status line for each area.

Figure 12.5.
An example of an image map in JavaScript.

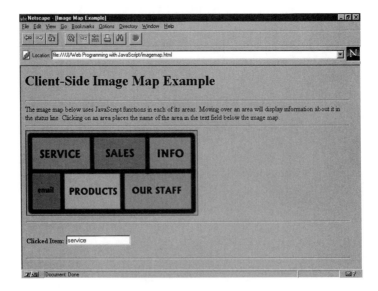

Listing 12.5. (IMAGEMAP.HTM) Using a client-side image map with JavaScript.

```
<HTML>
<HEAD>
<TITLE>Image Map Example</TITLE>
<SCRIPT LANGUAGE="JavaScript">
```

```
function update(text) {
    document.form1.text1.value = text;
}
</SCRIPT>
</HEAD>
<BODY>
<MAP NAME="map1">
<AREA SHAPE=RECT COORDS="14,15,151,87" HREF="javascript:update('service');"
 onMouseOver="window.status='Service Department'; return true;">
<AREA SHAPE=RECT COORDS="162,16,283,85" HREF="javascript:update('sales');"
 onMouseOver="window.status='Sales Department'; return true;">
<AREA SHAPE=RECT COORDS="294,15,388,87" HREF="javascript:update('info');"
 onMouseOver="window.status='Information'; return true;">
<AREA SHAPE=RECT COORDS="13,98,79,178" HREF="javascript:update('email');"
 onMouseOver="window.status='Email Us'; return true;">
<AREA SHAPE=RECT COORDS="92,97,223,177" HREF="javascript:update('products');"
 onMouseOver="window.status='Products'; return true;">
<AREA SHAPE=RECT COORDS="235,98,388,177" HREF="javascript:update('our staff');"
 onMouseOver="window.status='Our Staff'; return true;">
<AREA SHAPE=default HREF="javascript:update('No item selected.');"
 onMouseOver="window.status='Please select an item.'; return true;">
</MAP>
<h1>Client-Side Image Map Example</h1>
<hr>
The image map below uses JavaScript functions in each of its areas. Moving over
an area will display information about it in the status line. Clicking on an
area
places the name of the area in the text field below the image map.
<hr>
<IMG SRC="imagemap.gif" USEMAP="#map1">
<hr>
<FORM NAME="form1">
<b>Clicked Item:</b>
<INPUT TYPE="text" NAME="text1" VALUE="Please select an item.">
</FORM>
<hr>
</BODY>
</HTML>
```

This program uses a single JavaScript function called `update()`; this function simply places an item in the text field `form1.text1`. The text is sent directly by the link in each area definition.

Workshop Wrap-Up

In this chapter, you explored several uses of JavaScript in working with graphics, and you learned the following:

❏ How to create graphic back and forward buttons

❏ How to use the dynamic images technique to change images "on the fly"

❏ Applications of dynamic images, including a clock and a method for rotating advertisements

❏ How to use JavaScript with client-side image maps

Next Steps

You should now understand how JavaScript works with images. Continue with one of the following:

❑ To review the rest of the objects in the object hierarchy, see Chapter 5, "Accessing Window Elements as Objects."

❑ To add more multimedia features, such as sound and video, see Chapter 13, "Working with Multimedia and Plug-Ins."

❑ To learn techniques for debugging JavaScript programs and review the differences between browser versions, see Chapter 14, "Debugging JavaScript Programs."

❑ For an example of a complete graphical application in JavaScript, see Chapter 15, "Real-Life Examples III."

Q&A

Q: I need to eliminate an image entirely, rather than changing its source. Is there a way to do this?

A: Not officially; you can't remove an image. However, you can replace it with a blank image of the same size, which should produce the same effect—and a one-color GIF is a very small file. Remember, you can't do anything that would change the layout of the text.

Q: I created a JavaScript program on a page with images, and my event handlers don't seem to be working. What's wrong?

A: JavaScript requires you to use HEIGHT and WIDTH attributes on all IMG tags. Adding these will most likely make the event handlers work properly. See Chapter 14 for other debugging techniques.

Q: I'd like to create a clock using text instead of graphics. This should be easy, right?

A: It's easy, but only if you use a text field in a form. As for normal text in the page, there's no way to change it. You could keep the clock in a separate frame, though, and update the entire frame. An example in Chapter 9, "Using Frames, Cookies, and Other Advanced Features," does exactly that.

THIRTEEN

Working with Multimedia and Plug-Ins

"Multimedia" is probably the oldest buzzword in the computer industry, and its definition keeps changing. In the 80s, decent graphics and sound were enough to make a multimedia computer system. Now the term includes such things as CD-ROM, CD-quality audio, and full-motion video.

As far as the Web is concerned, multimedia generally means having more than the usual media—text and images—on your Web page. Alternate forms of media can be supported on a Web page in two key ways:

❏ Helper applications are the traditional solution. These give a browser added capabilities, such as playing sounds or displaying video images. The file you link to is downloaded completely, then passed to the helper application.

❏ Plug-ins are a new solution, developed by Netscape. These are custom applications that work within the browser, using a special programmer's interface (API). Using plug-ins, alternate media can be displayed directly in the browser window.

Graphics are also an essential part of multimedia. Read Chapter 12, "Working with Graphics in JavaScript," for information about graphics.

Although JavaScript is a simple language, it can work with multimedia. In this chapter, you'll explore what it can—and can't—do. You'll start with a look at sounds and their use in JavaScript, then continue with a discussion of plug-ins.

Using Sound in JavaScript

JavaScript doesn't include any special functions to play sounds. However, it's easy to force a sound to load and play in JavaScript. You can do this by setting the `window.location.href` property—the same thing you set when forcing the user to load another page.

The result is the same as if the user clicks on a link to the sound. The file is downloaded, and after the download is complete, the sound player application plays the sound.

By using this technique, you can play a sound at any time during the execution of your JavaScript application. This could be as an event handler, as an alternative to an `alert` message, or just to annoy the user.

TIP: Speaking of annoying the user, keep in mind that network connections aren't always fast. It's best to stick to small, easily downloaded sounds to keep things fast and smooth.

Configuring a Sound Player

Most of the recent versions of Netscape automatically install a helper application for sounds (`.wav` and .au files) called the Netscape Audio Player, or NAPLAYER.EXE. If you don't have a player configured, you can choose NAPLAYER.EXE from the NETSCAPE\PROGRAMS directory.

There is one problem with Netscape's audio player: it stays on top after it finishes playing the sound, so keep in mind that some users will have to close the Audio Player window after each sound is played. You may wish to recommend a sound player that exits after playing the sound; one program that does this is the shareware `WPLANY.EXE`.

Playing Sounds on Events

As an example of sounds in JavaScript, the application in Listing 13.1 uses events to trigger sounds. The example sounds used in this application are included on the accompanying CD-ROM.

Listing 13.1. (SOUNDS.HTM) An application that plays sounds on various JavaScript events.

```
<HTML>
<HEAD>
<TITLE>Sounds on JavaScript Events</TITLE>
<SCRIPT LANGUAGE="JavaScript">
function playsound(sfile) {
// load a sound and play it
window.location.href=sfile;
}
</SCRIPT>
</HEAD>
<BODY
  onLoad="playsound('zap.wav');"
  onUnload="playsound('click.wav');" >
<H1>Sounds on JavaScript Events</H1>
<HR>
The following are some examples of JavaScript event handlers used to
play sounds. You should have also heard a sound play when this page
loaded; you'll hear another one when you unload this page.
<HR>
<a href="#" onClick="playsound('zap.wav');">
 Click here for a sound
</a>
<FORM NAME="form1">
<INPUT TYPE="button" VALUE="Button to Play a Sound"
onClick="playsound('click.wav');">
</FORM>
</BODY>
</HTML>
```

Figure 13.1 shows this example in action, complete with the Netscape Audio player. To truly appreciate it, though, you need to try it yourself—although your Web page can include sound, this book can't.

Figure 13.1.
The output of the sound player example.

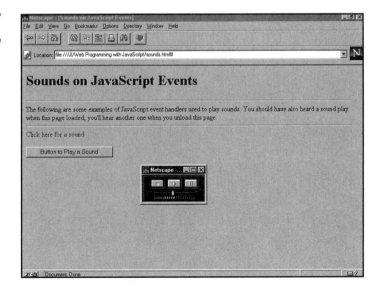

Overview: Netscape Plug-Ins

Plug-ins are a new alternative to helper applications, developed by Netscape for Navigator 2.0. There are currently a wide variety of plug-ins available for various types of files. Even Microsoft has gotten into the act; the latest version of Microsoft Internet Explorer (MSIE) also supports Netscape-compatible plug-ins.

Plug-ins are developed by third parties (or by browser developers, in some cases) using an API available from Netscape. The plug-in is able to use the resources of the browser and display its output within the browser window.

Here is a sampling of the plug-ins currently available, most at little or no charge:

TIP: I don't have room to list all the available plug-ins here; such a list could probably fill its own book. See Appendix C, "Online JavaScript Resources," for a list of online resources for plug-ins.

- ❑ Adobe's Acrobat Plug-in (Amber) enables Portable Document Format (PDF) documents to be displayed in the browser window.
- ❑ Macromedia's Shockwave plug-in enables Director movies and animations to be displayed inline.
- ❑ The QuickTime plug-in displays QuickTime movies inline.
- ❑ A wide variety of plug-ins support Virtual Reality Markup Language (VRML). This enables you to create interactive 3D sites. JavaScript can also work with VRML—see Appendix C for a pointer to information about VRMLScript.
- ❑ The NCompass plug-in, from ExCITE, enables Netscape to support ActiveX (OLE) controls. You'll learn about ActiveX in Chapter 18, "Using ActiveX and Microsoft Internet Explorer."
- ❑ The RealAudio plug-in enables you to listen to real-time audio; the sound is played as it is downloaded. Netscape includes its version of this, LiveAudio, in the latest version.
- ❑ The Pointcast (PCN) plug-in displays news stories, stock information, and press releases.

NOTE: Plug-ins are *not* platform-independent. If a plug-in manufacturer wants to support multiple platforms, it has to create a separate version of the plug-in for each platform. Many plug-ins are available exclusively for Windows or for the Macintosh.

You can place a plug-in document in a Web page using the <EMBED> tag, an extension to HTML. For example, the following HTML tag inserts a PDF file at the current location in the page:

```
<EMBED SRC="doc.pdf">
```

For plug-ins that take up an area of the screen, such as video players and graphics, you can specify HEIGHT and WIDTH attributes to limit the size of the embedded object, as with an ordinary image. For example, the following PDF document is limited to a 200-by-100-pixel square:

```
<EMBED SRC="doc1.pdf" WIDTH=200 HEIGHT=100>
```

Plug-Ins and JavaScript

JavaScript enables you to work with plug-ins in a number of ways:

❑ You can access the list of plug-ins installed on the user's browser.

❑ You can check for a particular plug-in and modify the page accordingly.

❑ You can generate a list of the available plug-ins or MIME types.

❑ Using the LiveConnect features of Netscape 3.0, you can control a plug-in with JavaScript.

You'll look at each of these capabilities in the following sections.

Objects Related to Plug-Ins

The plug-in features were added in Netscape version 3.0 beta. Two objects are available, as children of the navigator object, that can give you information about plug-ins. All properties of these objects are read-only.

❑ The navigator.plugins object is an array that contains information for each installed plug-in.

❑ The navigator.mimeTypes object is an array with information about each of the MIME types currently supported.

These objects are explained in detail in the next sections.

The plugins Object

The navigator.plugins object is an array with one entry for each of the available plug-ins. You can find out how many plug-ins are installed with the expression navigator.plugins.length.

Each element of the `plugins` array is an object in itself, called a `plugins` object. The `plugins` object has the following properties:

❏ `name` is the name of the plug-in.

❏ `filename` is the executable file that was loaded to install the plug-in.

❏ `description` is a description of the plug-in. The plug-in developer supplies this description.

❏ `mimeTypes` is an array of `mimeType` objects, each representing a MIME type that the plug-in can handle. This works similarly to the `navigator.mimeTypes` object, described in the section, The `mimeTypes` Object, later in this chapter.

Refreshing the Plug-In List

The `plugins` object has a single method, `refresh`. This method enables you to update the installed plug-ins list without exiting Netscape. For example, if the user has installed a new plug-in, this will add it to the list. The syntax is simple:

```
navigator.plugins.refresh();
```

You can add a single argument (true) to the `refresh` method to change its behavior. If the parameter is true, Netscape will also automatically reload any page that requires the plug-in.

This makes it possible for you to check for a plug-in and display a link to download it if it is not installed. Your program can then refresh the plug-ins list and reload the page automatically. See the task later in this chapter for an example of checking for a plug-in.

The `mimeTypes` Object

The `navigator.mimeTypes` array contains an element for each MIME type currently supported by Netscape or by a plug-in. Each element of the array is a `mimeType` object, which includes the following properties:

❏ `type` is the MIME type name, such as `text/html` or `video/mpeg`.

❏ `description` is a description of the MIME type.

❏ `enabledPlugin` is the name of the plug-in that is currently supporting the type.

❏ `suffixes` is a listing of the extensions that can be used for documents of this MIME type.

LiveConnect: Controlling a Plug-In

LiveConnect and Java are explained in more detail in Chapter 16, "Integrating JavaScript with Java."

Along with getting information about plug-ins, JavaScript can actually exercise some control over them. This is provided as part of LiveConnect, Netscape's system for communication between JavaScript, Java applets, and plug-ins.

In order for this to work, a plug-in developer must include LiveConnect features in the plug-in. These can allow the following:

❏ The plug-in can have methods that JavaScript can call.

❏ The plug-in can have properties that JavaScript can use or modify.

Because LiveConnect is in its infancy at this writing, there are few plug-ins that work this way yet. One example that has been announced is the LiveAudio plug-in, which ships with Netscape Navigator 3.0. This plug-in can play sounds, and you can control it with JavaScript. For example, this HTML tag embeds a sound:

```
<EMBED SRC="click.wav" NAME="click" VOLUME=100 HIDDEN=true AUTOSTART=false>
```

Once the sound is embedded, its methods become accessible to JavaScript:

❏ `document.click.play()` plays the sound.

❏ `document.click.stop()` aborts the playback.

❏ `document.click.stopall()` aborts all currently playing sounds.

Watch this book's Web site (listed in the introduction) for a full-scale JavaScript application that works with embedded sounds.

Listing Plug-Ins

Using the `navigator.plugins` object, you can easily make a program to display a list of currently available plug-ins. Listing 13.2 is such a program. The name, filename, and description for each plug-in are listed in a table.

Listing 13.2. (PLUGINS.HTM) A program to list available plug-ins.

```
<HTML>
<HEAD>
<TITLE>List of Plug-Ins</TITLE>
</HEAD>
<BODY>
<H1>List of Plug-Ins</H1>
<HR>
The following is a list of the plug-ins installed in this
copy of Netscape, generated using the JavaScript
navigator.plugins object:
<HR>
<TABLE BORDER>
<TR><TH>Plug-in Name</TH>
```

continues

Listing 13.2. continued

```
<TH>Filename</TH>
<TH>Description</TH>
</TR>
<SCRIPT LANGUAGE="JavaScript">
for (i=0; i<navigator.plugins.length; i++) {
   document.write("<TR><TD>");
   document.write(navigator.plugins[i].name);
   document.write("</TD><TD>");
   document.write(navigator.plugins[i].filename);
   document.write("</TD><TD>");
   document.write(navigator.plugins[i].description);
   document.write("</TD></TR>");
}
</SCRIPT>
</TABLE>
</BODY>
</HTML>
```

This program should be easy to understand. It uses the `navigator.plugins.length` property to determine the number of plug-ins. For each one, it displays table cells containing the properties. Figure 13.2 shows the list generated by this program.

Figure 13.2.

The list of available plug-ins as generated by the example program.

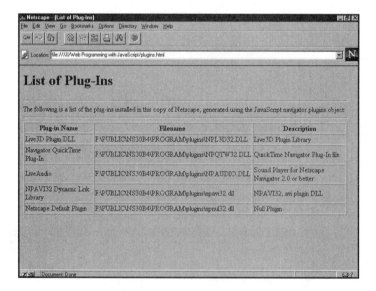

Listing MIME Types

Similarly, you can create a program to list the available MIME types on your system. Listing 13.3 shows a program that lists each type in a table along with its description, the plug-in that handles that type, and the suffixes used for that type of file.

Listing 13.3. (MIMETYPE.HTM) A program to display a list of available MIME types and their properties.

```
<HTML>
<HEAD>
<TITLE>List of MIME Types</TITLE>
</HEAD>
<BODY>
<H1>List of MIME Types</H1>
<HR>
The following is a list of the MIME types installed in this
copy of Netscape, generated using the JavaScript
navigator.mimeTypes object:
<HR>
<TABLE BORDER>
<TR><TH>MIME Type</TH>
<TH>Description</TH>
<TH>Current Plug-in</TH>
<TH>Extensions</TH>
</TR>
<SCRIPT LANGUAGE="JavaScript">
for (i=0; i<navigator.mimeTypes.length; i++) {
   if (navigator.mimeTypes[i].type.indexOf("zz") == -1) {
      document.write("<TR><TD>");
      document.write(navigator.mimeTypes[i].type);
      document.write("</TD><TD>");
      document.write(navigator.mimeTypes[i].description);
      document.write("</TD><TD>");
      document.write(navigator.mimeTypes[i].enabledPlugin);
      document.write("</TD><TD>");
      document.write(navigator.mimeTypes[i].suffixes);
      document.write("</TD></TR>");
   }
   if (i > 55) break;
}
</SCRIPT>
</TABLE>
</BODY>
</HTML>
```

This program works in the same fashion as the previous example. It iterates through the `navigator.mimeTypes` array and displays the properties for each type. The list generated by this program is shown in Figure 13.3.

Figure 13.3.
*The list of available
MIME types as
generated by the
example program.*

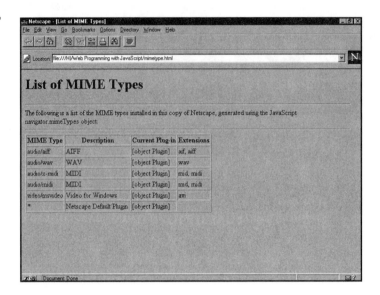

List of MIME Types

The following is a list of the MIME types installed in this copy of Netscape, generated using the JavaScript navigator.mimeTypes object:

MIME Type	Description	Current Plug-in	Extensions
audio/aiff	AIFF	[object Plugin]	auf, aiff
audio/wav	WAV	[object Plugin]	wav
audio/x-midi	MIDI	[object Plugin]	mid, midi
audio/midi	MIDI	[object Plugin]	rmd, midi
video/msvideo	Video for Windows	[object Plugin]	avi
*	Netscape Default Plugin	[object Plugin]	

 ## Testing for a Plug-In

Often, all you need to do with JavaScript is decide whether to attempt to display a plug-in document. You can check for support of the required plug-in, and if it isn't found, you can insert alternate content, or simply advise the user that the plug-in is needed.

For example, this code checks for the Shockwave plug-in. If it's installed, the Director movie is embedded in the document; otherwise, a message about the plug-in is displayed.

```
test = navigator.plugins["Shockwave"];
if (test)
   document.writeln("<EMBED SRC='test.dir' HEIGHT=50 WIDTH=100>")
else
   document.writeln("The Shockwave Plug-in is required for this part of the
➥page.")
```

You are simply displaying a message that the plug-in is required. As noted earlier, you could also provide a link to download the plug-in, then use the `refresh` method of the `plugins` object to add it to the plug-ins list and reload the document.

Workshop Wrap-Up

You should now understand how to use JavaScript to work with multimedia. You've learned the following:

❏ The difference between helper applications and plug-ins

❏ How to use JavaScript to play sounds on events

❏ The basics of the plug-in standard

❏ The plug-ins included with Netscape 3.0 and their uses

❏ Using JavaScript to detect or list plug-ins

❏ Accessing the list of available MIME types

Next Steps

Continue your studies of JavaScript with one of the following:

❏ To add dynamic images and simple animation to your multimedia Web page, see Chapter 12, "Working with Graphics in JavaScript."

❏ To learn about common errors in JavaScript programs and how to avoid them, see Chapter 14, "Debugging JavaScript Programs."

❏ For an example of a large-scale JavaScript application, see Chapter 15, "Real-Life Examples III."

❏ To learn to further enhance your Web pages with Java, see Chapter 16, "Integrating JavaScript with Java."

Q&A

Q: If users don't have a plug-in that my page requires, is there any way to make their browsers automatically download and install it?

A: Not presently, and this probably won't be a JavaScript feature in the future. However, Netscape is considering a similar feature to be built in to a future version of Navigator (probably version 4.0).

Q: Is there any possibility of true integration of JavaScript with plug-ins—for example, being able to add event handlers to parts of a video image or PDF document?

A: Not at present, and trying to do this would open quite a can of worms for Netscape—particularly because each of the plug-in vendors would have to add JavaScript support.

Q: Is there any disadvantage to using plug-ins on my pages?

A: Yes. First of all, you'll be restricting the page to users of plug-in compatible browsers; second, they will need the plug-in itself installed. Many users will consider this too much work just to view one Web page.

FOURTEEN

Debugging JavaScript Programs

So far, you've learned the basics of JavaScript and several advanced techniques. You have explored several examples, all of which were tested and debugged for publication in this book.

At this point, you're probably interested in creating your own unique JavaScript applications, and you may have run into some problems. In this chapter, you'll explore some common errors and misconceptions in JavaScript programming.

You'll also look at some tools and techniques you can use to debug your programs. Finally, you'll explore some problems that aren't your fault—bugs in various implementations of JavaScript. You'll also consider the impact of these bugs and explore ways of working around them.

Common Errors in JavaScript Programming

> Don't be discouraged if your program doesn't work the first time— they rarely do.

Although JavaScript is one of the simplest programming languages, there are still some statements, functions, and techniques that can be confusing. You will explore some of the most common errors you might make, and their symptoms, in the next sections.

Syntax Errors

> Syntax errors are often simple typing errors.

Some of the most common errors you might make in a JavaScript program are syntax errors—errors in the punctuation, object names, and such that make up a program.

Some syntax errors are obvious. For example, you might miss a comma or period, or spell the name of an object wrong. Netscape recognizes most of these errors and will point them out to you.

Unfortunately, some of the easiest syntax errors to make can be the hardest to detect. Netscape won't detect them, and the program may even work—but produce the wrong result. You'll explore the most difficult syntax errors in the following sections.

Assignment and Equality

One of the most common errors people make in JavaScript is to confuse the assignment (=) operator with the equality (==) operator. This can often be one of the hardest errors to spot in your source code. If you've done any programming in C or Perl, you'll recognize this as one of the most common errors in those languages also.

Luckily, JavaScript is able to detect this error better than most languages. For example, the following line of JavaScript code mistakenly uses the assignment operator:

```
if (a = 5) window.status="a is 5";
```

When the JavaScript interpreter encounters this line, it recognizes that it was probably intended as an equality test and gives you an error message indicating this (see Figure 14.1). The interpretation of the program continues and treats the line as if it were an equality test. (Of course, you should still fix it.)

If you make the opposite mistake—using == when you should have used =—the error message isn't quite as clear. In fact, you may not receive an error message. For example, this program will generate an error message:

```
a == 5;
if (a == 5) window.status="a is 5";
```

Figure 14.1.

Netscape recognizes when you have used an assignment operator by mistake.

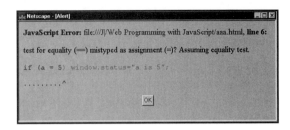

The first statement is considered an error because you are trying to compare the variable a with a value, but a currently has no value. The error message produced by this example is shown in Figure 14.2.

Figure 14.2.

The error message produced when you used the equality error by mistake.

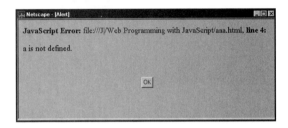

However, consider the following modified version of the example:

```
a = 7;
a == 5;
if (a == 5) window.status="a is 5";
```

In this example, the variable a has been defined and assigned a value, before the equality operator is used. This makes a == 5 an expression that simply evaluates to true, doing nothing. No error message is produced, but the correct action is not performed.

Naming Objects Correctly

Another common error in JavaScript is to leave out some details of an object's name—for example, in the following form definition:

```
<FORM name="form1">
<INPUT TYPE="text" NAME="text1">
</FORM>
```

If you want to access the value of the text1 text field, the correct syntax is this:

```
document.form1.text1.value
```

It's often tempting to refer to the object as simply text1, but it won't work without the document and form name. If the previous form was defined in a different frame, you would also need to refer to the proper frame:

```
parent.frames[1].document.form1.text1.value
```

Obviously, things can get complicated, especially when you're working with multiple documents, windows, and frames. If you have used the incorrect name, you will usually get the same error message: *name* has no properties. Figure 14.3 shows an example of the error message when the form name has been left out.

Figure 14.3.
The error message you usually get when using the incorrect name for an object.

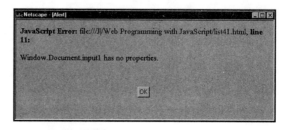

Using Proper Punctuation and Capitalization

A few common errors involve punctuation. These usually result in an error message when the page is first loaded, and include the following:

❑ Be sure to use parentheses after a method name, even if you are not passing any parameters—for example, date1.getSeconds() accesses a method of the date object. Similarly, be sure not to use parentheses with a property name.

❑ If you want to use the value of a variable as the name of a property, be sure to use brackets ([]) rather than the period syntax. With a period, the variable name is used as the property name. For example, object[var] accesses a property with the value of var as its name; object.var looks for a var property.

❑ Be sure to use parentheses around the condition in the if statement and anywhere else you use a conditional expression.

You should also keep close watch on your capitalization, because JavaScript variable, method, function, object, and property names are case-sensitive. For example, this statement is invalid because the random() method should not be capitalized:

```
a = Math.Random();
```

TIP: If JavaScript gives you an error message saying that a name is invalid, doesn't exist, or has no properties, look for a punctuation or capitalization error.

HTML Issues

Because a JavaScript program is embedded within an HTML document, errors in the actual HTML can affect your program. HTML is a complicated language in itself, and this book can't cover all of it here; however, here are some common HTML errors that can affect JavaScript programs:

- ❏ Be sure to use the NAME attribute for all forms, form elements, and frames. This makes it easy to access the objects from JavaScript.

- ❏ Be sure to enclose JavaScript code within <SCRIPT> tags, except when defining event handlers.

- ❏ Use quotation marks around an entire event handler, and be sure to use single quotation marks (apostrophes) instead within the event handler itself.

- ❏ Avoid using too many statements in an event handler; if you have a complex need, define a function and call the function in the event handler.

- ❏ If you are using HTML comments to hide JavaScript code from older browsers, you have to be careful; using the greater-than (>) or decrement (−) symbols anywhere in the script can cause the comment to end prematurely. For tips on working around this problem, see Chapter 1, "Creating Simple JavaScript Programs."

Using Correct Objects

Some of the objects and properties in JavaScript can be confusing. The best example of this is that the document and the window both have a location property. These are very different things:

- ❏ window.location is a location object that defines the location of the current window (or the specified window). You can change this location to cause a new document to be loaded by changing its properties, such as window.location.href.

- ❏ document.location is a simple text property that indicates the location of the document. This may be different from the value of window.location.href if the document was redirected from a different location.

A common error is to attempt to set document.location to send the user to a new URL. This doesn't generate an error message, but also doesn't accomplish anything. You should always use window.location.href to load a new URL.

Another area of confusion is the history object. Some references, such as Netscape's own documentation, refer to the history object as a property of document. However, it is actually a property of the window object. Each window has its own history.

For example, to go back to the previous document, you should use the `window.history.back()` method, or simply `history.go()`. To go back to the previous document in the `frame1` frame, you would use `parent.frame1.history.back()`. Using `document.back()` results in an error.

> # NOTE:
> You can omit the `window` keyword if you are referring to an object (such as `history`) in the current window. If you are referring to a different window, you need to use its name. You cannot omit the `document` keyword.

Timing Problems

A number of potential JavaScript programming errors are caused by failure to understand various timing factors—the order in which a document loads and JavaScript code executes. Here are some examples of problems of this nature:

❏ You must always define a function before calling it. If you place your function definitions in the `<HEAD>` section of the HTML document, they will always be loaded first. Otherwise, the script section that defines the function must be located before the section that uses it.

❏ The window's `onLoad` event handler can be triggered before the entire document loads. This is particularly true of images. This means that you should be careful when working with the `images` array, because some images may not be loaded yet. You can use each image's `onLoad` event handler to verify this.

❏ Another situation when `onLoad` doesn't always work is in using frames. The best way to verify that an object you need to use is loaded is to check its value. If it isn't there, use `setTimeout` to pause before trying again.

❏ Multiple `setTimeout` calls do not override each other. If the timeouts use different variables, they will execute independently.

Variable Problems

Variables and scope are introduced and explained in Chapter 2, "Working with Larger Programs and Variables."

Sometimes variables can create problems. One of the most confusing aspects of JavaScript is the scope of variables—in other words, where a variable can be used. As you have learned, there are basically two variable scopes in JavaScript:

❏ Global variables are those you define outside a function, or by using the `var` keyword. These can be used anywhere in the HTML file where they are defined.

❏ Local variables are those you define within a function, or without using the var keyword. They apply only to the function or set of <SCRIPT> tags where they are defined.

Problems can occur when you cut and paste JavaScript routines between two pages. You might be using a global variable for one routine with the same name as a local variable used in another routine. Any time a variable's value changes unexpectedly, suspect this type of problem.

NOTE: Two different local variables (local to two different functions) can have the same name without causing a problem.

Reserved Words

JavaScript has a list of reserved words—words that you can't use as variable names because they serve an important purpose within JavaScript. Because this list includes all the object properties in the object hierarchy, it can be quite long.

This can create problems if you choose a name that matches a reserved word. For example, suppose you created an order form that includes a name, address, and phone number. You might choose the obvious names name, address, and phone for those text fields. However, because form.name is a predefined property that holds the name of the form, this can create conflicts.

In some cases, the property might not work the way you expect it to, or change value unexpectedly, because the internal JavaScript property has priority. In other cases, your new property might override the built-in property, causing a different set of problems.

TIP: Refer to Appendix B for a complete list of JavaScript reserved words.

Platform-Specific Issues

JavaScript is designed as a platform-independent language. In other words, the Windows, Macintosh, and UNIX versions of Netscape should run a script in exactly the same way.

For the majority of JavaScript features, this is true; however, there are still a few differences in the way JavaScript works on the different platforms. Here are a few common platform-specific problems:

❏ For some Macintosh versions of Netscape, dates in `Date` objects are one day in the future compared to other versions.

❏ For some UNIX and Macintosh versions, the `document.lastModified` property returns an incorrect value—or causes a crash.

❏ The `parseInt()` and `parseFloat()` functions return `0` to indicate that the result is not a number in Windows platforms; on other platforms, they return `"NaN"` (not a number).

There are many other minor differences between platforms. Worse, when the current version of Netscape is a beta version, there may be different bugs for different platforms, or the version may not be available for a particular platform yet.

How do you keep up? The differences are usually minor, so you can usually avoid these issues. Because most of us don't have several computers handy to test a program on every platform, the best you can do is put it on the Web—you'll get feedback from users if there's a problem.

TIP: If you use much JavaScript in your pages and change it frequently, you may wish to find at least one user on each platform to use as a beta tester. Send that user a note when you change your pages, to make sure the user works on all platforms.

Techniques for Debugging

Let's look at two techniques you can use in the process of debugging your JavaScript programs. Either of these methods can be used to test the value of a variable at intermittent points and follow the data through the program.

Using Alerts to Display Values

The simplest way of adding debugging information to a JavaScript program is to use the `window.alert()` method to display a value. For example, the following section of code includes an alert to test the value of the `text` variable:

```
text = document.form1.text1.value;
window.alert("Value:" + text);
```

Remember that because JavaScript is a loosely typed language, you can include numeric variables, string variables, and floating-point variables in the `alert` text. Here's an example:

```
a = 5.66;
b = 2;
window.alert("a is " + a + " and b is " + b);
```

In the process of debugging a JavaScript program, you might add statements like this several times to find the cause of a problem. After determining the problem, you can remove the `alert` statement.

TIP:
You can also use the status line to view debugging information. However, the value you display there might be erased by Netscape or by your program.

Debugging with a Temporary Window

For larger-scale debugging needs, you can open a new window and use it to display debugging information. The following is an example of a statement to create a new window called `bug` to display debug information in:

```
bug = window.open("","bug","status=0 toolbar=0");
```

After opening the debug window, you can use a simple function to write data to it:

```
function debug(text) {
   bug.document.writeln(text);
}
```

You can now use the `debug()` function to display debug messages in the new window. Listing 14.1 shows a detailed example of this technique, and Figure 14.4 shows the output in the debug window.

Figure 14.4.
Using a temporary window to display debugging information.

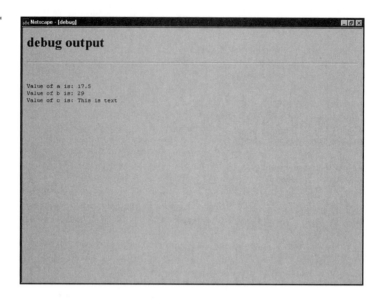

Listing 14.1. (TEMPWIN.HTM) A simple program that displays debug information in a temporary window.

```
<HTML>
<HEAD><TITLE>Test of Debugging Window</TITLE>
<SCRIPT>
//open the debug window
bug = window.open("","bug","status=0 toolbar=0 height=100 width=400");
    bug.document.write("<HTML><HEAD><TITLE>debug</TITLE></HEAD>");
    bug.document.write("<BODY><h1>debug output</h1><hr><PRE>");
//function to write to debug window
function debug(text) {
    bug.document.writeln(text);
}
a = 17.5;
b = 29;
c = "This is text";
debug("Value of a is: " + a);
debug("Value of b is: " + b);
debug("Value of c is: " + c);
</SCRIPT>
</HEAD>
<BODY>
<h1>Test of Debugging Window</h1>
<hr>
this is a test.
</BODY>
</HTML>
```

Tools for JavaScript Debugging

At present, JavaScript has limited debugging features.

If you've programmed with C, Perl, or another full-scale programming language, you might be used to the benefits of a complete debugger, which enables you to step through programs, test variables, and perform other helpful tasks automatically.

JavaScript is a simple language and is not equipped with a debugger. However, you're not entirely alone in your task of debugging a JavaScript program. You will learn about two tools in the next sections that can help:

❏ The JavaScript command line, built into Netscape, can be useful for testing JavaScript commands.

❏ The JavaScript Trace Facility is a third-party tool that can be helpful in developing complex JavaScript applications.

Using the JavaScript Command Line

Although you won't find any mention of it in Netscape's documentation, there is a debugging tool of sorts built into Netscape Navigator (all versions that support JavaScript). It has no official name, but it's called the *JavaScript command line* here.

To access this tool, simply type `javascript:` in Netscape's Location field and press Enter. If you're a slow typist or enjoy coffee-related terms, you can type `mocha:` to access the same screen. The resulting screen is divided into two frames horizontally; the top one is blank, and the bottom frame includes a text field. The initial JavaScript command line screen is shown in Figure 14.5.

Figure 14.5.
The JavaScript command line: a simple debugging tool.

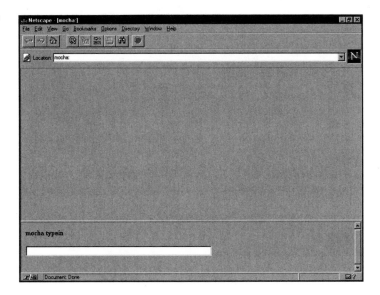

Testing JavaScript Commands Interactively

As you might guess, the JavaScript command line enables you to type a command into the blank. When you press Enter, the command is executed. The top frame is used to display the status of each of the commands in a scrolling list.

Although this won't help you debug an existing program, it can be very useful in the process of learning JavaScript or planning a project. You can test commands in this command line to find out easily how they work and what they return.

As an example, Figure 14.6 demonstrates the use of the command line to test the `window.confirm()` method. I have already tried it several times, and you can see the result (true or false) for each trial. The confirmation dialog is currently displayed along with the command that produced it.

Figure 14.6.
The result of several trials of the `window.confirm()` *method using the JavaScript command line.*

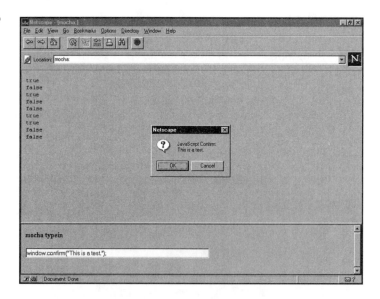

You don't have to use an actual statement in the command line. You can use any valid JavaScript expression. The result of evaluating the expression is shown in the upper frame. For example, Figure 14.7 shows the result of several trials of the `Math.random()` method.

Figure 14.7.
The result of several trials of the Math.random() *method using the command line.*

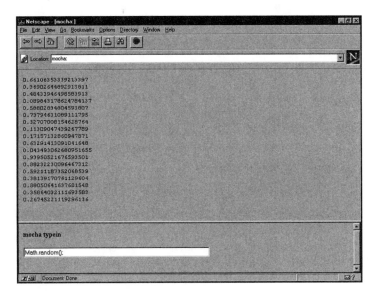

When you're working at the command line, you can use variables and even create functions. The only restriction is that anything you do has to fit in the text field. For example, you could define a simple function to add 5 to a number by typing this command:

```
function add5(num) {return num+5}
```

Once you've done that, you can type this expression:

```
add5(39)
```

and the result (44) will be displayed.

> **TIP:** You can also use the JavaScript command line as a convenient calculator. Type an expression, such as 5*30, and it will be evaluated. You can even define variables and use them in your calculations.

Using Commands in the URL

You can also skip a step and enter a JavaScript command directly into Netscape's Location field. Use javascript: (or mocha:) as the method before the command. For example, you can type the following into the Location field to display an alert message:

```
javascript:window.alert("This is an alert.");
```

You use this technique to work with image maps in Chapter 12, "Working with Graphics in JavaScript."

This makes it easy to test a statement or expression quickly. Using this method, however, you cannot define functions or perform other complex operations.

NOTE:

You can also use `javascript:` as a link destination to make links that execute a JavaScript statement or function. This is an alternative to event handlers. You saw some uses for this technique in Chapter 12.

The JavaScript Trace Facility

Obviously, the JavaScript command line leaves something to be desired as a debugger. It enables you to test statements, but it doesn't do much good in testing complete applications. The JavaScript Trace Facility is a third-party utility that allows a wide variety of options for testing a program.

The JavaScript Trace Facility was created by Fred Highland (`wwmfarm@fred.net`). It is copyrighted, but it can be copied for use in your own JavaScript programs.

 # Installing the JavaScript Trace Facility

To use the Trace Facility, you need to copy its functions into the HTML file with your script. You can also use the `<SCRIPT SRC=>` tag in later versions of Netscape to include it in your file.

To copy the Trace Facility functions, load the page at this URL:

```
http://www.fred.net/wwmfarm/javastra.htm
```

 # TIP:

The JavaScript Trace Facility is also included on the CD-ROM accompanying this book.

Once you've done this, you can use the functions for interactive debugging and tracing.

Using the Debug Form

The Trace Facility includes several functions that you can use for debugging and tracing. The first, `trace_form()`, creates a form to hold the results of the trace. In the call to this function, specify the width and length of the form. This example:

```
trace_form(60,5)
```

defines a form with 5 lines, 60 characters across.

The JavaScript Trace Facility debug form is shown in Figure 14.8. It includes the following components:

❑ The Expression or Object text field enables you to enter an expression, command, or object name to be evaluated.

❑ The Evaluate button evaluates the expression, similar to Mocha's command line.

❑ The Properties button lists the properties of the object you have named on the command line.

❑ The Clear button clears all the fields.

❑ The Result text field displays the result of the expression, the return code for a statement, or the properties of the object.

❑ The Trace Output window displays tracing messages. You can create these by using the trace functions, described in the next section.

❑ The Statistics button displays statistics for a function. This is used with the statistical functions described in the next section.

Figure 14.8.

The JavaScript Trace Facility debug form enables you to test values and trace the execution of your program.

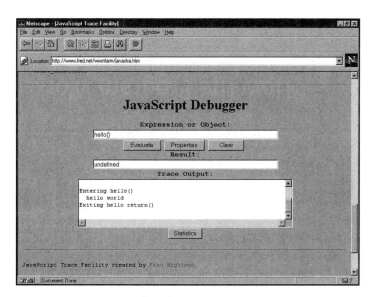

Using the Trace Functions

Along with the debug form, the JavaScript Trace Facility includes a variety of functions that you can use to track events in your program. The output of each of these commands appears in the Trace Output window of the debug form:

❑ `trace_entry(name,arguments)`: Use this function to trace the entry into a function. Specify the function's name and the arguments being passed to it in the parentheses. Place this function call at the beginning of your function definition to trace calls to the function.

❑ `trace_exit(name,value)`: Use this function to trace the exit from a function. Place this function call immediately before the `return` statement in the function. Specify the function's name and the value that you will return.

❑ `trace_msg(text)`: Use this function to display the text string you specify in the trace output field. You can use this to display any message you like.

❑ `trace_entry_stats(name)`: This function enables you to trace the entry to a function and collect statistics on the number of calls to the function and the time spent within it. The name you specify is used to identify the function. You must also use `trace_exit_stats`.

❑ `trace_exit_stats(name)`: This function ends the statistical trace of a function. Place this command at the end of the function and specify the same name as you did previously. After the function has been called at least once, you can press the Statistics button in the debug form to display the statistics.

CAUTION: All these trace functions will slow down your program, and they should be used only while debugging. The statistical functions are particularly time-consuming, and they may not work well with complex programs.

Dealing with Bugs and Crashes

Expect an occasional crash, especially when using JavaScript's latest features.

JavaScript is continually being developed and improved; because of this, you should always use the latest version of Netscape to test and debug your JavaScript applications. However, you're probably making your applications available to users all over the world via the Web, and there's no way to ensure that they have all upgraded.

In the next sections, you'll look at each of the versions of Netscape and Microsoft Internet Explorer that support JavaScript, their limitations and bugs. If users report a problem with your script, you should refer to this list to determine whether the problem is caused by their browsers.

NOTE: Bugs in JavaScript are still being fixed—and still being discovered. There is no way to guarantee that every possible bug is included, but I have tried to include all known problems at the time of this writing.

TIP: For more detailed information about each version of Netscape, including versions released after this book, refer to Netscape's release notes at this URL: `http://home.netscape.com/eng/mozilla/3.0/relnotes/index.html`.

Netscape Navigator 2.0

JavaScript was introduced in version 2.0 of Netscape Navigator. There were several beta versions of version 2.0 before the final version, and JavaScript progressed in these versions. You'll look at some of the problems in the beta versions, then in the released version.

You will also look at some memory problems in JavaScript in this section. These are not described by Netscape in the release notes, but have been discovered by users (usually causing a crash). You'll also look at some ways of avoiding the problem.

Beta Versions of Netscape 2.0

JavaScript was introduced in the first beta release of Netscape Navigator 2.0. It was originally called LiveScript, and the <SCRIPT> tag used "livescript" as its language value. It was also available only for the Windows platforms.

In version 2.0 beta 2, support was added for Macintosh and UNIX platforms. Improvements continued until version 2.0b6, the last beta release.

Several bugs are present in the beta versions. Here are some of the most important ones:

- ❏ The select() and focus() methods for input fields don't work properly.
- ❏ The selectedIndex property of a selection list doesn't receive the correct value.
- ❏ The window.close() method does not work in these versions.
- ❏ Attempting to use a window the user has closed can cause Netscape to crash.

Problems in the Release of Netscape 2.0

Although the final release of Netscape 2.0 is a much more stable product than any of the previous versions, it still has several JavaScript-related bugs and limitations:

- ❏ You must use the HEIGHT and WIDTH attributes for all images in a document that uses JavaScript. If they are not used, event handlers will not work correctly.

❏ The `onLoad` event may occur before the document and its images are completely loaded.

❏ The `lastIndexOf` string method does not work properly; it starts one character earlier than it should.

❏ You are not allowed to set the `form.method` property.

❏ Multiple form elements with the same name should be stored in an array. In some cases, this array will be indexed backward.

❏ The `document.close()` method can cause a crash if it is used with the default window.

❏ The `eval()` function causes crashes, particularly in the 16-bit Windows version of Netscape.

❏ Floating-point arithmetic has some inaccuracies.

❏ The `<SCRIPT SRC>` method of including JavaScript in an HTML file does not work.

Memory Problems

Along with these problems, Netscape 2.0 suffers from some memory leaks when JavaScript is used. This means that certain JavaScript code can use up memory, often resulting in an out-of-memory error or crash.

The most common cause of this problem is when you repeatedly assign a value to a string. JavaScript cannot modify the value of a string without re-creating the entire string. If you change a string's value repeatedly in a loop, memory will quickly disappear.

TIP: Some of the worst cases of memory leakage occur in scrolling-message programs, which assign a new value to a string every second or faster. The scrolling message program introduced in Chapter 8, "Improving a Web Page with JavaScript," avoids this problem.

Netscape Navigator 2.01

Netscape Navigator 2.01 did not add any new features (or bugs) to JavaScript. It did remove several features for security reasons, however. These include the following:

❏ You cannot use the `submit()` method with the `mailto:` action. This would enable scripts to send mail from you without your knowledge.

❏ You cannot access lists of files and directories (such as opening a local directory) within JavaScript.

❏ You cannot access the individual history items within the `history` object.

❏ If a document is loaded in another window from a different server, you can obtain only certain information about the window.

Netscape Navigator 2.02

This is an incremental release that fixed a number of bugs in version 2.01. The main bug was a problem with Daylight Savings Time, which caused pages to remain in the cache even when they had been changed. There were also some minor fixes to JavaScript:

❏ The `document.close()` method works properly.

❏ A fix prevents scripts from starting a file upload to the server without your permission.

Netscape Navigator 3.0 (Atlas)

At this writing, Netscape Navigator 3.0 is under development and several beta versions have been released. Some of these versions were released under the code name "Atlas." Many new features have been added in these versions.

New Features

Netscape 3.0 added many new features to JavaScript. In fact, many of the features you already learned about were added in this version. JavaScript didn't really "grow up" until version 3.0 was released. Here is a summary of the new features:

❏ JavaScript can now access a list of plug-ins, to determine which ones are available. You will use this feature in Chapter 13, "Working with Multimedia and Plug-Ins."

❏ JavaScript can now communicate with and access Java applets, and Java applets can access JavaScript. You'll explore these features in Chapter 16, "Integrating JavaScript with Java."

❏ The `Array` and `Object` keywords, which you looked at in Chapter 4, "Using Built-In Objects and Custom Objects," were added.

❏ The `images` array, which you looked at in Chapter 12, was added.

❏ Data tainting, explained in Chapter 10, "Working with Multiple Pages and Data," was added.

❏ The `focus()` method can now be used on external windows.

❏ The `<SCRIPT SRC>` tag can now be used to include JavaScript from a URL.

❏ The `<NOSCRIPT>` tag makes it easy to detect non-JavaScript browsers.

❏ You can modify the items in a selection list on the fly.

Remaining and New Bugs

Unfortunately, several bugs still plague the beta versions of Netscape 3.0. These should be fixed in a later release. These include the following:

❏ The `document.lastModified` property does not work on all platforms, and it sometimes causes a crash.

❏ The `click()` method of buttons, radio buttons, and checkboxes does not work properly.

❏ Forms or JavaScript code inside a nested table are not recognized properly.

❏ There are still several situations that can cause memory leaks.

Microsoft Internet Explorer

At this writing, Microsoft has begun to support JavaScript with an early alpha version of its Web browser, Microsoft Internet Explorer (MSIE) 3.0. At present, this support is very minimal.

Currently, few of the examples in this book will work in MSIE 3.0 at all, and many will cause a crash. My recommendation is not to attempt to support this browser until it is more finished; Microsoft has promised full JavaScript support in the final version of MSIE 3.0.

TIP: You'll take a closer look at MSIE, ActiveX, and VBScript in Chapter 18, "Using ActiveX and Microsoft Internet Explorer 3.0."

Workshop Wrap-Up

In this chapter, you explored some of the many ways JavaScript programs can fail, and what to do about them:

❏ You've looked at some of the most common errors JavaScript programmers make and how to avoid them.

❏ You have also looked at two techniques for displaying debug information: alerts and external windows. Each of these has its advantages.

❏ Next, you looked at two tools that may help the debugging process: Netscape's JavaScript command line, and the JavaScript Trace Facility by Fred Highland.

❏ Finally, you took a tour of the various versions of Netscape (and Microsoft Internet Explorer) that support JavaScript and some of the problems and bugs in each version.

Next Steps

You should now have a good understanding of the techniques you can use to debug even the most stubborn JavaScript program. Now move on with one of the following:

❏ To build a full-scale JavaScript application, see Chapter 15, "Real-Life Examples III."

❏ To learn issues involved when working with JavaScript and Java, see Chapter 16, "Integrating JavaScript with Java."

❏ To learn tips for debugging CGI programs used with JavaScript and forms, see Chapter 17, "Combining JavaScript, CGI, and SSI."

❏ To learn more about Microsoft Internet Explorer and its scripting capabilities, see Chapter 18, "Using ActiveX and Microsoft Internet Explorer 3.0."

❏ To learn about proposed and rumored features for future versions of Netscape, see Chapter 20, "The Future of JavaScript."

Q&A

Q: Are all the causes for Netscape crashes covered in this chapter?

A: By no means. I've tried to cover the most common causes, but there are still occasional crashes—in any program, not just Netscape—that can't be explained. Watch also for new bugs in any future version.

Q: What's the easiest way to avoid the problems with hiding JavaScript from older browsers with HTML comments?

A: Instead of using comments, use the `<SCRIPT SRC>` command and store the script in a separate file. This feature is supported in Netscape 3.0b5 and later versions.

Q: If the `onLoad` event doesn't necessarily happen after the document is finished loading, how can I be sure it's finished?

A: A simple workaround is to set a timeout in the `onLoad` handler to execute your function a few seconds later. Netscape has promised a method to verify this in a future version.

FIFTEEN

Real-Life Examples III

This chapter includes a single example program: a poker solitaire game written in JavaScript. This is the largest program presented in this book and illustrates the following concepts from previous chapters:

❏ Functions and event handlers (Chapter 3)
❏ Arrays, custom objects, and arrays of objects (Chapters 4 and 10)
❏ Forms (Chapter 6)
❏ Replacing inline images (Chapter 12)

In addition, it's a good demonstration of a large-scale JavaScript application. The next sections describe and present the program.

Planning the Program

The task for this example is to create a JavaScript poker solitaire game. The game board, at the start of a game, is shown in Figure 15.1. Here is a summary of how the game is played:

❏ The board consists of 25 squares in a 5-by-5 grid. A "draw" card is on the lower right corner.
❏ The computer deals cards one at a time. Each card appears in the draw pile. You can click on one of the 25 squares in the grid to move the card to the board.

❏ Scoring is based on poker hands. Each row, column, and diagonal is a separate hand, and is scored when it is completed. The total score is a combination of all of these.

❏ The game ends when 25 cards have been dealt. You can also click on the New Game link to start over.

Figure 15.1.

The Poker Solitaire game board at the start of a game.

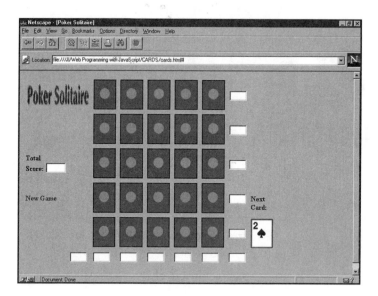

Before you move on to the program itself, let's look at a few of the challenges of planning a project of this size:

❏ The board consists of 25 squares. By including a title graphic, I conveniently made these the 1st through 25th images on the page—this will make them easy to access via the document.images array.

❏ I used a custom object, Card, to store information about the cards in the game. This object includes a number (1-13) and a suit (c, h, s, or d.)

❏ The deck of cards is stored in an array called deck; each element is a Card object.

❏ The cards currently on the board are placed in an array called board. Once again, these are Card objects.

❏ I created 52 images—one for each card—and a blank image to represent blank spaces on the board. These are all exactly the same size, so they can be easily swapped inline.

❏ The whole game board is laid out using a table. The first column includes a link to start a new game and the total score, columns 2 through 6 are the game board, and the last column and row are used for text fields. These will hold the score for each column, row, and diagonal.

TIP: You'll find the graphics you need for this example (cards, blank card, title) on the CD-ROM accompanying this book.

The Complete Application

Without further ado, Listing 15.1 shows the complete Poker Solitaire application, including all HTML and JavaScript functions.

Listing 15.1. (CARDS.HTM) The Poker Solitaire application (HTML and JavaScript).

```
<HTML>
<HEAD>
<TITLE>Poker Solitaire</TITLE>
<SCRIPT LANGUAGE="JavaScript">
// global variables
var tally = new Array(14)
var nextcard = 1;
var nexti = new Image(53,68);
// numeric comparison for sort () function numsort (a,b){
   return a-b;
   }
function InitGame() {
   nextcard = 1;
// clear scores
   for (i=0; i<5; i++) {
   document.form1.col[i].value = " ";
   document.form1.row[i].value = " ";
   document.form1.diag1.value = " ";
   document.form1.diag2.value = " ";
   document.form1.total.value = " ";
   }
// array for board contents
   board = new Array(26);
   for (i=1; i<26; i++) {
      board[i] = new Card(0,"x");
      document.images[i].src = "blank.gif";
   }

// fill the deck (in order, for now)
   deck = new Array(53);
   for (i=1; i<14; i++) {
     deck[i] = new Card(i,"c");
     deck[i+13] = new Card(i,"h");
     deck[i+26] = new Card(i,"s");
     deck[i+39] = new Card(i,"d");
   }
// shuffle the deck
   n = Math.floor(52 * Math.random() + 200);
```

continues

Listing 15.1. continued

```
          if (card1 != card2) {
             temp = deck[card2];
             deck[card2] = deck[card1];
             deck[card1] = temp;
          }
       }
// draw the first card on screen
    document.images[26].src = deck[nextcard].fname();
    nexti.src = deck[nextcard+1].fname();
// end InitGame
}

// place the draw card on the board where clicked

function PlaceCard(pos) {
    if (board[pos].suit != "x") {
       return;
    }
    document.images[pos].src = document.images[26].src;
    document.images[26].src = "blank.gif";
    board[pos] = deck[nextcard];
    nextcard++;
    Score();
    if (nextcard > 25) {
       EndGame();
    }
    else {
       document.images[26].src = deck[nextcard].fname();
// cache next image for draw pile
       nexti = new Image(53,68);
       nexti.src = deck[nextcard+1].fname();
    }
}

// check for completed rows and display row scores
function Score() {
    totscore = 0;
// rows
    for (x=0; x<5; x++) {
       r = x * 5 + 1;
       a = AddScore(board[r],board[r+1],board[r+2],board[r+3],board[r+4])
       if (a != -1) {
          document.form1.row[x].value = a;
          totscore += a;
       }
    }
// columns
    for (x=0; x<5; x++) {
       r = x + 1;
       a = AddScore(board[r],board[r+5],board[r+10],board[r+15],board[r+20])
       if (a != -1) {
          document.form1.col[x].value = a;
          totscore += a;
       }
    }
```

```
              totscore += a;
         }
    }
// diagonals
    a = AddScore(board[5],board[9],board[13],board[17],board[21])
    if (a != -1) {
       document.form1.diag1.value = a;
       totscore += a;
    }
    a = AddScore(board[1],board[7],board[13],board[19],board[25])
    if (a != -1) {
       document.form1.diag2.value = a;
       totscore += a;
    }
    document.form1.total.value = totscore;
}

// check for poker hands
function AddScore(c1,c2,c3,c4,c5) {
   straight = false;
   flush = false;
   pairs = 0;
   three = false;

// sorted array for convenience
   nums = new Array(5);
   nums[0] = c1.num;
   nums[1] = c2.num;
   nums[2] = c3.num;
   nums[3] = c4.num;
   nums[4] = c5.num;
   nums.sort(numsort);
// no score if row is not filled
   if (c1.num == 0 || c2.num == 0 || c3.num == 0
       || c4.num == 0 || c5.num == 0) {
      return -1;
   }
// flush
   if (c1.suit == c2.suit && c2.suit == c3.suit
      && c3.suit == c4.suit && c4.suit == c5.suit) {
      flush = true;
   }
// straight
   if (nums[0] + 4 == nums[1] + 3 == nums[2] +2
       == nums[3] + 1 == nums[4]) {
      straight = true;
   }
// royal flush, straight flush, straight, flush
   if (straight && flush && nums[4]==13) return 250;
   if (straight && flush) return 50;
   if (straight) return 4;
   if (flush) return 5;

// tally array is a count for each card value
   for (i=1; i<14; i++) {
      tally[i] = 0;
   }
   for (i=0; i<5; i++) {
```

continues

Listing 15.1. continued

```
    for (i=1; i<14; i++) {
// four of a kind
        if (tally[i] == 4) return 25;
        if (tally[i] == 3) three = true;
        if (tally[i] == 2) pairs += 1;
    }
// full house
    if (three && pairs == 1) return 8;
// two pair
    if (pairs == 2) return 2;
// three of a kind
    if (three) return 3;
// just a pair
    if (pairs == 1) return 1;
// nothing
    return 0;
// end AddScore()
}

// game over - final score
function EndGame() {
    document.images[26].src = "blank.gif";
    window.alert("Game Over");
}

// make a filename for an image, given Card object
function fname() {
    return this.num + this.suit + ".gif";
}

// constructor for Card objects
function Card(num,suit) {
    this.num = num;
    this.suit = suit;
    this.fname = fname;
}

</SCRIPT>
</HEAD>
<BODY>
<FORM NAME="form1">
<TABLE>
<tr>
  <td> <img src="title.gif" height=59 width=150> </td>
  <td> <a href="#" onClick="PlaceCard(1);">
      <img border=0 src="blank.gif" height=68 width=53></a>
  <td> <a href="#" onClick="PlaceCard(2);">
      <img border=0 src="blank.gif" height=68 width=53></a>
  <td> <a href="#" onClick="PlaceCard(3);">
      <img border=0 src="blank.gif" height=68 width=53></a>
  <td> <a href="#" onClick="PlaceCard(4);">
      <img border=0 src="blank.gif" height=68 width=53></a>
  <td> <a href="#" onClick="PlaceCard(5);">
      <img border=0 src="blank.gif" height=68 width=53></a>
  <td> <INPUT TYPE="TEXT" SIZE=4 NAME="row"> </td>
  <td> </td>
</tr>
```

```
<tr>
  <td> </td>
  <td> <a href="#" onClick="PlaceCard(6);">
       <img border=0 src="blank.gif" height=68 width=53></a>
  <td> <a href="#" onClick="PlaceCard(7);">
       <img border=0 src="blank.gif" height=68 width=53></a>
  <td> <a href="#" onClick="PlaceCard(8);">
       <img border=0 src="blank.gif" height=68 width=53></a>
  <td> <a href="#" onClick="PlaceCard(9);">
       <img border=0 src="blank.gif" height=68 width=53></a>
  <td> <a href="#" onClick="PlaceCard(10);">
       <img border=0 src="blank.gif" height=68 width=53></a>
  <td> <INPUT TYPE="TEXT" SIZE=4 NAME="row"> </td>
  <td> </td>
</tr>
<tr>
  <td> <B>Total<BR>Score:</B>
       <INPUT TYPE="TEXT" SIZE=5 NAME="total"></td>
  <td> <a href="#" onClick="PlaceCard(11);">
       <img border=0 src="blank.gif" height=68 width=53></a>
  <td> <a href="#" onClick="PlaceCard(12);">
       <img border=0 src="blank.gif" height=68 width=53></a>
  <td> <a href="#" onClick="PlaceCard(13);">
       <img border=0 src="blank.gif" height=68 width=53></a>
  <td> <a href="#" onClick="PlaceCard(14);">
       <img border=0 src="blank.gif" height=68 width=53></a>
  <td> <a href="#" onClick="PlaceCard(15);">
       <img border=0 src="blank.gif" height=68 width=53></a>
  <td> <INPUT TYPE="TEXT" SIZE=4 NAME="row"> </td>
  <td> </td>
</tr>
<tr>
  <td> <a href="#" onClick="InitGame();">
       <b>New Game</b></a>
       <br><b><a href="psoldoc.html">Instructions</a></b></td>
  <td> <a href="#" onClick="PlaceCard(16);">
       <img border=0 src="blank.gif" height=68 width=53></a>
  <td> <a href="#" onClick="PlaceCard(17);">
       <img border=0 src="blank.gif" height=68 width=53></a>
  <td> <a href="#" onClick="PlaceCard(18);">
       <img border=0 src="blank.gif" height=68 width=53></a>
  <td> <a href="#" onClick="PlaceCard(19);">
       <img border=0 src="blank.gif" height=68 width=53></a>
  <td> <a href="#" onClick="PlaceCard(20);">
       <img border=0 src="blank.gif" height=68 width=53></a>
  <td> <INPUT TYPE="TEXT" SIZE=4 NAME="row"> </td>
  <td> <b><BR>Next<BR>Card:</b></td>
</tr>
<tr>
  <td> </td>
  <td> <a href="#" onClick="PlaceCard(21);">
       <img border=0 src="blank.gif" height=68 width=53></a>
  <td> <a href="#" onClick="PlaceCard(22);">
       <img border=0 src="blank.gif" height=68 width=53></a>
  <td> <a href="#" onClick="PlaceCard(23);">
       <img border=0 src="blank.gif" height=68 width=53></a>
  <td> <a href="#" onClick="PlaceCard(24);">
       <img border=0 src="blank.gif" height=68 width=53></a>
```

continues

Listing 15.1. continued

```
<td> <a href="#" onClick="PlaceCard(25);">
    <img border=0 src="blank.gif" height=68 width=53></a>
  <td> <INPUT TYPE="TEXT" SIZE=4 NAME="row"> </td>
  <td> <img src="blank.gif" height=68 width=53></td>
</tr>
<tr>
  <td align=right> <INPUT TYPE="TEXT" SIZE=4 NAME="diag1"> </td>
  <td> <INPUT TYPE="TEXT" SIZE=4 NAME="col"> </td>
  <td> <INPUT TYPE="TEXT" SIZE=4 NAME="col"> </td>
  <td> <INPUT TYPE="TEXT" SIZE=4 NAME="col"> </td>
  <td> <INPUT TYPE="TEXT" SIZE=4 NAME="col"> </td>
  <td> <INPUT TYPE="TEXT" SIZE=4 NAME="col"> </td>
  <td> <INPUT TYPE="TEXT" SIZE=4 NAME="diag2"> </td>
</TABLE>
</FORM>

</BODY>
</HTML>
```

How the Program Works

The HTML for this application is nearly as complicated as the JavaScript code, but it's easy because it's repetitive. Each of the images in the game board includes an `onClick` event handler that calls the `PlaceCard()` function, described later.

In the next few sections, you'll take a look at how the program works.

Initializing the Game

The `InitGame()` function, shown in Listing 15.2, is called when the page loads and also when you use the New Game link. It performs the following tasks:

❏ Stores 52 `Card` objects, in order, in the `deck` array

❏ Initializes the `board` array with null values

❏ Shuffles the deck by swapping a random number of random cards

❏ Places the first card on the draw pile (otherwise known as `document.images[26]`)

Listing 15.2. The `InitGame()` function begins a new game.

```
function InitGame() {
   nextcard = 1;
// clear scores
   for (i=0; i<5; i++) {
   document.form1.col[i].value = " ";
   document.form1.row[i].value = " ";
   document.form1.diag1.value = " ";
   document.form1.diag2.value = " ";
   document.form1.total.value = " ";
   }
// array for board contents
   board = new Array(26);
   for (i=1; i<26; i++) {
      board[i] = new Card(0,"x");
      document.images[i].src = "blank.gif";
   }

// fill the deck (in order, for now)
   deck = new Array(53);
   for (i=1; i<14; i++) {
     deck[i] = new Card(i,"c");
     deck[i+13] = new Card(i,"h");
     deck[i+26] = new Card(i,"s");
     deck[i+39] = new Card(i,"d");
   }
// shuffle the deck
   n = Math.floor(52 * Math.random() + 200);
   for (i=1; i<n; i++) {
      card1 = Math.floor(52*Math.random() + 1);
      card2 = Math.floor(52*Math.random() + 1);
      if (card1 != card2) {
         temp = deck[card2];
         deck[card2] = deck[card1];
         deck[card1] = temp;
      }
   }
// draw the first card on screen
   document.images[26].src = deck[nextcard].fname();
   nexti.src = deck[nextcard+1].fname();
// end InitGame
}
```

Placing Cards

Once the `InitGame()` function is finished, the program isn't running at all—that's the beauty of event-based programming. The next step is up to the user, who should click on one of the squares of the game board.

When a square is clicked, the `PlaceCard()` function, shown in Listing 15.3, is called. This function moves the card from the draw pile to the appropriate square. Because it's already in the cache, this happens instantly. An `image` object is then created to preload the next card. Figure 15.2 shows a game in progress with several cards placed.

Listing 15.3. The `PlaceCard()` function places the next card.

```
function PlaceCard(pos) {
   if (board[pos].suit != "x") {
      return;
   }
   document.images[pos].src = document.images[26].src;
   document.images[26].src = "blank.gif";
   board[pos] = deck[nextcard];
   nextcard++;
   Score();
   if (nextcard > 25) {
      EndGame();
   }
   else {
      document.images[26].src = deck[nextcard].fname();
// cache next image for draw pile
      nexti = new Image(53,68);
      nexti.src = deck[nextcard+1].fname();
   }
}
```

Figure 15.2.
The Poker Solitaire game in progress.

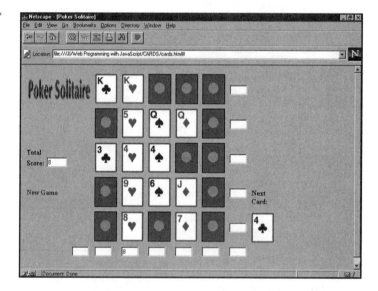

Scoring the Game

The Score() function, shown in Listing 15.4, is called each time a card is placed. This routine scans through the five rows and five columns and the two diagonals. The cards for each row are passed to the AddScore() function, which does the tricky part—finding poker hands and scoring them.

Listing 15.4. The Score() function scores the rows and columns.

```
function Score() {
   totscore = 0;
// rows
   for (x=0; x<5; x++) {
      r = x * 5 + 1;
      a = AddScore(board[r],board[r+1],board[r+2],board[r+3],board[r+4])
      if (a != -1) {
         document.form1.row[x].value = a;
         totscore += a;
      }
   }
// columns
   for (x=0; x<5; x++) {
      r = x + 1;
      a = AddScore(board[r],board[r+5],board[r+10],board[r+15],board[r+20])
      if (a != -1) {
         document.form1.col[x].value = a;
         totscore += a;
      }
   }
// diagonals
      a = AddScore(board[5],board[9],board[13],board[17],board[21])
      if (a != -1) {
         document.form1.diag1.value = a;
         totscore += a;
      }
      a = AddScore(board[1],board[7],board[13],board[19],board[25])
      if (a != -1) {
         document.form1.diag2.value = a;
         totscore += a;
      }
      document.form1.total.value = totscore;
}
```

The following scores are assigned to the various poker hands, based on their relative probability:

Poker hand	Score
Pair	1
2 pair	2
3 of a kind	3
Straight	4
Flush	5
Full house	8
4 of a kind	25
Straight flush	50
Royal Flush	250

Ending a Game

The EndGame() function, shown in Listing 15.5, is called when 25 cards have been played. This function is simple; it "blanks out" the draw card and informs you that the game is over with an alert. Because the total score is updated continuously, there's no need to worry about it here.

Listing 15.5. The EndGame() function ends the game.

```
// game over - final score
function EndGame() {
   document.images[26].src = "blank.gif";
   window.alert("Game Over");
}
```

Figure 15.3 shows the screen after a reasonably successful game. That's it! I hope this example shows you how much you can do with JavaScript and inspires you to even bigger things.

Figure 15.3.

The Poker Solitaire game display after all cards have been played.

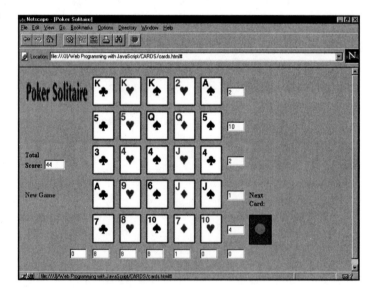

P A R T

V

JavaScript Alternatives and the Future

SIXTEEN

Integrating JavaScript with Java

As I mentioned in Chapter 1, there's not much relation between Java and JavaScript—except for the name. However, they can both be useful on your Web pages—sometimes at the same time. This chapter begins with an introduction to the Java language and its capabilities.

JavaScript also includes functions to control Java applets, and Java applets can access JavaScript functions. By integrating these two Web languages, you can have the best of both worlds, allowing for many complicated applications.

An Overview of Java

Let's begin with a tour of the Java language, the development process for Java applets, and the way Java and HTML interact. If you're unfamiliar with Java, this will give you a quick start and help you understand how Java and JavaScript can work together.

Consult Chapter 1, "Creating Simple JavaScript Programs," for details about the differences between Java and JavaScript.

NOTE: Java is a complex language—much more so than JavaScript. This chapter introduces Java, but can't explain it in detail. If you want to learn more about Java, consult the online resources listed in Appendix C, or pick up a copy of the bestselling *Teach Yourself Java in 21 Days*, by Laura Lemay, also from Sams.net publishing.

How Java Works

The Java language is both compiled and interpreted.

Some languages, such as C, are compiled into executable programs before they can be run. Others, such as JavaScript, are interpreted directly from the source code. Java is something in between.

A Java program starts out as source code and is then run through the Java compiler. The compiler doesn't produce true machine code, though—instead, it produces code for a *virtual machine*. This virtual machine code can then be interpreted by an implementation of the virtual machine, such as Netscape.

NOTE: To complicate things even more, the latest versions of Netscape and MSIE include Java compilers. Called *just-in-time compilers*, these compile Java virtual machine code into executable code before running the applet. This greatly increases the speed of applets.

There are actually two types of Java programs:

❑ A Java *application* is a complete program, such as a Web browser.

❑ A Java *applet* is a program that is meant to run within a Web browser. All Java programs you can run from the Web are applets. The next sections focus on applets.

The Java Language

The Java language is similar to C++. You may also notice a similarity to JavaScript; Netscape loosely based the JavaScript syntax on that of Java.

Like JavaScript, Java includes statements and functions. It also includes objects, properties, and methods. You will look at a simple example of a Java applet in the section titled Creating Your Own Java Applets later in this chapter.

Java Objects and Classes

All Java applets are subclasses of the `Applet` object.

Java is an object-oriented language—much more so than JavaScript. A Java applet is actually a class; running an applet means creating an instance of the class. Technically, applets are subclasses of the `Applet` object.

There are also several object classes you can import into a Java program. These provide functions such as graphics, fonts, working with strings, and so on. You'll look at a class later that enables Java to access JavaScript objects.

Integrating Java with HTML

Unlike JavaScript, Java code is never included in the HTML file itself. Instead, a special HTML tag, `<APPLET>`, is used to embed the applet in the Web page. Here is a simple example of an applet:

```
<applet code="Applet1.class" width=55 height=68>
</applet>.
```

Notice that both opening and closing `<APPLET>` tags are required. Between them, you can use optional `<PARAM>` tags to give parameters to the applet. The parameters required depend on the applet. Each `<PARAM>` tag includes a variable name and value:

```
<PARAM name=height value=100>
```

TIP: You can also use JavaScript to choose between a Java or non-Java version of a page. Use the `Navigator.javaEnabled` property, described in Chapter 4, "Using Built-In Objects and Custom Objects."

The next section presents a complete HTML file with an embedded applet. For examples of embedding public domain Java applets into your pages, see Chapter 19, "Real-Life Examples IV."

NOTE: Currently, most complicated Java applets are a bit slow. If you include one in your Web page, be sure you test it carefully; you may also wish to warn users that an applet is loading.

Creating Your Own Java Applets

The JDK is all you need to create your own Java applets.

To create your own Java applets, you use the Java Development Kit (JDK). This includes the Java compiler, example applets, and an applet viewer. The JDK is available at no charge from Sun.

 TIP: The JDK is also included on the CD-ROM that accompanies this book, along with a variety of sample applets.

The JDK is available for the following platforms:

- ❏ Windows 95
- ❏ Windows NT
- ❏ UNIX (SPARC or x86 Solaris only)
- ❏ Macintosh (Power Mac only)

NOTE: Currently, there is no version of the JDK for Windows 3.1 or 68000-series Macintosh. You will need to use a different platform to compile Java applets, although you can still view applets in Netscape. If you have a shell account with your Internet provider, you may be able to use the JDK from there.

The following tasks explain how to download and install the JDK, use it to create a simple Java applet, and compile and view the new applet.

Installing the Java Development Kit

To download the JDK, visit Sun's Java Web page at the following address:

`http://java.sun.com/`

and follow the appropriate links. At this writing, the latest version of the JDK is 1.02. Once you've downloaded it, the installation process depends on your platform:

- ❏ For Windows 95 or NT, start a DOS session. Copy the self-extracting archive file to the directory or drive you wish to install the JDK in, and execute it. It will be unpacked into a `java` directory with several subdirectories. The JDK needs about 5M of space to unpack.

❏ For Solaris, the JDK comes in a compressed `tar` file. You can expand it into the directory of your choice with this command:

```
/usr/bin/zcat JDK-1_0_2-solaris2-sparc.tar.Z ¦ tar xf -
```

❏ For Macintosh, the JDK is available in MacBinary or hqx format. Expand the file with a utility such as StuffIt, DeHQX, or BinHex4. Run the installer program, which will create a folder on your desktop for the JDK.

Creating a Simple Java Applet

Now let's try creating a simple Java applet. Listing 16.1 shows a Java applet that displays a message in a large font.

Listing 16.1. (JavaTest.java) A simple Java applet that displays a message.

```
import java.applet.Applet;
import java.awt.Graphics;
import java.awt.Font;

public class JavaTest extends Applet {
Font f = new Font("TimesRoman", Font.BOLD, 60);
public void paint(Graphics g) {
  g.setFont(f);
  g.drawString("Text from Java", 15, 50);
  }
}
```

Here is a brief explanation of the program. The first three lines are Java `import` statements. These specify three classes (libraries) used by the applet:

❏ `java.applet.Applet` is a standard class that must be imported for any applet.

❏ `java.awt.Graphics` is part of the AWT API, which handles the GUI for Java. This library includes functions for graphics.

❏ `java.awt.Font` includes functions to handle text with fonts.

Next, the class definition begins with the `public class JavaTest` statement. You're defining a class called `JavaTest`, which is a subclass of the `Applet` class (as all applets are).

Like JavaScript, Java includes a variety of objects for interacting with the user.

The next statement, `Font f = new Font`, defines an instance of the `Font` object, an object used to store information about a font and size. The `new Font` object is called `f`. (Notice the similarity to the `new` keyword for defining objects in JavaScript.)

The next statement begins the `paint` function, which is the main program. This also defines a new `Graphics` object called `g`. The next two statements are methods of the `Graphics` object; methods in Java work much like JavaScript.

The g.setFont() method sets the font to be used when drawing text, and the g.drawString() method draws the text on the screen in the applet's area.

 # Compiling and Viewing a Java Applet

Now that you have a simple Java applet, you need to compile it and use it in an HTML page. Be sure you have placed the applet source code in a file called JavaTest.java.

First, compiling the applet is simple. Type the following command from the directory where you installed the JDK:

```
bin\javac JavaTest.java
```

The compilation process should take only a few seconds. If no errors were found, the compiler won't display any messages. After the compilation, you should have a file in the same directory called JavaTest.class. This is the Java class file that you can use on a Web page.

NOTE: Just about everything in Java is case-sensitive—source files, class files, and the <APPLET> tag. Be sure you use the exact names.

Chapter 19 presents another example of creating and using a Java applet.

To test the new applet, you need to embed it in an HTML page. Listing 16.2 shows a simple HTML page that includes the applet created previously. Create this HTML file in the same directory as the class file or copy the class file into its directory.

Listing 16.2. (JAVA1.HTM) An HTML file to test the new Java applet.

```
<HTML>
<HEAD>
<TITLE>Simple Java Test</TITLE>
</HEAD>
<BODY>
<h1>test</h1>
<hr>
An applet is included below to display some text.
<hr>
<APPLET CODE="JavaTest.class" WIDTH=450 HEIGHT=125>
</APPLET>
<hr>
applet finished... here's the rest of the page.
</BODY>
</HTML>
```

The <APPLET> tag in this file includes the filename of the JavaTest class and a width and height. Be sure to include the closing </APPLET> tag, although there may be nothing between the two tags.

The applet viewer shows an applet's output, but doesn't display HTML documents.

Now that you have an HTML file, you need to test it. A simple way to do this is with the *applet viewer*, included with the JDK. You can start the applet viewer by typing the following command in the JDK directory:

```
bin\appletviewer file:\Java\JavaTest.html
```

TIP: You may need to modify this command to work on your system. You can also add the java\bin directory to your path to avoid typing `bin\` before each command.

Although you started the applet viewer from a command line, the actual output is shown in a graphical window. Figure 16.2 shows the applet viewer in action, using the example applet.

Figure 16.1.
The Java applet viewer in action.

Notice that the applet viewer shows the output of the Java applet, but does not include the text from the HTML file itself. This may be useful when you're debugging a Java applet. To see the entire HTML file including the applet, you'll need to use a browser, such as Netscape.

To test the applet in Netscape, simply use the `Open` command to load the HTML file created previously. Figure 16.2 shows the applet example as viewed by Netscape.

NOTE: Once you've created and debugged a Java applet, you'll probably want to publish it on the Web. To do this, simply place the class file for the applet in the same directory as the HTML file on the Web server.

Figure 16.2.

The Java applet in action, as viewed by Netscape.

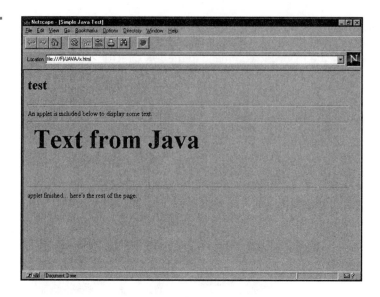

Using Java Classes with JavaScript

In Navigator 3.0b4 Netscape introduced a new feature called LiveConnect, which provides the following capabilities:

❏ JavaScript programs can communicate with and control Java applets.

❏ Java applets can access JavaScript objects, properties, and methods.

❏ JavaScript programs can control Netscape plug-ins.

Plug-ins, and the corresponding LiveConnect features, are explained in Chapter 13, "Working with Multimedia and Plug-Ins."

You will look at the first capability in this section: accessing Java classes (applets) from within JavaScript. You will look at the opposite method in the section titled Calling JavaScript functions from Java, later in this chapter.

Calling Java Methods

Some public-domain Java applets can be controlled through JavaScript.

You can call Java methods directly from JavaScript. This means you can treat methods as if they are JavaScript statements themselves. For example, this statement prints a message to the Java console:

```
java.lang.System.err.println("This is a test.");
```

This will be most useful if you are an experienced Java programmer. If you are not, you can use JavaScript to take advantage of features of existing Java applets, as described in the next section.

The `applet` Object

Each Java applet you embed in a Web page is made available to JavaScript as an `applet` object, with the same name as the applet's class name. The `applet` object resides in the object hierarchy under the `document` object. For example, a Java applet called `Scroll` would be accessed through an object called `document.Scroll`.

The objects, properties, and methods of the applet are then available to JavaScript, provided the Java programmer has made them public. You will use this technique to control a Java applet in the task later in this section.

NOTE: There is an exception to the rule: any Java method that communicates over the network can't be called from JavaScript. This limitation exists for security reasons.

Making the Java Applet Accessible

From the Java programmer's point of view, there are a few things that need to be done to make an applet accessible to JavaScript:

❑ Define the methods you want to make accessible as public methods.

❑ Be sure the Netscape package is included in your `CLASSPATH` environment variable when the applet is compiled.

Once you've made sure of these things, you should be able to access the applet from within JavaScript. The next section gives an example of an applet that is controllable by JavaScript.

Controlling a Java Applet

Let's create a Java applet that can be manipulated from within JavaScript. Listing 16.3 shows the Java source code. This is an expanded version of the example in Listing 16.1.

Listing 16.3. (ControlJava.java)A Java applet that can be controlled via JavaScript.

```
import java.applet.Applet;
import java.awt.Graphics;
import java.awt.Font;

public class ControlJava extends Applet {
Font f = new Font("TimesRoman", Font.BOLD, 60);
String Message;
```

continues

Listing 16.3. continued

```
public void init() {
  Message = new String("Java Test");
}

public void SetMessage(String MsgText) {
    Message = MsgText;
    repaint();
}

public void paint(Graphics g) {
  g.setFont(f);
  g.drawString(Message, 15, 50);
  }
}
```

This applet now includes a SetMessage() method to change the text in the display. Listing 16.4 shows the HTML and JavaScript document used to control the applet.

Listing 16.4. (CJAVA.HTM) The JavaScript program to control the Java applet.

```
<HTML>
<HEAD>
<TITLE>Control a Java Applet</TITLE>
</HEAD>
<BODY>
<H1>Control a Java Applet</H1>
<HR>
The Java applet below displays text in a large font. You can enter
new text to display in the form below, and JavaScript will call the
Java applet to change the text.
<HR>
<FORM NAME="form1">
<INPUT TYPE="TEXT" NAME="text1">
<INPUT TYPE="BUTTON" VALUE="Change Text"
onClick="document.ControlJava.SetMessage(document.form1.text1.value);">
</FORM>
<HR>
<APPLET NAME="ControlJava" CODE="ControlJava.class" WIDTH=450 HEIGHT=125>
</APPLET>
<HR>
End of page.
</BODY>
</HTML>
```

This uses a simple event handler to call the Java applet's SetMessage() method. The string you enter in the text field is passed to the applet and displayed in place of the original string. Figure 16.3 shows this application in action after the text has been changed.

Figure 16.3.

JavaScript has changed the text by accessing the Java applet.

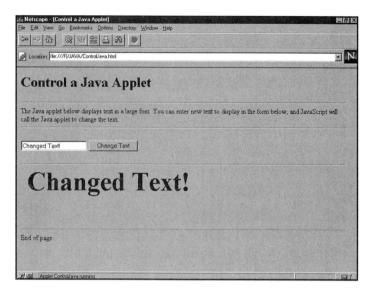

Calling JavaScript Functions from Java

Java can also call JavaScript functions and access JavaScript objects.

It's also possible to call JavaScript functions, and access JavaScript objects and properties, from within Java. This enables you to use JavaScript's unique capabilities, such as reading the values of form elements, in powerful Java applications.

To make JavaScript functions accessible from Java, you need to configure things both in JavaScript and in Java. You'll look at the required steps in the next sections.

Java programmers can also access JavaScript's capabilities.

Steps for the JavaScript Programmer

It's possible for a Java applet to do things you don't want it to, so you must give permission for it to access your JavaScript program and objects. To do this, add the MAYSCRIPT attribute to the <APPLET> tag that embeds the applet:

```
<APPLET CODE="Script.class" NAME="TestApp" MAYSCRIPT>
</APPLET>
```

Steps for the Java Programmer

For the Java programmer, there are also some important steps before you can access JavaScript. First, you need to include the netscape.javascript package, which provides these functions, in your imported classes:

```
import netscape.javascript.*
```

Next, you need to create a handle for the JavaScript window. To do this, define a variable of type JSObject and use the getWindow method to assign it:

```
JSObject js = new JSObject;
js = JSObject.getWindow(this);
```

Accessing JavaScript Objects

Once you have a handle for the JavaScript window, you can get the objects you need to access. To do this, you need to call the getMember method for each property. For example, to make the text1 field on the form1 form accessible:

```
js = JSObject.getWindow(this);
   JSObject document = (JSObject) js.getMember("document");
   JSObject form1 = (JSObject) document.getMember("form1");
   JSObject text1 = (JSObject) form1.getMember("text1");
```

You are creating an object of type JSObject for the document, then for each object underneath it.

Calling JavaScript Functions

You can also call JavaScript functions and methods from within Java, using the same technique. The two methods you use for this purpose are call and eval. For example, this statement calls a JavaScript method to display an alert message:

```
js = JSObject.getWindow(this);
js.call("window.alert('This is a test.');");
```

Workshop Wrap-Up

In this chapter you learned about Java and how it can work with JavaScript:

- ❏ The basics of how the Java language and compiler work
- ❏ Where to get the Java Development Kit (JDK) and how to install it
- ❏ How to create and compile a simple Java applet
- ❏ How to embed a Java applet in an HTML page
- ❏ How to use JavaScript and LiveConnect to control a Java applet
- ❏ Using JavaScript objects, functions, and methods from within a Java applet

Next Steps

You can continue exploring JavaScript and Java with one of the following chapters:

- ❏ To learn how to combine JavaScript with other popular Web languages— CGI and SSI—turn to Chapter 17, "Combining JavaScript, CGI, and SSI."

❏ To learn about Microsoft Internet Explorer, ActiveX, and VBScript, turn to Chapter 18, "Using ActiveX and Microsoft Internet Explorer."

❏ To see examples of using Java applets and controlling them via JavaScript, see Chapter 19, "Real-Life Examples IV."

❏ To learn about the future of JavaScript, Java, and other Web languages, turn to Chapter 20, "The Future of JavaScript."

Q&A

Q: Can I access third-party Java applets from JavaScript, particularly those that were created without JavaScript in mind?

A: Usually not. The applet must include the Netscape package, which includes the required functions for JavaScript and Java communication.

Q: Can I use more than one Java applet in a Web page?

A: Yes. However, note that this may cause severe slowdowns (and sometimes crashes) in some versions of Netscape.

Q: Judging by the examples in this chapter, Java isn't very similar to JavaScript. Why on earth do they have similar names?

A: JavaScript was originally called LiveScript, but was renamed after Java. Although some of the syntax is based on Java, it's a very different language.

SEVENTEEN

Combining JavaScript, CGI, and SSI

In the beginning, the Web was a read-only medium—you could browse all sorts of information and link from site to site, but you couldn't really contribute anything yourself, except by clicking on an e-mail address.

In this chapter, you

- ❏ Learn the basics of the CGI specification and how CGI programs interact with the browser
- ❏ Learn how SSI works at the server
- ❏ Write a simple CGI program and install it on the server
- ❏ Use SSI and JavaScript together to expand JavaScript's capabilities

Tasks in this chapter:

- ❏ Creating a Simple CGI Program
- ❏ Installing a CGI Script
- ❏ Creating JavaScript Functions with SSI

You first explored CGI and interactive forms in Chapter 6, "Using Interactive Forms."

The Common Gateway Interface (CGI) specification was the first step in making the Web more interactive. With new languages such as JavaScript and Java adding interactivity, you might wonder whether CGI has become obsolete. At the moment, this is far from true—CGI bears little resemblance to these languages, and can perform tasks impossible to other languages.

Because this is a book about JavaScript, this chapter doesn't go into detail about CGI —it's complicated enough to have merited a few books of its own. You will take a look at the basics of how CGI works, along with its close relative, SSI. This chapter presents a few examples of simple CGI scripts and explains how you can install scripts on your server. Finally, you'll learn how CGI, SSI, and JavaScript can work together to improve your Web pages.

NOTE: There are many books about CGI. I recommend *Teach Yourself CGI Programming in Perl* by Herrmann, and *HTML & CGI Unleashed* by December, Ginsburg et al., both published by Sams.net.

Choosing the Right Tool for the Job

CGI and JavaScript enhance Web pages in different ways.

Although CGI may become obsolete in the future, it won't be JavaScript that replaces it—they're very different things, and each has its uses. Here are the main differences:

❏ JavaScript executes on the client (like Java), and CGI executes on the server.

❏ CGI returns an entire document, and JavaScript may act on a tiny part of the page, such as a text field or the status line.

❏ CGI has access to information, such as the user's IP address, which JavaScript cannot access.

❏ JavaScript has access to information that CGI can't access—the links and anchors in the current page, for example.

Comparing JavaScript with CGI

To illustrate the difference between JavaScript and CGI programs, let's look at one program that could be written using either—a program to display a random quotation when you load the page. I happen to have examples of both handy:

❏ I created a CGI program called the Random Quotations Page, which you can access at

`http://www.starlingtech.com/quotes/randquote.cgi`.

The output of this program is shown in Figure 17.1.

❑ A JavaScript program to display a random quotation was created in Chapter 7, "Real-Life Examples I." The output of this program is shown in Figure 17.2.

Figure 17.1.

A Web page with random quotations, produced by a CGI program.

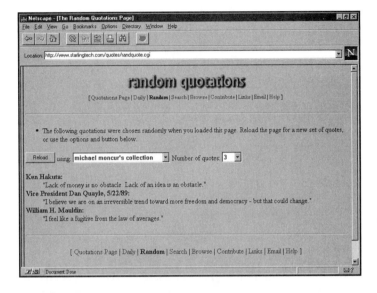

Figure 17.2.

A random quotation page using JavaScript.

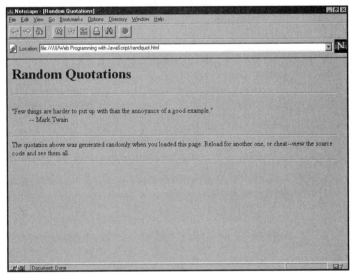

Using these pages as an example, here are a few comparisons of the capabilities of JavaScript and CGI:

JavaScript can be used
in any Web page, but
CGI must be supported
by the server.

❑ My CGI version has about 20,000 quotes available, all stored in a database on the server. This wouldn't be practical with JavaScript, because all the possible quotations would have to be loaded with the Web page.

❑ The JavaScript version is much, much faster, and it places no more load on the server than an ordinary Web page.

❑ The CGI version requires a server that supports CGI, access to it, and available disk space—things a low-priced Internet account may not provide. The JavaScript version, on the other hand, works even without a server—for example, you can load the file directly from the CD-ROM included with this book.

❑ The CGI version will work with any browser, but the JavaScript version requires Netscape, MSIE, or another JavaScript-compatible browser.

❑ If the quotation was displayed in a text field, the JavaScript version could update it at the touch of a button, without even reloading the page. CGI can't update part of a page.

As you can see, both JavaScript and CGI have advantages and disadvantages. Which you choose for a particular job will depend on what you need to do and what resources you and your users will have available.

The Basics of CGI

CGI is a specification,
not a language.
Common languages for
CGI include Perl and C.

CGI is a specification that enables programs to run on a Web server, accept data from the browser, and send data back in the form of a Web page. CGI programs can be written in any language the server understands.

> **TIP:** CGI programs are sometimes referred to as *CGI scripts*, because many of the languages used for CGI are considered scripting languages.

When you're browsing the Web, you can access a CGI program in one of two ways:

❑ You can access it directly with an URL. The URL will often end in .cgi or .pl, although this is not a requirement.

❑ You can press the SUBMIT button on an HTML form. This sends the data you have entered in the form's elements to the CGI program on the server.

Unlike JavaScript, CGI
can send only an entire
Web page as its output.

In technical terms, a *request* is being sent to the HTTP server to run the CGI program. After you send your request using either method, the CGI program can send output back to you in the form of a Web document. An entire document is always sent.

GET and POST Requests

The HTML attributes to
specify these methods
are described in
Chapter 6.

The requests sent to the server are sent using one of two methods. The difference between these lies in the way that data from your browser, or from form elements you filled out, are sent to the server. The two methods are the following:

❏ The GET method sends data in the URL itself. If you enter the URL of a CGI program directly, you are accessing it with the GET method. Forms can also use this method.

❏ The POST method sends data in a stream (standard input) after the request. This method enables larger amounts of data to be sent. The POST method is used exclusively by forms.

Defining Requests in Forms

When you define an HTML form, you specify a CGI script to process the information and the method that will be used. You can do this using the following attributes to the <FORM> tag in HTML:

❏ ACTION specifies the URL of the CGI program that will receive the data when the SUBMIT button is pressed. You can also specify a mailto action here.

❏ METHOD specifies the request method and can be either GET or POST. Your CGI program will need to read the data using the same method.

As an example, the following <FORM> definition uses the POST method and sends the data to a program called data.cgi:

```
<FORM NAME="form1" ACTION = "data.cgi" METHOD = "POST">
```

NOTE: A JavaScript program cannot be used as the ACTION of a form, but it can work with the data before it is sent to the CGI program. Chapter 6 describes the use of JavaScript with forms.

Name and Value Pairs

Like JavaScript, CGI can
access the data you
enter into a form.

A CGI program receives the data from the form as a group of name and value pairs. Each of these includes a name for the item and the item's value. For example, if the user entered "Fred" into a text field called text1, the name/value pair would have the name text1 and the value Fred.

Part of the work of a CGI program is to decipher these name/value pairs. Depending on the method used, the program receives the data in one of two ways:

- For the GET method, the data is stored in an environmental variable called QUERY_STRING.
- For the POST method, the data is sent via the standard input.

In both cases, the data appears as a single large string, and you must separate it into names and values. For example, the following is how a request with two variable values might appear:

```
name=Fred&Address=123+Elm+Street
```

The & characters separate each name/value pair, and the = symbol separates each name from its value. In addition, notice that the spaces the user entered were replaced by + symbols. This is called *URL encoding*, and a CGI program must also take this into account. Along with replacing spaces with +, URL encoding replaces nonalphanumeric characters with escape codes; for example, the tilde (~) character becomes %7E.

Using URL Encoding and Decoding

CGI sends data to the server using URL encoding, and you may need to encode data you are sending. You may also run into this encoding using JavaScript; for example, data you send using the mailto: method is encoded this way. URLs sometimes include encoded characters, and you may need to decode them.

JavaScript includes two functions to let you work with encoding:

- The escape() function converts a string to URL-encoded form.
- The unescape() function converts a URL-encoded string to normal text.

With either function, simply use the text to be converted as the function's parameter.

Environmental Variables

Along with the name/value pairs, a CGI program also receives information in environment variables. These include a variety of items about the server and the browser. Here are a few of the most common ones:

- SERVER_SOFTWARE is the version of the Web server in use.
- REMOTE_ADDR is the user's IP address.
- REMOTE_HOST is the user's host name.
- REQUEST_METHOD is the form's method, either GET or POST.
- QUERY_STRING is used to store the name/value pairs if the GET method is used.

❏ `HTTP_USER_AGENT` is the name of the browser the user is using (similar to JavaScript's `Navigator` object).

As you can see, these include some information that is not available to JavaScript. You'll see a way to make this information available to JavaScript in the task Creating JavaScript Functions with SSI, later in this chapter.

How CGI Programs Generate Output

The final step in a CGI program is to display data back to the user. This may be as simple as a confirmation that the data was received, or it could be a complete Web page that is created based on the form data. The output of a CGI program is always displayed on a new, blank Web page.

You learn about various MIME types and their uses in Chapter 13, "Working with Multimedia and Plug-Ins."

Before a CGI program sends its output to the client, it must specify the type of document that will be created. These are MIME document types, and they can be of any type. Most CGI programs return an HTML document, using the `text/html` type.

The first line a CGI program outputs is a header that indicates the MIME type. The following header indicates an HTML document:

```
Content-type: text/html
```

NOTE: The `Content-type` header must always be followed by a blank line, before the actual output of the program begins.

Optionally, a CGI program can send the user to an existing Web page, rather than outputting a document of its own. This is done using the `Location:` header, as in this example:

```
Location: http://www.starlingtech.com/books/javascript/
```

You should now have an understanding of the basics of CGI programming. You'll look at the specific languages a CGI program can use later in this chapter and also see an example of a CGI program.

SSI: CGI Within a Web Page

Like CGI, SSI is a specification—not a language in itself.

An alternative to CGI is *Server-Side Includes (SSI)*. These are special directives recognized by some Web servers, which enable you to execute a program or perform another function at any point within a Web page. SSI enables you to produce output as part of a Web page—in this way, it's similar to JavaScript.

An SSI program is similar to a CGI program—in some cases, the same program can be used. The main difference is in the way the program is called. An SSI program is called using an SSI directive in the HTML of the page. You'll look at the various directives that can be used in the next section.

Another difference between CGI and SSI is that an SSI program does not have access to form elements. It executes while the page is being sent to the client. An SSI program does, however, have access to the same environmental variables as CGI, as listed in the section titled Environmental Variables, earlier in this chapter.

Server-Side Include Directives

SSI directives are interpreted by the server before being sent to the browser. Thus, they will be invisible to the user; only the output of an SSI program shows up in the HTML source.

Here is an example of an SSI directive that executes a program:

```
<-#exec program.ssi>
```

The following are the available commands for the latest SSI specification, called SSI+ 1.0:

- ❏ `echo` displays the value of an environmental variable.
- ❏ `include` adds the contents of another HTML document to the current document.
- ❏ `fsize` displays the size of a file; this is handy for images or downloadable programs.
- ❏ `fLastMod` displays the last-modified date for the current page.
- ❏ `exec` executes a CGI program.
- ❏ `email` sends an e-mail message.
- ❏ `if` enables you to include different text depending on the contents of a variable.
- ❏ `goto`, `label`, and `break` enable you to transfer control within a page.

Enabling Server-Side Includes

To use SSI in a Web page, you need to enable the feature in the Web server. Because the server must preparse each document and interpret the SSI commands, the server can be slowed down, so it is usually not enabled by default.

The exact process to enable SSI for your pages will depend on the server software and on how the administrator has configured it. You may have to do one of the following:

- ❏ Use a command in the server's configuration file, or a local .htaccess file, to enable server-side includes.
- ❏ Make the HTML document executable, as with the UNIX command chmod o+x document.
- ❏ Consult your administrator to see whether the feature is available for your documents.

Languages for CGI and SSI

As mentioned before, CGI isn't a language in itself—just a specification. CGI and SSI programs can be in any language the server (and the page developer) understands.

Several languages are commonly used for CGI and SSI. You'll look at a few of the most common ones in the sections that follow.

Perl

Perl is a simple but powerful language and is popular for CGI.

Perl is by far the most common language used for CGI programs today. Perl is a versatile scripting language available for UNIX, DOS, and Windows NT platforms; practically every Web server has Perl available.

Like JavaScript, Perl is an interpreted language, so programs you download or create in Perl will not require compiling.

Perl's syntax is unique and can be confusing; however, you'll find that it has much in common with JavaScript. Many books are available that explain Perl fully; you can also refer to Appendix C, "Online JavaScript Resources," for Web pages with information about Perl.

C and C++

C and its object-oriented counterpart, C++, are also a popular choice for CGI. Unlike Perl, these languages must be compiled. If you download a public-domain program in these languages, you need to compile it to run on your particular server.

Other Languages

Simple shell languages, such as sh and csh, are a common choice for simple CGI programs on UNIX platforms. Other possibilities include Python and TCL. Any language you know can be used, provided it's available on your server.

TASK

Creating a Simple CGI Program

Although we won't explain every detail about Perl and CGI in this chapter, you may find this example helpful. The program in Listing 17.1 is a Perl program that sends the data entered in a form via e-mail.

Listing 17.1. (EMAIL.PL) An example of a Perl CGI program to e-mail a form's data.

```perl
#!/usr/bin/perl

MAIN:  {
    $sendmail = "|/usr/bin/sendmail user@address";
    open(MAIL, $sendmail);
# Read POST data from standard input.
# The CONTENT_LENGTH variable tells us how
# many bytes to read.
    read(STDIN, $request, $ENV{'CONTENT_LENGTH'});
# Split request into name/value pairs
    %rqpairs = split(/[&=]/, $request);
# Convert URL syntax to ASCII
    foreach (%rqpairs) {
        tr/+/ /;
        s/%(..)/pack("c",hex($1))/ge;
    }
# headers for mail message
    print MAIL "From: web@server\n";
    print MAIL "To: user@address\n";
    print MAIL "Subject: Form submission\n";
# Add each name/value pair to mail message
    while (($key,$value) = each %rqpairs) {
        print MAIL "$key = $value\n";
    }
close MAIL;
# Output an HTML document
print "Content-type: text/html\n\n";
    print "<HTML><HEAD><TITLE>Mail sent</TITLE>";
    print "</HEAD><BODY>";
    print "<H1>Mail sent</H1>";
    print "Your mail was sent successfully.";
    print "</BODY></HTML>";
exit 0;
}
```

This program reads the name and value pairs from a POST request and decodes them, then sends them in an e-mail message. This program may require minor changes to work on your server. You'll look at the process of installing a CGI program on a server in the next section.

TIP: Like JavaScript, Perl allows comments. The lines beginning with # in Listing 17.1 are comments, and they describe the purpose of each section of the program.

 # Installing a CGI Script

Whether you learn to write CGI programs yourself or decide to use one of the many available public-domain CGI programs, you'll need to install it on your Web server to use it. This section explores the steps you follow to do this.

Depending on your situation, you might need to cooperate with the administrator of your server to perform these tasks. Some Internet providers do not allow CGI programs at all; you should check with the staff if you have any doubts or if the following steps don't work.

Here are the steps for installing a CGI program:

1. After creating or downloading the program, transfer it to the server. You will use an FTP program to do this. Depending on your Internet provider, the administrator may need to do this for you.

2. You may need to place the program in a specific directory, such as cgi-bin, to make it work. In addition, you may need to rename it with an extension such as .cgi. Again, this will depend on your Web server.

3. You will need to set the permissions correctly so that users can run the program. The UNIX command `chmod a+x filename` will usually work for this purpose.

4. Determine the URL for the program. This will depend on your server's configuration and the directory in which you have placed the program.

5. Place the correct URL in your HTML form and test the CGI program by submitting the form.

NOTE: Additional steps may be necessary, depending on the configuration of your Web server. Check with your administrator if the previous steps don't work.

Creating JavaScript Functions with SSI

Here's an example of how SSI and JavaScript can work together. This case uses an SSI directive to create JavaScript "on the fly," in much the same way that JavaScript can create HTML "on the fly."

You learned earlier in this chapter that the CGI variables, such as REMOTE_HOST, are not available in JavaScript; using SSI, though, you can make them available to JavaScript. Listing 17.2 shows an HTML document that uses this feature.

Listing 17.2. (SSIVAR.HTM) Combining SSI and JavaScript.

```
<HTML>
<HEAD><TITLE>SSI and JavaScript</TITLE>
</HEAD>
<BODY>
<H1>CGI variables in JavaScript</H1>
<HR>
This program displays your current host in a
JavaScript dialog box.
<HR>
<SCRIPT LANGUAGE="JavaScript">
Host = "<-#echo var=REMOTE_HOST->";
window.alert("Your host is: " + Host);
</SCRIPT>
</BODY>
</HTML>
```

This JavaScript program simply sets a variable to the host name and displays it to the user by using the window.alert() method. The tricky part is that you have assigned the Host variable using an SSI echo directive.

The SSI will be interpreted by the host before sending the HTML document to the browser, so when the browser interprets it, the actual host will be in place of the #echo directive.

Workshop Wrap-Up

In this chapter you learned about CGI and SSI, and how they can work with JavaScript:

- ❏ The basics of the CGI specification
- ❏ The environmental variables and name/value pairs sent to a CGI program
- ❏ The basics of the SSI specification
- ❏ How to write a simple CGI program and install it on the server
- ❏ How to use SSI and JavaScript together to expand JavaScript's capabilities

Next Steps

Move on with one of the following:

- ❏ To learn to use JavaScript to validate a form before sending it to a CGI program, see Chapter 6, "Using Interactive Forms."
- ❏ To learn about another Web language—Java—and how it can work with JavaScript, see Chapter 16, "Integrating JavaScript with Java."
- ❏ To see examples of the techniques in this chapter, see Chapter 19, "Real-life Examples IV."
- ❏ To learn how JavaScript's capabilities may improve in the future, see Chapter 20, "The Future of JavaScript."

Q&A

Q: Can I use JavaScript to create SSI commands depending on a variable?

A: No. By the time the browser sees the page, the SSI commands have already been parsed by the server. You can use SSI to create JavaScript, but not the other way around.

Q: When I install a CGI script and try to use it, I get an error indicating that the program doesn't exist. What's the solution?

A: This is a common error in CGI, but it can have many causes. It can mean that your program actually doesn't exist, that it has the wrong permissions or is in the wrong place, or that the `Content-type:` header is not being sent correctly by the script.

Q: Can I include a JavaScript program in the output of a CGI program?

A: Yes. This can be useful for creating JavaScript programs based on data entered in a form.

Q: Aside from using a form, is there any other way to send data to a CGI program from JavaScript?

A: You could also send data in the URL. Use the `escape()` function to convert it, then add it to the CGI program's URL as a query using a question mark: `prog.cgi?var1=John+Smith` sends the name `var1` and the value `John Smith` to the program. Set the `location.href` property to activate the script. CGI programs can also set cookie values you set using JavaScript.

EIGHTEEN

Using ActiveX and Microsoft Internet Explorer 3.0

In this chapter, you're taking a bit of a detour from JavaScript. You will be looking at Microsoft's answer to scripting. This includes the following topics:

❑ Using the Microsoft Internet Explorer (MSIE) Web browser, and how it works with JavaScript

❑ ActiveX controls, which can be placed on Web pages

❑ VBScript, a scripting language supported exclusively (for now) by MSIE

In this chapter, you

❑ Learn about Microsoft Internet Explorer 3.0, its features, and its JavaScript support

❑ Use ActiveX controls to spice up a Web page, and learn how they work

❑ Learn about VBScript and create a simple script

Tasks in this chapter:

❑ Downloading and Installing Internet Explorer 3.0

❑ Using an Existing ActiveX Control

❑ Using the ActiveX Control Pad

❑ Creating a Simple VBScript Application

Downloading and Installing Internet Explorer 3.0

Microsoft Internet Explorer (MSIE) is Netscape's greatest competition, and for good reason—it includes many enhancements and is completely free. However, it doesn't support JavaScript completely. Here are some highlights of the features in the latest version:

❏ The entire HTML 3.2 specification is supported. In addition, MSIE supports *style sheets*—a supplement to HTML that enables you to precisely control the way a page is laid out, without violating the HTML standard. Netscape has planned support for style sheets for Navigator 4.0.

❏ Along with JavaScript support, which is still being perfected at this writing, MSIE 3.0 supports ActiveX and VBScript, which you'll look at later in this chapter.

❏ MSIE 3.0 supports the Netscape plug-in specification; most Netscape plug-ins will work just as well with MSIE. You learned about plug-ins in Chapter 13, "Working with Multimedia and Plug-Ins."

❏ This is the first version of MSIE to fully support frames and cookies, which you learned about in Chapter 9, "Using Frames, Cookies, and other Advanced Features."

❏ An extension to frames enables *floating frames*—frames that can be anywhere on the page, rather than simply dividing the screen. They can also overlap.

❏ It includes intranet-specific features, such as enabling an administrator to limit which functions users can access.

❏ You can follow links without using the mouse. This sounds minor, but it's something I've wanted to see in Netscape for years.

TIP: For more information about MSIE 3.0, ActiveX, and VBScript, take a look at *Internet Explorer 3 Unleashed*, published by Sams.net.

To begin, you need to download the latest version of MSIE. You can find the appropriate link to download it by starting at this URL:

```
http://www.microsoft.com/ie/
```

The Windows version of MSIE comes in a self-extracting archive file. To begin the installation, simply click on the file. Note that, in the current version, MSIE installs on drive C, whether you want it to or not.

NOTE: MSIE is available for Windows 95, Windows 3.1, and Macintosh platforms at this writing, although not all platforms have all features available. Consult Microsoft's Web page for further information.

Once installed, you will find an icon to run MSIE on the desktop. When you first run MSIE, the Microsoft Network page will be loaded by default, as shown in Figure 18.1. Luckily, you can change the default page.

Figure 18.1.
The initial display of MSIE includes Microsoft's Web page.

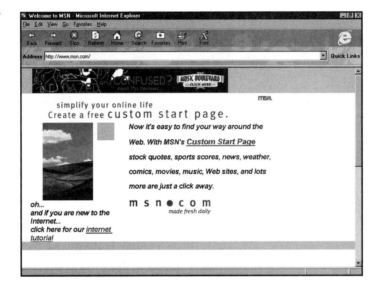

Internet Explorer and JavaScript

In this section, you'll take a look at the support for JavaScript in MSIE. Currently, some JavaScript is supported, but not all—perhaps half of the examples in this book will work with MSIE. Here are some of the key features that are missing:

❏ Event handlers don't seem to work properly in some cases.

❏ New features, such as data tainting (see Chapter 10, "Working with Multiple Pages and Data") and dynamic images (Chapter 12, "Working with Graphics in JavaScript") have not been implemented.

❏ Although the latest MSIE supports Java, the Java/JavaScript connection feature (LiveConnect) is not implemented.

❏ Any very complicated JavaScript application is likely to have problems, at least for now.

These problems apply to the current version of MSIE (3.0 beta). Of course, future versions may implement JavaScript better. Because Netscape is still developing JavaScript, Microsoft can't get everything right until it's finished.

NOTE:

Bear in mind that this book is based on Netscape 3.0's implementation of JavaScript, but MSIE's support more closely matches that of Netscape 2.0. A future version of MSIE will undoubtedly address the 3.0 features.

As one example, Figure 18.2 shows MSIE displaying the Fictional Software Company Web page with the scrolling message example from Chapter 8, "Improving a Web Page with JavaScript." The scrolling status-line message works fine, but the onMouseOver events to display friendly link descriptions don't.

Figure 18.2.
MSIE shows the FSC home page from Chapter 8.

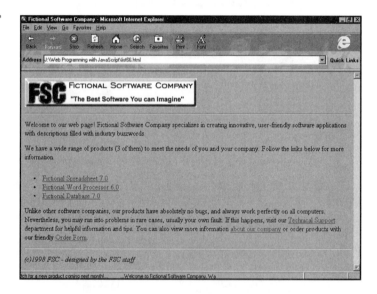

Using ActiveX Controls

ActiveX controls can also be used in non-Internet applications.

One of the latest buzzwords on the Internet today is ActiveX. ActiveX was developed by Microsoft and is a standard for *controls*—self-contained devices with their own functions—that can be placed on Web pages.

If you've heard of Object Linking and Embedding (OLE), you already know about ActiveX, because they're the same thing. OLE controls were called OCX controls for a while and are now called ActiveX controls. By the time you read this, they may already have a new name.

Regardless of the name, ActiveX controls can be powerful additions to a Web page. Better still, you can use them without necessarily knowing how they work. Currently, MSIE is the only browser to support ActiveX controls, but this will change—a plug-in for Netscape to support them is already in development, and Netscape has announced that it will support them in a future version.

NOTE: As you may have guessed, ActiveX is a Windows-only feature—at least for now. It is unknown whether Microsoft will support other platforms; ActiveX controls rely heavily on the Windows API, so this may never happen.

How ActiveX Controls Work

Java is explained in Chapter 16, "Integrating JavaScript with Java."

You can use an ActiveX control anywhere in a Web page using the `<OBJECT>` tag, which you learn about in the next section. ActiveX controls work similarly to Java—they are embedded in the page and perform a specific function. Compared to Java, though, they're more integrated with HTML.

Unlike Java, an ActiveX control can be permanently installed on your machine, making it available for future use. When you access a page with a control, it attempts to use an installed control. If you don't have the control installed, it downloads and installs it automatically. (It does inform you that it's doing this.)

Also unlike JavaScript and Java, ActiveX controls are purely executable code—they are handled by the operating system directly, and little work is done by the browser.

Netscape plug-ins are explained in detail in Chapter 13.

These controls can be quite large and complicated. They can be used to add functionality to the browser, similar to Netscape plug-ins. For example, the current version of MSIE implements the Java virtual machine as an ActiveX control.

You can create your own ActiveX controls—however, it's not as easy as JavaScript, or even Java. You need to use the Microsoft C compiler under Windows to create them.

 ## Using an Existing ActiveX Control

Microsoft added the `<OBJECT>` tag to its implementation of HTML to support ActiveX controls. This tag works like Java's `<APPLET>` tag—it specifies the control to load and can optionally include parameters to be sent to the control.

As an example, Listing 18.1 shows an HTML file that embeds an ActiveX control. This control is the gradient control, which displays a range of colors in an area. Figure 18.3 shows the result of loading this page in MSIE.

Listing 18.1. (GRADIENT.HTM) An HTML document including an embedded ActiveX control.

```
<HTML>
<HEAD>
<TITLE>The ActiveX Gradient Control</TITLE>
</HEAD>
<BODY>
<H1>Gradient Control (ActiveX)</H1>
<HR>
<OBJECT
id=iegrad1
type="application/x-oleobject"
classid="clsid:017C99A0-8637-11CF-A3A9-00A0C9034920"
codebase="http://www.microsoft.com/ie/download/activex/
➥iegrad.ocx#Version=4,70,0,1086"
width=500 height=50 >
<param name="StartColor" value="#ff0000">
<param name="EndColor" value="#0000ff">
<param name="Direction" value = "0">
</OBJECT>
<HR>
The above is a gradient, produced by the MSIE 3.0 gradient control.
</BODY>
</HTML>
```

Figure 18.3.

MSIE shows the HTML document with the embedded gradient control.

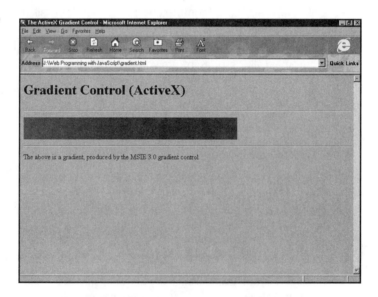

Here is an explanation of the parameters used here:

❑ The <OBJECT> tag begins the object definition.

❑ The id is an identifying name for the object, and type is the MIME type (for an OLE object).

❑ classid is the class ID—a rather large number specific to this control.

❑ codebase is where the control can be downloaded from, in case the user doesn't have it.

❑ width and height allocate an area for the control. This works the same as the corresponding attributes in an image tag.

❑ StartColor, EndColor, and Direction are parameters to be passed to the control. In this case, they control the starting and ending colors and the direction of the gradient.

A Sampling of ActiveX Controls and Features

It would be difficult to cover all the available ActiveX controls, because there are so many—and more are being developed daily. In this section, you'll take a look at some of the controls available from Microsoft. This should give you an idea of the types of things that are possible with ActiveX:

❑ Animated Button enables you to include buttons with animated displays in a page. For example, the button might look "pressed in" when you click on it.

❑ Chart displays pie, line, and other types of charts within a Web page. The data to be charted is stored in a separate file on the Web server. Figure 18.4 shows an example of this control in action on one of Microsoft's Web pages.

Figure 18.4.

The ActiveX Chart control enables you to display graphs and charts within Web pages.

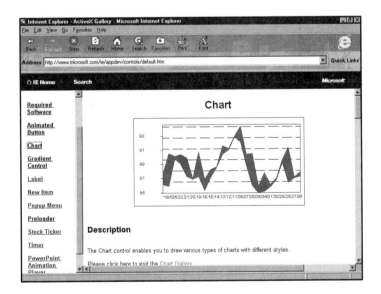

❑ Gradient displays a block of color, ranging from one color to another. This control was used in the example in the previous section.

❑ Label displays text, but at any angle, or even a curve. This can be useful for labeling a figure or control.

❑ New Item enables you to display "new" icons automatically next to links on your page. A parameter enables you to specify a date, and after that date the icon is not displayed.

❑ Pop-up Menu displays a pop-up menu of options. Selecting an option causes an event, which can be used with VBScript or JavaScript.

❑ Pre-loader enables a page to be loaded into the cache, but not displayed until you specifically request it.

❑ Stock Ticker downloads data from the URL you specify at regular intervals and displays it in an area of the page. This is useful for changing information, such as stock prices.

❑ Timer waits a specified time, then causes an event. This is similar to the `setTimeout` method in JavaScript.

❑ PowerPoint Animation Player plays Microsoft PowerPoint animations within a page—an easy way to make animations, if you have PowerPoint.

NOTE:
All the controls listed are available from Microsoft's Web site. See Appendix C, "Online JavaScript Resources," for a listing of other pages with downloadable controls.

As you can see, just about anything can be done with ActiveX controls. There's a price, however—some of the controls can be quite slow, and downloading a new control can be even slower. You'll also have to consider whether you want non-Windows users to be able to view your page.

 ## Using the ActiveX Control Pad

You don't have to understand ActiveX—or even HTML—to use an ActiveX control in a Web page of your own. Microsoft has made it easy with a product called the ActiveX Control Pad. This includes a text editor for the HTML page, as well as dialogs to control the properties of ActiveX controls.

To find out more about the ActiveX Control Pad and download it, see this page at Microsoft's Web site:

`http://www.microsoft.com/workshop/author/cpad/tutorial-f.htm`

Here's what you'll need to use the ActiveX Control Pad:

❑ The ActiveX Control Pad works only on Windows 95 or Windows NT 4.0.

❑ You must install MSIE 3.0 (beta 2 or later) before you install the control pad.

Once you install the control pad, you can begin to use it. Note that it's best to be online while using it so that it can access ActiveX control definitions if necessary.

The main screen includes a text editor; you can load any HTML page into this window. You can use the Insert ActiveX Control command from the Edit menu to insert a control. If you already have an existing control in the page, an icon will be shown next to the <OBJECT> tag.

Clicking a control's icon shows the control in action, along with a dialog that lists the properties for the control and enables you to change them. This is shown in Figure 18.5.

Figure 18.5.

The ActiveX Control Pad shows an HTML document, ActiveX control, and properties list.

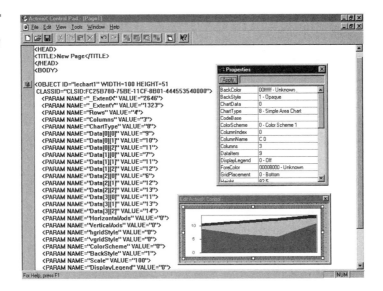

Once you accept the properties you have selected, the appropriate tags are inserted into the HTML document to set those parameters for the control. It's that simple.

NOTE: The ActiveX Control Pad can be used with any ActiveX control. However, you must be licensed to use the control. Many controls can be used freely; with others, you may have to purchase a license to use them in your own pages.

Developing ActiveX Controls

Anyone can develop ActiveX controls, although it's not as easy as JavaScript. If you've programmed in C++ before, you will find it easy. Here's what you need to develop your own ActiveX controls:

❏ You can write ActiveX controls in any language—if you have an ActiveX-compatible compiler. Currently, the only such compiler is Microsoft Visual C++ version 4.1.

❏ The ActiveX SDK (Software Development Kit) includes everything you need (except the compiler) to get started. It's available at no cost from Microsoft.

❏ Currently, the SDK works with Windows 95 or Windows NT 4 (currently in beta).

For more information about ActiveX and the SDK, see Microsoft's ActiveX information at this URL:

```
http://www.microsoft.com/intdev/sdk/
```

An Introduction to VBScript

One of the latest weapons in Microsoft's war with Netscape is VBScript. VBScript is meant to compete directly with JavaScript, and it includes many of the same features.

You might have noticed that this book takes 17 chapters to explain JavaScript—of course, VBScript can't be fully explained in one chapter. This section presents the basics of VBScript and shows you how to create a simple VBScript application. You'll also look at some of the key differences between JavaScript and VBScript.

NOTE: To learn more about VBScript, consult Microsoft's online documentation or get a copy of *Teach Yourself VBScript in 21 Days* by Brophy and Koets, published by Sams.net. Appendix D of this book includes a list of online references to get you started.

Creating a Simple VBScript Application

Like JavaScript, VBScript is included directly in an HTML file, and it is delimited with the <SCRIPT> tag. A script tag for a VBScript application looks like this:

```
<SCRIPT LANGUAGE="VBScript">
```

The actual language is a bit less complex in syntax than JavaScript; there is less punctuation, and many commands are simpler. Like JavaScript, VBScript can have functions, statements, and event handlers.

Because VBScript is a subset of Visual Basic, you may find it easy to learn if you've used Visual Basic before. However, there are many differences, so don't assume you already know everything.

As an introduction to VBScript, Listing 18.2 shows a simple VBScript application. The page includes a button; pressing the button causes an alert box (or message box, in VBScript lingo) to be displayed.

Listing 18.2. (VBSCRIPT.HTM) A simple VBScript application.

```
<HTML>
<HEAD><TITLE>A simple VBScript program</TITLE>
</HEAD>
<BODY>
<H1>VBScript Example</H1>
<hr>
The button below triggers a VBScript function which displays
an alert box.
<hr>
<INPUT TYPE=BUTTON VALUE="Test Button" NAME="Button1">
<SCRIPT LANGUAGE="VBScript">
Sub Button1_OnClick
MsgBox "You pressed the button.", 0, "Window title."
End Sub
</SCRIPT>
<hr>
End of VBScript function
</BODY>
</HTML>
```

Figure 18.6 shows this program in action, with the message box displayed. Notice that rather than using an event handler attribute on the button tag, the procedure's name specifies the button's name and the event handler name.

Figure 18.6.
The VBScript example in action.

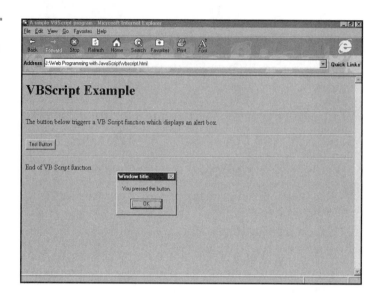

VBScript Versus JavaScript

Finally, let's take a quick look at some of the key features of JavaScript and how VBScript compares. This will give you some idea of what you're in for if you decide to learn VBScript as your next Web language.

Punctuation and Syntax

An obvious difference between JavaScript and VBScript is in its use of basic punctuation and syntax. VBScript does not use semicolons or brackets at all. Function declarations and other blocks of code, such as loops, are enclosed with beginning and ending statements. For example, here is a procedure definition:

```
Sub Message(text)
  MsgBox text
End Sub
```

This syntax is used for a *procedure*—a function that doesn't return a value. The Function keyword is used for functions that do return a value.

Variables

Like JavaScript, VBScript is a loosely typed language. There is one variable type, called Variant, that can hold a number, a string, or other types of values. Variables must be declared with the Dim statement (similar to var in JavaScript). This example declares a variable and assigns a string value to it:

```
Dim Answer
Answer = "The answer is 42."
```

VBScript and Forms

Like JavaScript, VBScript can access all the elements in a form—in fact, the syntax is strikingly similar. This is the VBScript syntax to refer to the `text1` input field in the `form1` form:

```
val = Document.form1.text1.value
```

VBScript can be used for form validation and can prevent form submission while fields are not filled in correctly.

Object-Oriented Features

Although VBScript can access form elements and ActiveX controls as objects, it is not as object-oriented as JavaScript. There is currently no way to create new objects or add properties to existing ones. These may be added in a future version.

ActiveX and VBScript

VBScript can access and control ActiveX controls, similar to the way JavaScript can work with Java. Each ActiveX control is available as an object to scripts in that page. Objects can generate events, and they can call VBScript functions when the events occur.

Workshop Wrap-Up

In this chapter, you learned about Microsoft Internet Explorer, ActiveX, and VBScript:

- ❏ How to download, install, and run MSIE
- ❏ How MSIE handles (or doesn't handle) JavaScript programs
- ❏ What ActiveX controls are, and how they are used
- ❏ How to embed an ActiveX control in a Web page
- ❏ What VBScript is, and how it compares to JavaScript
- ❏ How to create a simple VBScript program

You also explored a sampling of the available ActiveX controls.

Next Steps

Move on with one of the following:

❏ To see another example of an ActiveX control in action, see Chapter 19, "Real-Life Examples IV."

❏ To learn about other alternatives to JavaScript and the future of scripting on the Web, turn to Chapter 20, "The Future of JavaScript."

❏ To learn about Java, another powerful Web language, turn to Chapter 16, "Integrating JavaScript with Java."

❏ To find online resources related to JavaScript and VBScript, see Appendix C, "Online JavaScript Resources."

Q&A

Q: If MSIE supports JavaScript and Netscape will support VBScript, which language will be the standard?

A: Honestly, it's anyone's guess. Of course, Netscape wants JavaScript to be the standard, and Microsoft wants VBScript to be the standard. However, on the Web right now there are many sites using JavaScript and very few using VBScript. Will this change? Who knows.

Q: Can VBScript be used with Java, as JavaScript can?

A: Yes, according to Microsoft. The Java support in the latest MSIE is still in beta, though, and I haven't seen a working example of this yet.

Q: Which language should I use in my Web pages?

A: Because both MSIE and Netscape support it, at least to a point, JavaScript seems the clear choice right now. JavaScript is also more sophisticated than VBScript. Although MSIE is gaining rapidly, Netscape is still used by about 90 percent of Web users at this writing.

NINETEEN

Real-Life Examples IV

This chapter presents three example applications that apply the techniques you learned in Part V, "JavaScript Alternatives and the Future," of this book. These include the following:

❏ **Example 1: Manipulating a Java Applet.** You looked at a simple example of accessing Java from JavaScript in Chapter 16, "Integrating JavaScript with Java." This is a more complicated example.

❏ **Example 2: Creating JavaScript Dynamically.** This uses SSI, which you looked at in Chapter 17, "Combining JavaScript, CGI, and SSI," to modify a JavaScript program before the page is sent to the browser.

❏ **Example 3: Using an ActiveX Control.** You looked at ActiveX in Chapter 18, "Using ActiveX and Microsoft Internet Explorer 3.0." This example uses an ActiveX control to include a chart in a Web page.

Example 1: Manipulating a Java Applet

You learned a simple example of accessing the methods of a Java applet from within JavaScript in Chapter 16. For this example, let's create a more complicated example with extra features. This example demonstrates the following concepts:

- ❏ Preparing a Java program to be used from JavaScript
- ❏ Creating and compiling a Java applet
- ❏ Controlling Java from JavaScript with event handlers

For this example, I have expanded the ControlJava applet created in Chapter 16. It now includes a new method, SetFont(), which enables the font name and size to be changed. This is a public method, so it can be accessed through JavaScript. The Java source code for the applet is shown in Listing 19.1.

Listing 19.1. (ControlJava2.java) The Java source code for the Java applet to be controlled from JavaScript.

```java
import java.applet.Applet;
import java.awt.Graphics;
import java.awt.Font;

public class ControlJava2 extends Applet {
Font f = new Font("TimesRoman", Font.BOLD, 60);
String Message;

public void init() {
  Message = new String("Java Test");
}

public void SetMessage(String MsgText) {
   Message = MsgText;
   repaint();
}

public void SetFont(String NewFont, int NewSize) {
   f = new Font(NewFont,Font.BOLD,NewSize);
   repaint();
}

public void paint(Graphics g) {
  g.setFont(f);
  g.drawString(Message, 15, 50);
  }
}
```

This source code should be placed in a file called ControlJava2.java. Once you've done that, you can compile it into a Java class with this command:

```
bin\javac ControlJava2.java
```

NOTE: Be sure you have included the Netscape packages when you compile this applet. See Chapter 16 for details.

You now have a working applet that should work within any HTML file—but to access the new options you will need JavaScript. Listing 19.2 shows the HTML document with JavaScript functions to change the text, font, and size for the applet.

Listing 19.2. (JAVA2.HTM) An HTML form and JavaScript functions to update the Java applet.

```
<HTML>
<HEAD>
<TITLE>Control a Java Applet</TITLE>
<SCRIPT LANGUAGE="JavaScript">
function setfont() {
   x = document.form1.font.selectedIndex;
   font = document.form1.font.options[x].value;
   x = document.form1.fontsize.selectedIndex;
   size = document.form1.fontsize.options[x].value;
   document.applet1.SetFont(font,parseInt(size));
}
</SCRIPT>
</HEAD>
<BODY>
<H1>Control a Java Applet</H1>
<HR>
The Java applet below displays text in a large font. You can enter
new text to display in the form below, and JavaScript will call the
Java applet to change the text. You can also change the font and size.
<HR>
<FORM NAME="form1">
<INPUT TYPE="TEXT" NAME="text1">
<INPUT TYPE="BUTTON" VALUE="Change Text"
onClick="document.applet1.SetMessage(document.form1.text1.value);">
<BR>
<b>Font:</b>
<SELECT NAME="font">
<OPTION VALUE="TimesRoman">Times New Roman
<OPTION VALUE="Arial">Arial
<OPTION VALUE="Wingdings">WingDings
<OPTION VALUE="Courier">Courier New
<OPTION VALUE="Terminal">Terminal font
</SELECT>
 <b>Size:</b>
<SELECT NAME="fontsize">
<OPTION VALUE="10">10
<OPTION VALUE="15">15
<OPTION VALUE="20">20
<OPTION VALUE="25">25
<OPTION VALUE="30">30
<OPTION VALUE="48">48
<OPTION VALUE="60">60
</SELECT>
```

continues

Listing 19.2. continued

```
<INPUT TYPE="BUTTON" VALUE="Change Font"
onClick="setfont();">
</FORM>
<HR>
<APPLET NAME="applet1" CODE="ControlJava2.class" WIDTH=450 HEIGHT=125>
</APPLET>
<HR>
End of page.
</BODY>
</HTML>
```

Figure 19.1 shows this JavaScript application in action. Here is a breakdown of how it works:

- ❏ A new button and two select lists have been added. These enable the user to select a new font and font size.
- ❏ The Change Text button calls the Java applet's SetMessage method directly to change the text.
- ❏ The Change Font button calls a JavaScript function called setfont().
- ❏ The setfont() function calculates the selected value for the font and size and passes them to the Java applet's SetFont method for processing. Like the text change, this change should take effect immediately.

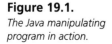

Figure 19.1.

The Java manipulating program in action.

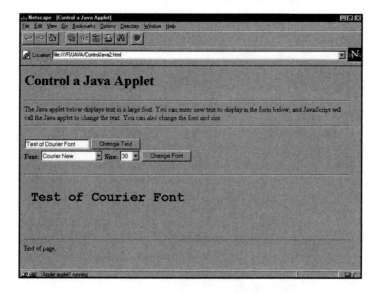

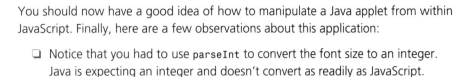

You should now have a good idea of how to manipulate a Java applet from within JavaScript. Finally, here are a few observations about this application:

❑ Notice that you had to use `parseInt` to convert the font size to an integer. Java is expecting an integer and doesn't convert as readily as JavaScript.

❑ Because the JavaScript `select` object has no direct method or property for returning the currently selected value, you had to calculate it using `selectedIndex`.

❑ Because the Java applet is restricted to a certain height and width, some combinations of fonts and sizes might be cut off.

❑ There's no way for JavaScript to know which fonts are installed on your computer. The fonts I included in Listing 19.2 should be available on most Windows systems; for Macintosh and others, you need to substitute an accurate list of your fonts.

Example 2: Creating JavaScript Dynamically

This is an example of using SSI to generate JavaScript. It uses the following techniques:

❑ Using SSI in a Web page

❑ Combining SSI with JavaScript

❑ Writing a simple Perl program

One of the most common items on the Web these days is a hit counter—a simple counter that displays the amount of visitors a page has received. They're a bit of a cliché right now, but many users can't live without them.

One thing is certain about counters, though—you can't make one using JavaScript alone, because JavaScript can't store any information on the server. You could count how many visits a particular user has made with cookies, but there's not much use for that.

As a solution, let's combine JavaScript with SSI. A simple SSI program will be used to insert the counter into the page; it will be inserted in the form of a JavaScript assignment statement, so the counter can be used in any JavaScript function.

To begin, Listing 19.3 shows the SSI program, written in Perl, for the counter.

Listing 19.3. (COUNT.PL) The Perl SSI program for the counter example.

```
#!/usr/local/bin/perl

MAIN: {
    print "Content-type:text/html\n\n";
    $count = 'cat count.dat';
    $count += 1;
    open(LAST,">count.dat");
    print LAST $count;
    close LAST;

    print "count = ",$count, "\n";
}
```

Here is a brief explanation of this program:

❑ The MAIN function is the primary function for this Perl program (and the only function).

❑ The first print statement provides the required MIME type for the output of the SSI program.

❑ The counter variable, $count, is read from a file on the server called count.dat. It is then incremented and output back to the same file.

❑ Finally, the counter is printed, with count = before it. This will serve as the JavaScript statement to initialize the counter.

Next, you will need a JavaScript program to use the counter. The HTML document, complete with JavaScript and the SSI directive, is shown in Listing 19.4.

Listing 19.4. The HTML document with JavaScript functions for the counter example.

```
<HTML>
<HEAD>
<TITLE>Counter Test in JavaScript and SSI</TITLE>
<SCRIPT LANGUAGE="JavaScript">
<!--#exec cgi="count.cgi"-->
</SCRIPT>
</HEAD>
<BODY>
<H1>A counter using SSI and JavaScript</H1>
<HR>
This page includes a counter using SSI, and made available to JavaScript.
<HR>
The count is:
<SCRIPT LANGUAGE="JavaScript">
document.write(count);
</SCRIPT>
<HR>
```

```
Press button for an alert with the count.
<FORM NAME="form1">
<INPUT TYPE="BUTTON" VALUE="Click for Count"
 onClick="window.alert('The count is' + count);">
</FORM>
<HR>
</BODY>
</HTML>
```

This example is shown in Netscape in Figure 19.2. Here are a few notes about how this program works:

❏ The SSI-inserted line of JavaScript assigns the current value to the JavaScript count variable in the header of the program.

❏ The document.write method is used to work with the counter in the body of the document.

❏ As a demonstration of using an event handler, the button provides another method of displaying the count—this time with a dialog box.

Figure 19.2.

The counter example, as displayed by Netscape.

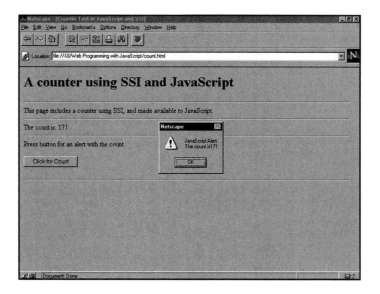

This example should give you some food for thought. By combining SSI with JavaScript, you can combine the advantage of SSI—being connected with the server— with the friendliness and versatility of JavaScript.

Example 3: Using an ActiveX Control

This is an example of using an ActiveX control within a Web page, and it will work only with Microsoft Internet Explorer 3.0. You looked at MSIE 3.0 and ActiveX in Chapter 18. This example uses the following techniques:

❏ Using the <OBJECT> tag

❏ Using ActiveX controls

❏ Modifying a control's properties

This example uses the Chart control, provided free from Microsoft. You may need to download this control if you don't have it already; MSIE will prompt you if you need to. Listing 19.3 shows the example.

Listing 19.3. An example of an ActiveX control and properties in HTML.

```
<HTML>
<HEAD>
<TITLE>Graph Example</TITLE>
</HEAD>
<BODY>
The following graph was created using the ActiveX
Graph control.
<HR>

<OBJECT ID="iechart1" WIDTH=599 HEIGHT=203
 CLASSID="CLSID:FC25B780-75BE-11CF-8B01-444553540000">
    <PARAM NAME="_ExtentX" VALUE="15849">
    <PARAM NAME="_ExtentY" VALUE="5371">
    <PARAM NAME="Rows" VALUE="4">
    <PARAM NAME="Columns" VALUE="2">
    <PARAM NAME="ChartType" VALUE="14">
    <PARAM NAME="Data[0][0]" VALUE="9">
    <PARAM NAME="Data[0][1]" VALUE="10">
    <PARAM NAME="Data[1][0]" VALUE="7">
    <PARAM NAME="Data[1][1]" VALUE="11">
    <PARAM NAME="Data[2][0]" VALUE="6">
    <PARAM NAME="Data[2][1]" VALUE="12">
    <PARAM NAME="Data[3][0]" VALUE="11">
    <PARAM NAME="Data[3][1]" VALUE="13">
    <PARAM NAME="HorizontalAxis" VALUE="0">
    <PARAM NAME="VerticalAxis" VALUE="0">
    <PARAM NAME="hgridStyle" VALUE="0">
    <PARAM NAME="vgridStyle" VALUE="0">
    <PARAM NAME="ColorScheme" VALUE="0">
    <PARAM NAME="BackStyle" VALUE="1">
    <PARAM NAME="Scale" VALUE="100">
    <PARAM NAME="DisplayLegend" VALUE="0">
    <PARAM NAME="BackColor" VALUE="16777215">
    <PARAM NAME="ForeColor" VALUE="32768">
</OBJECT>
<HR>
```

```
Now, back to the Web page.
</BODY>
</HTML>
```

The <OBJECT> tag includes quite a list of <PARAM> tags. These specify that the chart is a bar chart with two data items and four rows. Figure 19.3 shows this example in action in MSIE 3.0.

Figure 19.3.
The ActiveX control example.

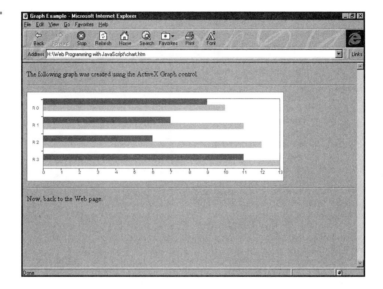

You can modify the <PARAM> tags to produce exactly the type of graph you wish. You could also use the ActiveX Control Pad, described in Chapter 18, to modify these values easily.

TWENTY

The Future of JavaScript

In this chapter, you

- ❏ Look at the future of Netscape and JavaScript
- ❏ Explore a "wish list" of changes for JavaScript
- ❏ Take a look at other languages on the Web and how they might affect JavaScript

Welcome to the final chapter! If you've made it this far, you should be approaching JavaScript Expert status. For this chapter, you'll take a look at what the future may bring for Netscape and JavaScript. You'll look at new features that are planned and those that would sure be nice. Finally, you'll examine some of the alternatives to JavaScript—both present and future.

Planned New Features

Although Netscape hasn't made any formal announcements, the developers have mentioned some upcoming fixes and improvements to the language. At this writing, Netscape 3.0 is nearly final; most of the new features will have to wait for version 4.0.

Here are some of the improvements you can expect to see in future releases:

- ❏ Event handlers will be able to include arguments. One useful example will be the capability of receiving x and y values from image maps.
- ❏ You'll be able to enable and disable elements within a form—and possibly, add new ones.
- ❏ A wider variety of events will be available for JavaScript.

❑ Most importantly, bugs will be fixed. Once Netscape 3.0 is stable, you can expect JavaScript to increase in popularity as features such as dynamic images become widespread on the Web.

Aside from JavaScript, Netscape 4.0 is expected to include many new features. By the time you read this, a beta version will probably be available. Here are some of the likely features:

❑ Support for HTML style sheets. These will enable you to specify exact spacings, fonts, and layout for HTML elements, while staying compatible with older browsers.

❑ Special features to enable collaboration between users, especially in corporate intranets.

❑ Frames will be improved to include "floating" frames, which can overlap each other and don't always include borders or scrollbars.

❑ Some basic form validation capabilities and automatic computations will be added as HTML attributes—without necessarily using JavaScript.

❑ Netscape's e-mail program will include MIME support and support for secure, encrypted e-mail.

LiveConnect

You learned about LiveConnect in Chapter 13, "Working with Multimedia and Plug-Ins," and Chapter 16, "Integrating JavaScript with Java." This is the recently introduced feature that enables integration between JavaScript, Java, and Netscape plug-ins.

Although LiveConnect is already available, I'm considering it part of the future because it isn't well-supported yet. Once it is, you'll be able to enjoy the following benefits:

❑ A wide variety of public-domain Java applets will be available, which include public methods that can be accessed with JavaScript.

❑ With any luck, plug-in authors will begin to widely support LiveConnect. This will enable you to use JavaScript to manipulate and control new types of data—3D objects, VRML, video, real-time audio, and many more.

A JavaScript Wish List

It's impossible to know exactly which features will be added to JavaScript in the future. For that matter, with the ephemeral nature of the Internet, it's impossible to know whether JavaScript will become a completely different language or be replaced with something else.

Rather than try to predict the future—an impossible task in a constantly changing industry—I'll focus on the things that I would like to see changed in JavaScript (and Netscape's implementation of it) in the future. The next sections outline a wish list of changes for which we can all hope.

Language Features

As noted in this book, the JavaScript language is limited in many ways. Although its simplicity is one of its greatest advantages, it can be difficult to create complex programs. Here are a few language features that would make JavaScript an even better language:

❏ Objects could be improved with a truly object-oriented implementation—for example, an object could be defined as based on another object and automatically inherit its characteristics.

❏ As noted in Chapter 14, "Debugging JavaScript Programs," JavaScript's error messages can be downright infuriating at times. It would be nice to have a JavaScript debugger of some sort—or at least some more accurate error messages.

Interactive Forms

As noted previously, Netscape intends to add the capability of enabling and disabling form elements. It would also be nice if you could modify a form after it was loaded—for example, changing the width of a text field. Another interesting feature would be the capability of modifying event handlers of form elements "on the fly."

Graphics and Multimedia

As you learned in Chapter 12, "Working with Graphics in JavaScript," the dynamic image feature made JavaScript truly useful for graphic applications—but it could be better. For example, images of different sizes could be supported. An object to handle sounds would also be very useful.

User Interfaces and Frames

Frames provide for some complicated JavaScript programs, and the new floating frames will make things that much more complicated. Anything to simplify working with frames would be an improvement. In addition, there is currently no way to read or change the values of JavaScript variables in another frame.

Java and Plug-Ins

As mentioned previously, LiveConnect would be very useful if supported by more Java applet and plug-in developers, and this is bound to happen in the near future. It would also be very helpful if JavaScript could dynamically load and unload Java applets, similar to the dynamic images feature.

New Applications for JavaScript

Currently, JavaScript is something of a novelty on the Web—by far, the most common use is to scroll a message. I believe that more serious applications will become more common in the future:

❏ JavaScript can be used for form validation, but few sites currently do so. Validated forms will become more common as the general public starts to accept JavaScript as part of the Web.

❏ There are a few good JavaScript games—recall the one in Chapter 15, "Real-Life Examples III"—but I believe the potential for games in JavaScript is largely untapped. Hopefully, as features such as dynamic images become common knowledge, more complex games will be developed.

❏ MSIE supports ActiveX, and Netscape can support it with the NCompass plug-in (see Appendix C). JavaScript can be used to add scripting and control to ActiveX controls, and this use will increase in the future—especially if MSIE turns out to be serious competition for Netscape Navigator.

❏ As LiveConnect becomes more widely supported, JavaScript will become a tool for manipulating Java applets and plug-ins dynamically.

JavaScript Development Environments

Another possibility in JavaScript's future is dedicated development environments. Currently, several tools for creating Java applets are available, but none dedicated to JavaScript.

A JavaScript integrated development environment (IDE) would enable you to use drag-and-drop tools to create a complex JavaScript application, without much actual programming. This may become especially useful as hybrid Java/JavaScript applications become more common.

A step in the right direction is that several of the available HTML editors now include features for inserting JavaScript tags (event handlers and the <SCRIPT> tag). Netscape's Navigator Gold is a WYSIWYG editor, and also enables you to use JavaScript.

Alternatives to JavaScript

Finally, let's take a quick look at the Web languages that are currently giving JavaScript a run for its money—or can be used along with it.

Java

Java was the first of the client-side Web languages, and is still among the most powerful. You looked at Java in detail in Chapter 16 and explored ways of integrating it with JavaScript.

Java has become widely accepted on the Web—more so than JavaScript, as a matter of fact. There are already over a thousand publicly available Java applets, and more are being developed constantly.

Java is a bit ahead of JavaScript, and it has already moved beyond the novelty stage. Although clocks, animations, and LED signs are still common Java applets, more and more sites are using it for interactive applications, games, and custom business-oriented applications for business intranets.

Microsoft has committed to supporting Java. It's already supported in the latest beta of Microsoft Internet Explorer, and rumor has it that Java will be involved in a big way in the next release of Windows.

Microsoft's concern is probably in response to the possibility of Network Computers (NCs)—dedicated consumer machines that use an Internet connection to access software and use Java as an operating system. NCs haven't become popular yet, but Java seems to be here to stay.

CGI

Chapter 17, "Combining JavaScript, CGI, and SSI," describes CGI and explains how it can work with JavaScript.

CGI was the first taste of interactivity for the Web. Despite the growth of Java, JavaScript, and plug-ins, CGI is doubtless still the most common type of program in use on the Web.

Any time you fill out a registration form, make an order, or answer a question on most Web pages, a CGI script is used. Some sites use CGI to read all pages from a database, so every page you read comes from CGI.

CGI is also one of the few parts of the Web that doesn't seem to be changing much. The CGI specification is much the same today as it was two or three years ago—and on the Internet, that's a very long time.

Some current CGI applications are being replaced with Java versions because it can communicate with the server and is more interactive; however, CGI will probably remain for a long time yet.

SSI

Server-side includes (SSI) is a way of embedding a CGI program directly in a Web page. Although less commonly used on the Web, it still provides features available in no other language.

Chapter 17 explains SSI in detail and also explains how to use it with JavaScript.

SSI is often used to add counters and dynamic information to pages, and it is used on some servers as a simple way of including the same text—for example, a copyright notice—on a Web page.

LiveWire: Server-Side JavaScript

You may not have heard of LiveWire, but it's a close relative of JavaScript. It was released by Netscape about the same time as the first version of JavaScript. (At the time, JavaScript was called LiveScript, so the names were similar.)

LiveWire has a similar syntax to JavaScript, but it is executed on the server instead of the client. This gives it many of the advantages of CGI and SSI. It can also communicate with client-side JavaScript, giving you the best of both worlds.

Sounds too good to be true? Well, it may be. There is one disadvantage of LiveWire— it works only on Netscape's Web server software. Because the majority of Web sites are run using the free servers—for example, Apache and NCSA httpd—LiveWire has had severe growing pains.

It is unknown whether Netscape will enable LiveWire to be supported on other server platforms, or whether anyone will attempt to do so; until then, it may be a useful tool if you happen to have a Netscape server.

Shockwave

Shockwave was one of the first plug-ins available for Netscape Navigator. It enables Director movies and animations to be displayed inline in a Web page, and it enables some measure of interactivity.

Shockwave, and plug-ins in general, were introduced in Chapter 13.

The Shockwave plug-in is available at no charge from MacroMedia. However, to create content for Shockwave, you need to use MacroMedia Director, which is not available for free. This has prevented Shockwave from being widespread, but there are already a wide variety of Shockwave sites available—and more are coming.

One reason sites avoid Shockwave, and other plug-in-based additions to the Web, is the concern that not all users will download the plug-in. Netscape has considered making plug-ins download automatically—something like ActiveX controls in MSIE— and this may solve the problem. In addition, future versions of Netscape may be bundled with plug-ins.

ActiveX

ActiveX controls are explained in more detail in Chapter 18, "Using ActiveX and Microsoft Internet Explorer."

ActiveX controls (previously known as OLE or OCX controls) are Microsoft's answer to dynamic Web content. These controls can be embedded in a Web page and add capabilities to the page—ranging from scrolling text to an entire spreadsheet.

The popularity of ActiveX in the future will depend on the popularity of MSIE, currently the only browser that supports these controls. In addition, a plug-in for Netscape, NCompass, supports ActiveX. Currently, Netscape does not plan to add ActiveX capabilities to Navigator directly.

NOTE: One limitation of ActiveX is that it works only on Windows platforms. This limits the audience and may prevent it from becoming widely accepted.

VBScript

You learned about VBScript in Chapter 18.

VBScript is the only currently available Web language that fits into the same niche as JavaScript. VBScript is implemented by MSIE, and it includes many of the same features of JavaScript. It's a simpler language and may be easier for beginners to understand.

Again, the popularity of VBScript will depend on the popularity of MSIE. However, MSIE already supports JavaScript, so users may simply keep using a language with which they're already familiar. On the other hand, Netscape may be adding support for VBScript in a future version.

NOTE: Currently, VBScript is supported only by MSIE. Netscape does not currently intend to support it. However, if MSIE becomes widespread, it may be forced to.

HTML Enhancements

If some uses of JavaScript become obsolete, it may not be another language that takes them over—additions to HTML itself may eliminate the need for JavaScript. Here are a few examples:

❑ Netscape intends to add simple form validation as an extension to HTML in a future version.

❑ Tricks now implemented by JavaScript, such as scrolling messages, may be built directly into HTML in the future.

❏ Style sheets, which will be supported in Netscape 4.0 and are already supported by MSIE, will give both designers and users control over a page's appearance, eliminating some needs for JavaScript (such as deciding whether to display a frame version).

As HTML improves, though, JavaScript will also improve—I'm confident that there will always be a use for it in Web pages. (But will there always be Web pages? That's another story.)

Workshop Wrap-Up

In this chapter, you took a look at the future of JavaScript:

❏ Features Netscape might add to JavaScript in the future, and to its Web browser

❏ A wish list of features that could make JavaScript more useful and powerful

❏ A look at the other languages on the Web, and how they might affect JavaScript's popularity in the future

Next Steps

If you've read this book in order, you've reached the end of the line. If not, you can learn more with the following:

❏ To learn about Java and how it can be integrated with JavaScript, see Chapter 16, "Integrating JavaScript with Java."

❏ To learn about CGI and SSI, turn to Chapter 17, "Combining JavaScript, CGI, and SSI."

❏ To learn more about ActiveX, VBScript, and MSIE, turn to Chapter 18, "Using ActiveX and Microsoft Internet Explorer."

❏ To see examples of integrating JavaScript with other Web languages, see Chapter 19, "Real-Life Examples IV."

Q&A

Q: Why did Microsoft implement JavaScript in its Web browser, if it wants VBScript to become a popular scripting language?

A: Microsoft needs people to accept MSIE as an alternative Web browser, and to do that it needs to support the latest Web features—JavaScript being one of them. Also, the ActiveX features of MSIE 3.0 make it easy to support a variety of scripting languages.

Q: Will ActiveX controls ever be available on anything but Windows platforms?

A: Doubtful, because they rely heavily on the Windows API. If they were implemented on other platforms, they would probably be slower and require large amounts of memory.

Q: Is every Web language listed in this chapter?

A: I've tried to list the most popular and controversial languages—those that are driving the future of the Web. However, there are always others. For example, there are well over a hundred plug-ins besides Shockwave that enable different types of interactive content.

Conclusion

I hope you've enjoyed this book, and that you're as excited as I am about the many possibilities for JavaScript. You're probably already thinking of some new ideas for JavaScript programs.

To keep up with JavaScript, you'll need to keep an ear to the ground, because the language is still changing. Appendix C lists some online resources that may be helpful—in addition, be sure to watch the Web site listed in the Introduction for updates, additions, and more examples.

If you create something new and exciting, I'd like to see it. Contact me at the address listed in the introduction. I'll also try to answer any questions about this book you may have.

I wish you well in your future tasks with JavaScript and other languages, and may all of your JavaScript programs be bug-free. (Or at least, may you not give up until they are.) Good luck!

P A R T

VI

Appendixes

A JavaScript Structure and Objects Reference

This appendix is a quick reference for JavaScript objects. It includes the built-in objects and the objects in the object hierarchy. For further information, refer to Part II, "Using JavaScript Objects and Forms," of this book.

Built-In Objects

The following objects are built in to JavaScript. Some can be used to create objects of your own; others can be used only as they are. Each is summarized in the following sections. See Chapter 4, "Using Built-In Objects and Custom Objects," for details and examples.

Array

You can create a new Array object to define an array—a numbered list of variables. (Unlike other variables, arrays must be declared.) Use the new keyword to define an array, as in this example:

```
students = new Array(30)
```

Items in the array are indexed beginning with 0. Refer to items in the array with brackets:

```
fifth = students[4];
```

Arrays have a single property, `length`, which gives the current number of elements in the array. They have the following methods:

- ❏ `join` quickly joins all the array's elements together, resulting in a string. The elements are separated by commas, or by the separator you specify.
- ❏ `reverse` returns a reversed version of the array.
- ❏ `sort` returns a sorted version of the array. Normally, this is an alphabetical sort; however, you can use a custom sort method by specifying a comparison routine.

String

Any string of characters in JavaScript is a `string` object. The following statement assigns a variable to a string value:

```
text = "This is a test."
```

Because strings are objects, you can also create a new string with the `new` keyword:

```
text = new String("This is a test.");
```

`string` objects have a single property, `length`, which reflects the current length of the string. There are a variety of methods available to work with strings:

- ❏ `anchor()` creates an HTML anchor within the current page.
- ❏ `indexOf()` finds an occurrence of a string within the string.
- ❏ `lastIndexOf()` finds an occurrence of a string within the string, starting at the end of the string.
- ❏ `link()` creates an HTML link using the string's text.
- ❏ `split()` splits the string into an array based on a separator.
- ❏ `substring()` returns a portion of the string.
- ❏ `toString()` can be used on non-string values and converts them to strings.
- ❏ `toUpperCase()` converts all characters in the string to uppercase.
- ❏ `toLowerCase()` converts all characters in the string to lowercase.

There are also a few methods that enable you to change a string's appearance when it appears in an HTML document:

❑ `big()` displays big text, using the `<BIG>` tag in HTML 3.0.

❑ `blink()` displays blinking text, using the `<BLINK>` tag in Netscape.

❑ `bold()` displays bold tag, using the `<B>` tag.

❑ `fixed()` displays fixed-font text, using the `<TT>` tag.

❑ `fontcolor()` displays the string in a colored font, equivalent to the `<FONTCOLOR>` tag in Netscape.

❑ `fontsize()` changes the font size, using the `<FONTSIZE>` tag in Netscape.

❑ `italics()` displays the string in italics, using the `<I>` tag.

❑ `small()` displays the string in small letters using the `<SMALL>` tag in HTML 3.0.

❑ `strike()` displays the string in a strikethrough font, using the `<STRIKE>` tag.

❑ `sub()` displays subscript text, equivalent to the `<SUB>` tag in HTML 3.0.

❑ `sup()` displays superscript text, equivalent to the `<SUP>` tag in HTML 3.0.

As an example, this statement prints the value of the `text` string in italics:

```
document.write(text.italics());
```

Math

The `Math` object is not a "real" object, because you can't create your own objects. Each property or method uses the built-in `Math` object. A variety of mathematical constants are available as properties of the `Math` object:

❑ `Math.E` is the base of natural logarithms (approximately 2.718).

❑ `Math.LN2` is the natural logarithm of two (approximately 0.693).

❑ `Math.LN10` is the natural logarithm of 10 (approximately 2.302).

❑ `Math.LOG2E` is the base 2 logarithm of e (approximately 1.442).

❑ `Math.LOG10E` is the base 10 logarithm of e (approximately 0.434).

❑ `Math.PI` is the ratio of a circle's circumference to its diameter (approximately 3.14159).

❑ `Math.SQRT1_2` is the square root of one-half (approximately 0.707).

❑ `Math.SQRT2` is the square root of two (approximately 2.7178).

The methods of the `Math` object enable you to perform mathematical functions. The methods are listed in the following sections in categories.

Algebraic Functions

- ❏ `Math.acos()` calculates the arc cosine of a number, in radians.
- ❏ `Math.asin()` calculates the arc sine of a number.
- ❏ `Math.atan()` calculates the arc tangent of a number.
- ❏ `Math.atan2()` calculates the polar coordinate angle (theta) for an *x, y* coordinate pair.
- ❏ `Math.cos()` calculates the cosine of a number.
- ❏ `Math.sin()` returns the sine of a number.
- ❏ `Math.tan()` calculates the tangent of a number.

Statistical and Logarithmic Functions

- ❏ `Math.exp()` returns *e* (the base of natural logarithms) raised to a power.
- ❏ `Math.log()` returns the natural logarithm of a number.
- ❏ `Math.max()` accepts two numbers and returns whichever is greater.
- ❏ `Math.min()` accepts two numbers and returns the smaller of the two.

For example, this statement assigns the `big` variable to the larger of x and y:

```
big = Math.max(x,y);
```

Basic Math and Rounding

- ❏ `Math.abs()` calculates the absolute value of a number.
- ❏ `Math.ceil()` rounds a number up to the nearest integer.
- ❏ `Math.floor()` rounds a number down to the nearest integer.
- ❏ `Math.pow()` calculates one number to the power of another.
- ❏ `Math.round()` rounds a number to the nearest integer.
- ❏ `Math.sqrt()` calculates the square root of a number.

As an example, the following statement assigns the x variable to the square root of 35:

```
x = Math.sqrt(25);
```

Random Numbers

`Math.random()` returns a random number between 0 and 1.

NOTE: The Math.random() method worked only on UNIX platforms until Netscape 3.0. Be sure you and your users use the latest version.

Date

The Date object is a built-in JavaScript object that enables you to work conveniently with dates and times. You can create a Date object any time you need to store a date and use the Date object's methods to work with the date:

NOTE: The Date object will not work with dates before January 1st, 1970.

- ❑ setDate() sets the day of the month.
- ❑ setMonth() sets the month. JavaScript numbers the months from 0 to 11, starting with January (0).
- ❑ setYear() sets the year.
- ❑ setTime() sets the time (and the date) by specifying the number of milliseconds since January 1st, 1970.
- ❑ setHours(), setMinutes(), and setSeconds() set the time.
- ❑ getDate() gets the day of the month.
- ❑ getMonth() gets the month.
- ❑ getYear() gets the year.
- ❑ getTime() gets the time (and the date) as the number of milliseconds since January 1st, 1970.
- ❑ getHours(), getMinutes(), and getSeconds() get the time.
- ❑ getTimeZoneOffset() gives you the local time zone's offset from GMT.
- ❑ toGMTString() converts the date object's time value to text, using GMT (Greenwich Mean Time, also known as UTC).
- ❑ toLocalString() converts the date object's time value to text, using the user's local time.
- ❑ Date.parse() converts a date string, such as "June 20, 1996" to a Date object (number of milliseconds since 1/1/1970).
- ❑ Date.UTC() is the opposite; it converts a Date object value (number of milliseconds) to a UTC (GMT) time.

navigator

The `navigator` object includes information about the current browser version. At present, it works only with Netscape browsers. Its properties include the following:

- ❏ `navigator.appCodeName` is the browser's code name, usually `"Mozilla"`.
- ❏ `navigator.appName` is the browser's name, usually `"Netscape"`.
- ❏ `navigator.appVersion` is the version of Netscape being used. Example: `"3.0(Win95;I)"`.
- ❏ `navigator.userAgent` is the user-agent header, which is sent to the host when requesting a Web page. It includes the entire version information—for example, `"Mozilla/2.0(Win95;I)"`.
- ❏ `navigator.javaEnabled` is either `true` or `false`, indicating whether Java (not JavaScript) is enabled on the browser.
- ❏ `navigator.plugins` is an array that contains information about each currently available plug-in (see Chapter 13, "Working with Multimedia and Plug-Ins).
- ❏ `navigator.mimeTypes` is an array containing an element for each of the available MIME types (see Chapter 13).

The JavaScript Object Hierarchy

The object hierarchy includes objects that represent the browser window, the current document, and its contents. These objects are summarized here and explained in detail in Chapter 5, "Accessing Window Elements as Objects."

window

The `window` object represents the current browser window. If multiple windows are open or frames are used, there may be more than one window object. These are given aliases to distinguish them:

- ❏ `self` is the current window, as is `window`. This is the window containing the current JavaScript document.
- ❏ `top` is the window currently on top (active) on the screen.
- ❏ `parent` is a window that contains frames. Each frame is also a `window` object under `parent`.
- ❏ Within a window you have created, `opener` refers to the window that opened the window.
- ❏ The `frames` array contains the `window` object for each frame. These can be addressed as `parent.frames[0]` through the number of frames, or with their individual names, as in `parent.docframe`.

Each `window` object includes the following properties:

❑ `defaultStatus` is the initial message displayed in the status line.

❑ `length` is the number of frames within a parent window.

❑ `name` is the name of the window.

❑ `status` is the current value of the status line.

The `window` object also has three child objects, which you'll look at in their own sections later:

❑ The `location` object stores the location (URL) of the document displayed in the window.

❑ The `document` object holds the Web page itself.

❑ The `history` object contains a list of sites visited before or after the current site in the window.

The `window` object includes the following methods:

❑ `alert()` displays an alert dialog.

❑ `blur()` removes focus from the window, sending it to the background.

❑ `close()` closes a window you have opened.

❑ `confirm()` displays a confirmation dialog and returns `true` or `false`.

❑ `focus()` gives the window focus, moving it to the top.

❑ `open()` opens a new window.

❑ `prompt()` prompts the user and returns the text entered.

❑ `scroll()` scrolls the window, either horizontally or vertically. The parameters are *x* and *y* (column and row) offset in pixels.

❑ `setTimeout()` sets a timeout to execute a statement and returns an identifier for the timeout.

❑ `clearTimeout()` clears the timeout you specify.

Finally, `window` objects have the following event handlers, which you can define in the document's `<BODY>` or `<FRAMESET>` tag:

❑ The `onLoad` event occurs when the document in the window is finished loading.

❑ The `onUnload` event occurs when another document starts to load, replacing the window's current document.

❑ The `onFocus` event occurs when the window receives focus.

❑ The `onBlur` event occurs when the window loses focus.

❑ The `onError` event occurs if the document in the window fails to load properly.

location

The `location` object contains information about the current URL being displayed by the window. It has a set of properties to hold the different components of the URL:

- ❏ `location.protocol` is the protocol (or method) of the URL.
- ❏ `location.hostname` specifies the host name.
- ❏ `location.port` specifies the communication port.
- ❏ `location.host` is a combination of the host name and port.
- ❏ `location.pathname` is the directory to find the document on the host, and the name of the file.
- ❏ `location.hash` is the name of an anchor within the document, if specified.
- ❏ `location.target` specifies the TARGET attribute of the link that was used to reach the current location.
- ❏ `location.query` specifies a query string.
- ❏ `location.href` is the entire URL.

The `location` object also has two methods:

- ❏ `location.reload()` reloads the current document; this is the same as the reload button on Netscape's toolbar.
- ❏ `location.replace()` replaces the current location with a new one; this is similar to setting the `location` object's properties.

history

The `history` object holds information about the URLs that have been visited before and after the current one in the window, and it includes methods to go to previous or next locations:

- ❏ `history.back()` goes back to the previous location.
- ❏ `history.forward()` goes forward to the next location.
- ❏ `history.go()` goes to a specified offset in the history list (negative numbers go back, positive numbers go forward).

document

The `document` object represents the current document in the window and is a child of the `window` object. It includes the following properties:

❏ `bgColor` is the background color, specified with the BGCOLOR attribute.

❏ `fgColor` is the foreground (text) color, specified with the TEXT attribute.

❏ `lastModified` is the date the document was last modified. This date is sent from the server along with the page.

❏ `linkColor` is the color used for nonvisited links, specified with the LINK attribute.

❏ `location` specifies the document's URL. Don't confuse this with the `window.location` object.

❏ `referrer` is the URL of the page the user was viewing prior to the current page—usually, the page with a link to the current page.

❏ `title` is the title of the current page, defined by the HTML <TITLE> tag.

❏ `vlinkColor` is the color for visited links, specified with the VLINK attribute.

The `document` object also includes the following child objects as properties:

❏ `document.forms` is an array with an element for each form in the document. These can also be addressed by name, as in `document.regform`. Form elements are child objects of the form object and are described in Chapter 6, "Using Interactive Forms."

❏ `document.links` is an array containing elements for each of the links in the document. It can also contain `area` objects, used for client-side image maps.

❏ `document.anchors` is an array with elements for each of the anchors in the document.

❏ `document.images` contains an element for each of the images in the current document. Chapter 12, "Working with Graphics and Games," explains this object in detail.

❏ `document.applets` is an array with references to each embedded Java applet in the document. This object is explained in Chapter 16, "Integrating JavaScript with Java."

The `document` object has no event handlers. It includes the following methods:

❏ `clear()` clears a document you have closed.

❏ `close()` closes a stream and displays any text you have written.

❏ `open()` opens a stream and clears the current document.

❏ `write()` writes text to the document window.

❏ `writeln()` writes text to the document window and adds a carriage return.

Creating and Customizing Objects

This is a brief summary of the keywords you can use to create your own objects and customize existing objects. These are documented in detail in Chapter 4, "Using Built-In Objects and Custom Objects."

Creating Objects

There are three JavaScript keywords used to create and refer to objects:

- ❏ `new` is used to create a new object.
- ❏ `this` is used to refer to the current object. `this` can be used in an object's constructor function or in an event handler.
- ❏ `with` makes an object the default for a group of statements. Properties without complete object references will refer to this object.

To create a new object, you need an object constructor function. This simply assigns values to the object's properties using `this`:

```
function Name(first,last) {
   this.first = first;
   this.last = last;
}
```

You can then create a new object using `new`:

```
Fred = new Name("Fred","Smith");
```

You can also create a generic object using the `Object()` constructor and define its properties later:

```
values = new Object();
```

Customizing Objects

You can add additional properties to an object you have created just by assigning them:

```
Fred.middle = "Clarence";
```

Properties you add this way apply only to that instance of the object, not to all objects of the type. A more permanent approach is to use the `prototype` keyword, which adds a property to an object's prototype (definition). This means that any future object of the type will include this property. You can include a default value:

```
Name.prototype.title = "Citizen";
```

You can use this technique to add properties to the definitions of built-in objects as well. For example, this statement adds a property called num to all existing and future string objects, with a default value of 10:

```
string.prototype.num = 10;
```

B
JavaScript Statements, Functions, Operators, and Keywords Reference

This appendix is a list of the statements and functions available in JavaScript and their uses. It also includes a complete list of the keywords that are reserved by JavaScript.

JavaScript Statements

This section contains an alphabetical listing of the statements available in JavaScript and their syntax.

Comments

Comments are used to include a note within a JavaScript program and are ignored by the interpreter. There are two different types of comment syntax:

```
//this is a comment
/* this is also a comment */
```

Only the second syntax can be used for multiple-line comments; the first must be repeated on each line.

break

This statement is used to break out of the current `for` or `while` loop. Control resumes after the loop, as if it had finished.

continue

This statement continues a `for` or `while` loop without executing the rest of the loop. Control resumes at the next iteration of the loop.

for

This statement defines a loop, usually to count from one number to another using an index variable. In this example, the variable `i` counts from 1 to 9:

```
for (i=1;i<10;i++;) { statements }
```

for...in

This is a different type of loop, used to iterate through the properties of an object or the elements of an array. This statement loops through the properties of the `Scores` object, using the variable `x` to hold each property in turn:

```
for (x in Scores) { statements }
```

function

This statement defines a JavaScript function that can be used anywhere within the current document. Functions can optionally return a value with the `return` statement. This example defines a function to add two numbers and return the result:

```
function add(n1,n2) {
   result = n1 + n2;
   return result;
}
```

if...else

This is a conditional statement. If the condition is true, the statements after the `if` statement are executed; otherwise, the statements after the `else` statement (if present) are executed. This example prints a message stating whether a number is less than or greater than 10:

```
if (a > 10) {
    document.write("Greater than 10");
}
else {
    document.write("10 or less");
}
```

A shorthand method can also be used for these types of statements, where ? indicates the `if` portion and : indicates the `else` portion. This statement is equivalent to the previous example:

```
document.write((a > 10) ? "Greater than 10" : "10 or less");
```

Conditional statements are explained further in Chapter 3, "Working with Objects and Events."

return

This statement ends a function and optionally returns a value. The `return` statement is necessary only if a value is returned.

var

This statement is used to declare a variable. If you use it within a function, the variable is guaranteed to be local to that function. If you use it outside the function, the variable is considered global. Here's an example:

```
var students = 30;
```

Because JavaScript is a loosely typed language, you do not need to specify the type when you declare the variable. A variable is also automatically declared the first time you assign it a value:

```
students = 30;
```

Using `var` will help avoid conflicts between local and global variables. Note that arrays are not considered ordinary JavaScript variables; they are objects. See the section titled The Array Object in Chapter 4, "Using Built-In Objects and Custom Objects," or Appendix A, "JavaScript Structure and Objects Reference," for details.

while

The `while` statement defines a loop that iterates as long as a condition remains true. This example waits until the value of a text field is `"go"`:

```
while (document.form1.text1.value != "go") {statements }
```

JavaScript Built-In Functions

The functions in the next sections are built into JavaScript, rather than being methods of a particular object.

eval

This function evaluates a string as a JavaScript statement or expression, and either executes it or returns the resulting value. In the example below, a function is called using variables as an argument:

```
a = eval("add(x,y);");
```

`eval` is typically used to evaluate an expression or statement entered by the user.

parseInt

This function finds an integer value at the beginning of a string and returns it. If there is no number at the beginning of the string, Windows platforms return `0`; other platforms return `"NaN"` (not a number).

parseFloat

This function finds a floating-point value at the beginning of a string and returns it. If there is no number at the beginning of the string, either `0` or `"NaN"` (not a number) is returned.

isNaN()

This function returns `true` if a value is not a number (`"NaN"`). This function works on UNIX platforms only.

escape()

This function converts a string to URL-encoded (escaped) form. All nonalphanumeric characters are converted to `%` and their ASCII value to hexadecimal.

`unescape()`

This function converts an escaped (URL-encoded) string to normal text. It can be used to convert characters in URLs.

`taint()`

This function taints (marks) a variable or property with the current script's taint code. Data tainting is explained in Chapter 10, "Working with Multiple Pages and Data."

`untaint()`

This function removes taint from (unmarks) a variable or property. This only works if the value carries the current script's taint code. If the value came from another script or another server, it cannot be untainted.

JavaScript Operators

JavaScript includes a variety of operators that can be used in expressions. The following operators are used for assignment:

- ❏ = uses the variable on the left to store the result of the expression on the right.
- ❏ += adds the number on the right to the variable on the left.
- ❏ -= subtracts the number on the right from the variable on the left.
- ❏ *= multiplies the variable by the number on the right.
- ❏ /= divides the variable by the number on the right.
- ❏ %= uses the modulo operator, described in the next section.

The following operators are used for mathematical expressions:

- ❏ + adds two numbers.
- ❏ - subtracts one number from another.
- ❏ * multiplies two numbers.
- ❏ / divides one number by another.
- ❏ % (modulo) is the remainder when two numbers are divided.
- ❏ - (unary minus) changes a number to its negative version (complement).
- ❏ ++ adds 1 to (increments) a variable. This can be used as either a prefix or a postfix.
- ❏ - subtracts 1 from (decrements) a variable. This can be used as either a prefix or a postfix.

A single operator works with string values: + concatenates (combines) two string values.

The following operators are used for conditions and comparisons:

- ❏ Equal (==)
- ❏ Not equal (!=)
- ❏ Less than (<)
- ❏ Greater than (>)
- ❏ Greater than or equal to (>=)
- ❏ Less than or equal to (<=)

The following operators are used for logical expressions using Boolean values:

- ❏ And (&&)
- ❏ Or (¦¦)
- ❏ Not (!)

These operators are used for binary and bitwise operations:

- ❏ And (&) returns one if both of the corresponding bits are one.
- ❏ Or (¦) returns one if either of the corresponding bits is one.
- ❏ Xor (Exclusive Or) (^) returns one if either, but not both, of the corresponding bits is one.
- ❏ Left shift (<<) shifts the bits in the left operand a number of positions specified in the right operand.
- ❏ Right shift (>>) shifts to the right, including the bit used to store the sign.
- ❏ Zero-fill right shift (>>>) fills to the right, filling in zeros on the left.

Finally, the following operators are used for working with variables and functions:

- ❏ `typeof` returns the type of a variable or literal. This is a string consisting of the values `number`, `string`, `boolean`, `function`, `object`, or `undefined`.
- ❏ `void()` can be used with a function definition to force it to evaluate to `undefined` instead of returning a value.

JavaScript Keywords

This is a list of all the keywords, or reserved words, in the JavaScript language. These may be statements, functions, or connecting words. Some of the words in this list are not currently used in JavaScript, but have been listed as reserved words by Netscape because they may be used in a future version.

The main reason for this list is to remind you of which words you cannot use as variable, function, or object names. Using them may result in unpredictable behavior.

❑ abstract
❑ boolean
❑ break
❑ byte
❑ case
❑ catch
❑ char
❑ class
❑ const
❑ continue
❑ default
❑ do
❑ double
❑ else
❑ extends
❑ false
❑ final
❑ finally
❑ float
❑ for
❑ function
❑ goto
❑ if
❑ implements
❑ import
❑ in
❑ instanceof

❑ int
❑ interface
❑ long
❑ native
❑ new
❑ null
❑ package
❑ private
❑ protected
❑ public
❑ return
❑ short
❑ static
❑ super
❑ switch
❑ synchronized
❑ this
❑ throw
❑ throws
❑ transient
❑ true
❑ try
❑ var
❑ void
❑ while
❑ with

Online JavaScript Resources

This appendix lists some useful resources for learning more about JavaScript—Web sites, newsgroups, and mailing lists. I have also included pointers to learn more about the other languages you encountered in this book—HTML, Java, Plug-ins, CGI, ActiveX, and VBScript.

A complete index of related Web sites could fill a book this size—in a recent Web search, I found nearly 75,000 Web pages containing the word "JavaScript." Rather than try to list everything, I've listed a few of the most useful sites for each topic—those I enjoy using myself. You can find additional sites by following links from the ones I've provided or by using your favorite search engine. If you don't have a favorite, I recommend Digital's Alta Vista:

```
http://altavista.digital.com/
```

Due to the constantly changing nature of the Web, a few of the sites on this list may have changed by the time you read this, and better ones may have sprung up. For an updated list of links, consult this book's Web site:

```
http://www.starlingtech.com/books/javascript/
```

JavaScript

This section presents some useful resources for JavaScript—newsgroups, mailing lists, and Web sites. You can use these to learn more about JavaScript, see many working examples, and help others with problems.

Newsgroups and Mailing lists

The following Usenet newsgroups are available for discussion of JavaScript topics:

❏ `comp.lang.javascript` was created for JavaScript discussions. If you have a question, it's a great place to ask it—many JavaScript experts frequent the group.

❏ `news://news.livesoftware.com/livesoftware.javascript.developer` is a JavaScript newsgroup maintained by Live Software. See the next list for its Web site.

There are also a few mailing lists for JavaScript:

❏ The JavaScript mailing list at `Inquiry.com`—one of the earliest JavaScript discussion groups. It gets a lot of traffic, but you'll find much useful information. Sign up by following the instructions on the Web page:

`http://www.inquiry.com/techtips/js_pro/maillist.html`

❏ `NETural.com` maintains another JavaScript mailing list. To sign up, see its Web page at this URL:

`http://www.NETural.com/javascript/`

❏ The JavaScript Talk mailing list was created for calm discussions about JavaScript, without the arguments found in the other lists. It also has a Web page with more information:

`http://www.farhorizons.com/jstalk/jstalk.html`

Web Sites

Hundreds of Web sites about JavaScript have sprung up since JavaScript became a popular Web language. I've listed some of the best ones (in my opinion) in the next sections. You'll also find links to many more sites.

Netscape's JavaScript Authoring Guide

The "user's manual" for JavaScript, this site explains everything in technical detail. You'll find information about the latest changes and updates to JavaScript here, along with a handy reference.

`http://home.netscape.com/eng/mozilla/3.0/handbook/javascript/`

Netscape 3.0 Features

Another useful page from Netscape is the list of features for Netscape 3.0. It includes links to information about each of the features, and it is also updated as new features are added:

```
http://home.netscape.com/comprod/products/navigator/version_3.0/index.html
```

The JavaScript Index

This was one of the first sites about JavaScript. Its maintainer, Andrew Wooldridge, has assembled a comprehensive directory of JavaScript-related sites and other resources, and he includes some useful examples of his own. Here's the address:

```
http://www.c2.org/~andreww/javascript/
```

JavaScript 411

This site is home to the original JavaScript FAQ (frequently asked questions) file. You'll also find some examples of JavaScript in use, and links to other sites here:

```
http://www.freqgrafx.com/411/
```

The JavaScript Resource Center

This site is maintained by Paul Colton of Live Software, author of *Java Unleashed,* also from Sams.net. It includes the JavaScript examples from that book, other examples, links to other sites, and newsgroups and chat areas:

```
http://jrc.livesoftware.com/
```

Yahoo! JavaScript Listings

Yahoo! is, of course, one of the most popular Web directories. You can use this URL to go directly to its listing of JavaScript resources:

```
http://www.yahoo.com/Computers_and_Internet/Languages/JavaScript/
```

The JavaScript Workshop

Last but not least, don't forget this book's own Web site. Here, you'll find updated versions of the examples in the book, other new examples, news about JavaScript and browsers, and updates to this book's text. You can also submit comments and questions about the book:

```
http://www.starlingtech.com/books/javascript/
```

HTML and the Web in General

Here are a few pointers to information about HTML, browsers, and the Web in general.

HTML Information

HTML is constantly being updated. To find the latest information about the HTML standard, see the W3C's pages at this address:

```
http://www.w3.org/
```

Currently the latest version is HTML 3.2. You can see a summary of the changes in HTML 3.2 at this page:

```
http://www.w3.org/pub/WWW/MarkUp/Wilbur/
```

Of course, not all tags you use in JavaScript pages are standard HTML. Consult Netscape's pages (listed below) for information about the extensions Netscape has made to HTML.

webreference.com

This is a useful reference for everything to do with the Web and HTML. One particularly useful feature is a comparison between Netscape's extensions and the HTML standard, which can be helpful when deciding which features to implement in your pages:

```
http://webreference.com/index.html
```

Validation Services

Of course, if you're interested in HTML standards, you'll want to make sure your pages follow them. Several validation services on the Web enable you to enter your URL and check it based on the HTML standard of your choice—or even Netscape's extended HTML. One of the most popular is the WebTechs Validation Service:

```
http://www.webtechs.com/html-val-svc/
```

You might find the results from most HTML validation services a bit confusing. If so, you should definitely check out an alternative, the "kinder, gentler validator" maintained by Gerald Oskoboiny. It's the one I use on my pages:

```
http://ugweb.cs.ualberta.ca/~gerald/validate/
```

Browser Manufacturers

To keep up with JavaScript, you'll want to stay informed about the latest new browser versions. Here are the addresses for the two browsers that currently support JavaScript:

❏ Netscape Navigator: `http://www.netscape.com/`

❏ Microsoft Internet Explorer: `http://www.microsoft.com/ie/`

Other Sites

Here are some other sites you should visit to stay tuned to the latest about HTML, browsers, and the Web:

❏ BrowserWatch—a great site with up-to-the-minute news about browser versions, plug-ins, and other Web technologies. This is usually the first place you'll hear about a new browser:

`http://browserwatch.iworld.com/`

❏ The Web Developers' Virtual Library: A comprehensive listing of sites that relate to HTML and the Web and tools you can use to develop Web pages:

`http://www.stars.com/Vlib/`

❏ BrowserCaps is a service that collects information by survey to find out just which HTML features each browser supports. You'll find information about nearly every existing browser here:

`http://www.pragmaticainc.com/bc/`

❏ The HTML Writers Guild is an international organization of HTML authors and other Internet professionals; you can find information on joining at its site:

`http://www.hwg.org/`

Java

We covered a bit of Java in Chapter 16, "Integrating JavaScript with Java." If you want to learn more, you can start with the online resources listed in the next sections.

Sun's Java Site

This is the original site for information about Java. You can find documentation and information about Java here, as well as example applets and the Java Developers Kit:

`http://java.sun.com/`

Gamelan

Gamelan is a huge directory of Java-related Web pages and publicly available applets. Currently, it includes links to over 3,000 resources. It also includes a section with links to JavaScript resources:

`http://www.gamelan.com/`

The Java Man

This site includes listings of Java job openings, a reference for the language, and a list of books and other references for Java:

`http://www.javaman.com/`

JavaWorld

JavaWorld is a monthly Web-based magazine about Java development. It also includes a monthly column on JavaScript:

`http://www.javaworld.com/`

Plug-Ins

Here are some useful resources for learning about plug-ins, which are introduced in Chapter 13, "Working with Multimedia and Plug-Ins."

Netscape's Plug-In Guide

This is Netscape's official site for information about plug-ins. You'll find information about the plug-in specification here, as well as information about using plug-ins with JavaScript and links to plug-in manufacturers:

`http://home.netscape.com/eng/mozilla/3.0/handbook/plugins/pguide.htm`

Plug-In Plaza

Part of BrowserWatch, mentioned above, this is a huge listing of available plug-ins with descriptions. It includes charts detailing which platforms each plug-in is available for:

`http://browserwatch.iworld.com/plug-in.shtml`

Shockwave

One of the most popular plug-ins is Macromedia's Shockwave, which enables users to view presentations, animations, and movies created with Macromedia Director on the Web. In addition, the latest version supports real-time CD-quality audio. See Macromedia's site for information and to download the plug-in:

```
http://www.macromedia.com/shockwave/
```

Adobe's Acrobat

One of the first available plug-ins was Adobe's Acrobat, which enables you to display PDF (Portable Document Format) documents on the Web. These documents can include graphics, fonts, and other features for great-looking presentation. See Adobe's site for information and to download the plug-in:

```
http://www.adobe.com/Amber/
```

QuickTime

QuickTime, developed by Apple, was one of the first standards for full-motion video on computers. The QuickTime plug-in enables you to view movies inline in Web pages. See Apple's site for information and downloads:

```
http://quicktime.apple.com/
```

Live3d

Live3d is one of the more popular VRML plug-ins for Netscape. It was developed by Netscape corporation, and it is bundled with the latest version (3.0). See its site for information:

```
http://home.netscape.com/comprod/products/navigator/live3d/download_live3d.html
```

NCompass

The NCompass plug-in by Excite has received a lot of attention lately, because it enables Netscape to support ActiveX—something Netscape doesn't plan to do anytime soon. See its site for information and downloads:

```
http://www.ncompasslabs.com/
```

CGI and SSI

You looked at CGI and SSI in Chapter 17, "Combining JavaScript, CGI, and SSI." Here are a few pointers to additional information.

NCSA's CGI Documentation

This is the official CGI documentation from the source—the National Center for Supercomputing Applications, where the Mosaic Web browser originated. The exact specifications are given, along with a tutorial:

```
http://hoohoo.ncsa.uiuc.edu/cgi/
```

CGI FAQ

This is a useful site with answers to frequently asked questions about CGI. It also includes links to other sites with further information:

```
http://www.best.com/~hedlund/cgi-faq/
```

Tools for Aspiring Web Weavers

This site includes a large collection of useful information about the WWW and HTML and many links to related sites. In addition, it includes a comprehensive section on CGI programming:

```
http://www.nas.nasa.gov/NAS/WebWeavers/weavers.html
```

Perl Information

Perl is the most popular language for CGI and SSI programming. You can learn more about it from Tom Christiansen's Perl page, which includes information about Perl, links to other sites, and an online version of the Perl manual:

```
http://www.perl.com/
```

Another useful site is the Perl 5 WWW Page, which includes information about the latest features of the Perl language, along with an archive of scripts and libraries:

```
http://www.metronet.com/perlinfo/perl5.html
```

Newsgroups

Here are a few Usenet newsgroups for discussions of CGI, SSI, and Perl:

- ❏ `comp.infosystems.www.authoring.cgi` is devoted to all aspects of CGI, in any language.
- ❏ `comp.lang.perl.misc` is a general newsgroup for information about the Perl language.

MSIE, ActiveX, and VBScript

Chapter 18, "Using ActiveX and Microsoft Internet Explorer 3.0," talks about ActiveX and VBScript, the new Web developments from Microsoft. You can find out more about both of these at the sites listed in the next sections.

Microsoft's Pages

You can find information direct from Microsoft at the Microsoft Developers' Workshop Web page, which includes specifications and tutorials for ActiveX, VBScript, and HTML. Here's the URL:

`http://www.microsoft.com/intdev/default.htm`

You can also learn about Microsoft Internet Explorer and its capabilities at this page:

`http://www.microsoft.com/ie/`

JScript

Microsoft recently announced JScript. Now, before you worry about learning another scripting language, don't panic—JScript is actually an implementation of JavaScript. Using the JScript implementation, you can use JavaScript to script just about any application; Microsoft will even license the source code, so you can expect it to be ported to other platforms. See this URL for information:

`http://www.microsoft.com/jscript/`

The ActiveX Arena

Yet another part of BrowserWatch, mentioned previously, is devoted to ActiveX controls. You'll find a comprehensive list of controls there, as well as news about the latest in ActiveX:

`http://www.browserwatch.com/activex/`

Miscellaneous Resources

In this section, you'll find pointers to Web sites with further information about some of the topics that were mentioned but not covered in this book.

VRML

VRML—the Virtual Reality Modeling Language—has been a buzzword for the past year as 3D environments have started to appear on the Web. Although VRML hasn't quite taken over the Web yet, it's worth learning about. Here's the URL for the VRML specification:

```
http://webspace.sgi.com/moving-worlds/spec/
```

Another reason to learn about VRML is that JavaScript is now its official scripting language. Using a different set of browser objects, you can use JavaScript in a 3D environment on VRML browsers. See this URL for information:

```
http://webspace.sgi.com/moving-worlds/spec/part1/javascript.html
```

GIF Animations

GIF animations are a good alternative to JavaScript animation, and they are fully supported by Netscape and MSIE. You can find out more about GIF animations at this site:

```
http://members.aol.com/royalef/gifanim.htm
```

Web Security

Because security has been an important issue on the Web recently, I conclude with some pointers to security information related to JavaScript, Java, and the Web in general:

❏ The US Department of Energy maintains the Computer Incident Advisory Capability (CIAC). The CIAC site includes up-to-the-minute information about computer viruses and security problems with software. Most of the security problems in JavaScript have been reported here:

```
http://ciac.llnl.gov/
```

❏ The World Wide Web Security Frequently Asked Questions (FAQ) list is maintained by Lincoln D. Stein. Here, you'll find information on what's secure and what isn't, and on how security is affecting the Web:

```
http://www.genome.wi.mit.edu/WWW/faqs/www-security-faq.html
```

❏ Yahoo! includes a listing for Web security-related links. You'll find many more sites listed there:

```
http://www.yahoo.com/Computers_and_Internet/Internet/World_Wide_Web/
Security/
```

D What's on the CD-ROM

On the *Laura Lemay's Web Workshop: JavaScript* CD-ROM, you will find all the sample files that have been presented in this book, along with a wealth of other applications and utilities.

NOTE: Please refer to the readme file on the CD-ROM for the latest listing of software.

Windows Software

Netscape Navigator

❏ Netscape Navigator 3 for Windows 3.1, 95, and NT

HTML Tools

❏ Microsoft Internet Assistants for Access, Excel, PowerPoint, Schedule+, and Word
❏ Hot Dog 32-bit HTML editor
❏ HoTMeTaL HTML editor
❏ HTMLed HTML editor
❏ HTML Assistant for Windows
❏ WebEdit Pro HTML editor

❑ Web Weaver HTML editor

❑ CSE 3310 NTML validator

❑ ImageGen

❑ W3E HTML editor

Graphics, Video, and Sound Applications

❑ Goldwave sound editor, player, and recorder

❑ MapThis imagemap utility

❑ MPEG2PLY MPEG viewer

❑ MPEGPLAY MPEG viewer

❑ Paint Shop Pro 3.12 graphics editor and graphic file format converter for Windows

❑ SnagIt screen capture utility

❑ ThumbsPlus image viewer and browser

ActiveX

❑ Microsoft ActiveX Control Pad and HTML Layout Control

❑ Sample controls

Java

❑ Sun's Java Developer's Kit for Windows 95/NT, version 1.02 with sample applets and scripts

❑ JFactory Java IDE

❑ JPad Java IDE ModelWorks Software

CGI

❑ CGI*StarDuo and CGI*StarDuo95

❑ CGI PerForm command language interpreter for Common Gateway Interface (CGI) application design

❑ Several sample CGI scripts and libraries

Perl

❑ Perl Version 5 build 109 for Windows NT

Utilities

- ❏ Microsoft Viewers for Excel, PowerPoint and Word
- ❏ Adobe Acrobat viewer
- ❏ Microsoft PowerPoint Animation Player & Publisher
- ❏ WinZip for Windows NT/95
- ❏ WinZip Self-Extractor is a utility program that creates native Windows self-extracting ZIP files

Electronic Books

- ❏ *Teach Yourself Web Publishing with HTML 3.2 in 14 Days,* Professional Reference Edition
- ❏ *Laura Lemay's Web Workshop: JavaScript*

Macintosh Software

Netscape Navigator

- ❏ Netscape Navigator 3 for Macintosh

HTML and Graphics Applications

- ❏ HTML Markup 2.0.1
- ❏ Web Painter b5

Java

- ❏ Sun's Java Developer's Kit for Macintosh v1.0b1 with sample applets and scripts

Utilities

- ❏ Adobe Acrobat reader

Electronic Books

- ❏ *Teach Yourself Web Publishing with HTML 3.2 in 14 Days*, Professional Reference Edition

About Shareware

Shareware is not free. Please read all documentation associated with a third-party product (usually contained with files named readme.txt or license.txt) and follow all guidelines.

INDEX

Symbols

– (minus sign)
  negation operator, 36
  subtraction operator, 36, 361
– – (double minus sign), decrement operator, 37
—> (HTML comment end tag), 18
! (exclamation point), Not operator, 38, 362
% (percent sign), modulo operator, 36, 361
& (ampersand), And operator, 39, 362
&& (double ampersand), And operator, 38, 362
* (asterisk), multiplication operator, 36, 361
+ (plus sign)
  addition operator, 36, 361
  concatenating strings, 38
  URL encoding, 300
++ (double plus sign), increment operator, 37
/ (slash), division operator, 36, 361
// (double slashes), single-line comments, 24
; (semicolon), 22
< (less than), conditional operator, 40, 362
<!! (HTML comment begin tag), 18
<= (less than or equal to), conditional operator, 40, 362
= (equal sign)
  assignment operator, 35, 361
  syntax errors, 246-247
== (double equal sign), 39, 362
  syntax errors, 246-247
> (greater than), conditional operator, 40, 362
>= (greater than or equal to), conditional operator, 40, 362

^ (caret), Xor operator, 39, 362
{} (braces), 22
| (vertical bar), Or operator, 39, 362
|| (double bar), Or operator, 38, 362

A

abstract keyword, 363
accessing Java applets, 289
Acrobat (Adobe), 236, 371
ACTION parameter (<FORM> tag), 113
ActiveX, 312-313, 339
  Animated Button control, 315
  Chart control, 315
  Control Pad, 316-317
  developing controls, 318
  example, 330-331
  Gradient control, 315
  Label control, 315
  New Item control, 316
  <OBJECT> tag, 313-315
  Pop-up Menu control, 316
  PowerPoint Animation Player, 316
  Pre-loader control, 316
  resources, 373
  Stock Ticker control, 316
  Timer control, 316
  VBScript, 321
The ActiveX Arena (Web site), 373
Add( ) function, 23
addition operator (+), 361
AddScore( ) function, 276
Adobe Acrobat, 236, 371
advertisement banners, 227-229
alert windows, 253
alert( ) method, 95
  window objects, 351
Alta Vista (search engine), 365
ampersand (&), And operator, 39, 362

anchor objects, 108-109
anchor( ) method, string objects, 81, 346
And operator, 39
And operator (&&), 362
Animated Button control (ActiveX), 315
<APPLET> tag (HTML), 283
applet objects, 289
applets (Java), 324-327
  accessing, 289
  compiling, 286-287
  creating, 284-286
  manipulating, 289-290
applications, 25
  creating in nested frames, 192-194
  future JavaScript application improvements, 336
  multiserver applications, data tainting, 198-199
  VBScript application, 319
arithmetic operators, 36-37
array objects, 48, 76, 345-346
  creating, 76-77
arrays
  creating, 30
  databases, 195
  frames array, 181
  images array, 221-222
assigning values
  properties, 49
  variables, 32
assignment operators, 35, 361
associative arrays, 48
  databases, 195
asterisk (*), multiplication operator, 36, 361
Audio Player (Netscape), 234
automatic totals in forms, 126-129
automating shipping addresses in forms, 129-131

B

back button, 220-221
<BASE> tag (HTML), 178
bgColor property, document
  objects, 353
big( ) method, string objects, 347
bitwise operators, 39, 362
blink( ) method, string objects, 347
blur( ) method, 99, 121
  frames, 182
  window objects, 351
<BODY> tag (HTML), 53
bold( ) method, string objects, 347
Boolean data type, 26-28
boolean keyword, 363
Boolean operators, 362
border property, images array, 222
braces ({}), 22
break command (SSI), 302
break keyword, 363
break statement, 64, 358
BrowserCaps (Web site), 369
browsers
  communication with HTTP
    server, 13
  compatibility with JavaScript, 18-19
  frames, 177
  Microsoft Internet Explorer, 7
  Netscape Navigator, 7
  resources, 369
  viewing script output, 18
BrowserWatch (Web site), 369
built-in objects, see objects
buttons on forms, 116
  properties, 125
byte keyword, 363

C

C/C++, 303
call method, 292
calling
  functions, 51
  Java methods, 288
  JavaScript functions from Java,
    291-292
caret (^), Xor operator, 39, 362
case keyword, 363

catch keyword, 363
CGI (Common Gateway Interface),
  112, 337
  C/C++, 303
  compared to JavaScript, 296-298
  cookies, 179, 187-188
  environmental variables, 300-301
  forms, 299-300
  GET method, 299
  installing scripts, 305
  integrating with JavaScript, 15
  Perl, 303
  POST method, 299
  program output, 301
  resources, 372
  sample program, 304-305
  SSI, 301-302, 338
    directives, 302
    enabling, 302-303
    generating JavaScript,
      327-329
    JavaScript functions,
      creating, 306
    resources, 371
  URL encoding, 300
  versus JavaScript, 9
CGI FAQ (Web site), 372
ChangeImg( ) function, 224
char keyword, 363
charAt( ) method, 79
Chart control (ActiveX), 315
checkboxes in forms, 115
  properties, 123
checked property, 123
CIAC (Computer Incident Advisory
  Committee), 11, 374
class keyword, 363
classes (Java), 283
clear( ) method, document objects,
  105, 353
clearTimeout( ) method, 98
  frames, 182
  window objects, 351
click( ) method
  checkboxes, 123
  radio buttons, 124
client-side image maps, 229
clock graphic, 225-227
Clock( ) function, 227

close( ) method
  document objects, 105, 353
  updating frames, 185
  window objects, 351
closing windows, 94
color, document objects, 104
command line, debugging, 255-258
commands, see statements
comments, 24-25, 358
Common Gateway Interface,
  see CGI
comparing VBScript with
  JavaScript, 320-321
comparison operators, 39-40
compiling Java applets, 286-287
complete property, images
  array, 222
Computer Incident Advisory
  Committee (CIAC), 11, 374
concatenating strings, 38
conditional expressions, 60-61
conditional operators, 362
configuring sound players, 234
confirm( ) method, 95
  window objects, 351
const keyword, 363
continue keyword, 363
continue statement, 64-65, 358
Control Pad (ActiveX), 316-317
controls, developing, 318
converting
  between Date objects, 83
  strings, 78
cookies, 179, 187-188
  example, 212-215
CopyAddress function, 129
customizing objects, 85-86, 354-355
  String, 86

D

data tainting, 196-198
  enabling, 197
  functions, 197-198
  multiserver application example,
    198-199
data types, 25-26
  Boolean values, 28
  floating-point decimal numbers, 27
  integers, 26-27
  number, 30-31

Live3d (Web site), 371
LiveConnect, 239, 288, 334
LiveWire, 338
local variables, 33
location objects, 101-102, 352
location property, 103
   document objects, 353
logical operators, 38
long keyword, 363
loops
   break statement, 64
   conditional expressions, 60-61
   continue statement, 64-65
   for keyword, 61-62
   for…in, 63
   if…else, 59-60
   infinite loops, 63-64
   looping through properties, 75
   while loops, 62-63
lowsrc property, images array, 222

M

Macromedia Shockwave, 236
mailing lists, 366
maintaining state information, 200
   questionnaires, creating, 200-202
Math objects, 83, 347-349
   generating random numbers, 84
   rounding decimal places, 83-84
Math.ceil( ) method, 83
Math.floor( ) method, 83

Math.round( ) method, 83
message boxes, displaying, 141-143
messages, scrolling, 163-166
   text fields, 167-169
METHOD parameter (<FORM> tag), 113
methods, 24, 55-56, 73
   alert( ), 95
   blur( ), 99
   call, 292
   calling Java methods, 288
   charAt( ), 79
   clear( ), document objects, 105
   clearTimeout( ), 98
   close( ), document objects, 105
   confirm( ), 95
   Date objects, 349
   defining, 56-57
   eval, 292
   focus( ), 99
   formatting strings, 80-81
   forms, 120
     text fields, 121
   frames, 182
   GET, 112, 299
   getTimeZoneOffset( ), 82
   history objects, 352
   indexOf( ), 79
   join( ), 76
   lastIndexOf( ), 80
   location objects, 352
   Math objects, 348
   open( ), document objects, 105
   POST, 112, 299
   prompt( ), 95
   refresh, 238
   retrieving Date object values, 82
   reverse( ), 76
   scroll( ), 99
   SetMessage( ), 290
   setTimeout( ), 97
   setting Date object values, 82
   sort( ), 76
   split( ), 79
   substring( ), 78
   toFMTString( ), 83
   toLocalString( ), 83
   toLowerCase( ), 56, 78

   toUpperCase( ), 78
   window objects, 93-94
   window.alert, 253
   writing HTML text with document objects, 104-105
   see also individual method names
Microsoft Internet Explorer, 7
   downloading, 310-311
   errors, 264
   installing, 310-311
   JavaScript support, 311-312
   plug-ins, 236
   resources, 373
MIME types, listing, 241
mimeTypes object, 238
minus sign (–)
   negation operator, 36
   subtraction operator, 36, 361
modulo operator (%), 36, 361
MSIE, *see* Microsoft Internet Explorer
multidimensional arrays (databases), 195
multiframe documents, testing, 184-185
multiple-line comments, 24
multiplication operator (*), 361
multiserver applications, data tainting, 198-199

N

NAME parameter (<FORM> tag), 113
name property
   checkboxes, 123
   file upload fields, 126
   frames, 182
   images array, 222
   radio buttons, 123
   selection lists, 124
   text fields, 121
   window objects, 351
naming
   objects, syntax errors, 247-248
   variables, 31-32
   Web subpages, 156
native keyword, 363
Navigate( ) function, 158

A V I A C O M   S E R V I C E

The Information SuperLibrary™

Bookstore

Search

What's New

Reference

Software

Newsletter

Company Overviews

Yellow Pages

Internet Starter Kit

HTML Workshop

Win a Free T-Shirt!

Macmillan Computer Publishing

Site Map

Talk to Us

CHECK OUT THE BOOKS IN THIS LIBRARY.

You'll find thousands of shareware files and over 1600 computer books designed for both technowizards and technophobes. You can browse through 700 sample chapters, get the latest news on the Net, and find just about anything using our massive search directories.

Macmillan Computer Publishing books are available at your local bookstore.

We're open 24-hours a day, 365 days a year.

You don't need a card.

We don't charge fines.

And you can be as **LOUD** as you want.

The Information SuperLibrary
http://www.mcp.com/mcp/   ftp.mcp.com

Laura Lemay's Web Workshop: Netscape Navigator Gold 3

—Laura Lemay & Ned Snell

Netscape Gold and JavaScript are two powerful tools for creating and designing effective Web pages. This book covers Web publishing, and details not only design elements, but also how to use the Netscape Gold WYSIWYG editor. The CD-ROM contains editors and code from the book, making the reader's learning experience a quick and effective one.

This book teaches you how to program within Navigator Gold's rich Netscape development environment; it also explores elementary design principles for effective Web page creation.

Price: $39.99 USA/$53.99 CDN   User Level: Casual-Accomplished
ISBN: 1-57521-128-9   Internet—General

Laura Lemay's Web Workshop: Graphics and Web Page Design

—Laura Lemay & James Rudnick

With the number of Web pages increasing daily, only the well-designed will stand out and grab the attention of those browsing the Web. This book illustrates, in classic Laura Lemay style, how to design attractive Web pages that will be visited over and over again.

The CD-ROM contains HTML editors, graphics software, and royalty-free graphics and sound files. This book teaches beginning and advanced level design principles and covers the Internet.

Price: $55.00 USA/$77.95 CDN   User Level: Accomplished
ISBN: 1-57521-125-4   Internet—Online/Communications

Laura Lemay's Web Workshop: Creating Commercial Web Pages

—Laura Lemay & Daniel Bishop

Filled with sample Web pages, this book shows how to create commercial-grade Web pages using HTML, CGI, and Java. In the classic clear style of Laura Lemay, author of the bestselling *Teach Yourself Java in 21 Days,* it details not only how to create the page, but how to apply proven principles of design that will make the Web page a marketing tool.

The CD-ROM includes all the templates in the book, plus HTML editors, graphics software, CGI forms, and more.

This book teaches how to use HTML, CGI, and Java, and illustrates the various corporate uses of Web technology—catalogues, customer service, and product ordering.

Price: $39.99 USA/$56.95 CDN   User Level: Accomplished
ISBN: 1-57521-126-2   Internet—Business

Laura Lemay's Web Workshop: Microsoft FrontPage

—Laura Lemay & Denise Tyler

This is a hands-on guide to maintaining Web pages with Microsoft's FrontPage. Written in the clear, conversational style of Laura Lemay, it is packed with many interesting, colorful examples that demonstrate specific tasks of interest to the reader.

This book teaches how to maintain Web pages with FrontPage, and includes all the templates, backgrounds, and materials on the CD-ROM.

Price: $39.99 USA/$56.95 CDN   User Level: Casual-Accomplished
ISBN: 1-57521-149-1   Internet—Web Publishing

Laura Lemay's Web Workshop: 3D Graphics and VRML 2.0

—Laura Lemay & Karl Jacobs

This book is the easiest way for readers to learn how to add three-dimensional virtual worlds to Web pages. It describes the new VRML 2.0 specification, explores the wide array of existing VRML sites on the Web, covers the Internet, and steps the readers through the process of creating their own 3D Web environments.

The CD-ROM contains the book in HTML format, a hand-picked selection of the best VRML and 3D graphics tools, plus a collection of ready-to-use virtual worlds.

Price: $39.99 USA/ $56.95 CDN   *User Level: Casual-Accomplished*
ISBN: 1-57521-143-2   *Internet—Graphics/Multimedia*

Teach Yourself Web Publishing with HTML 3.2 in 14 Days, Professional Reference Edition

—Laura Lemay

This is the updated edition of Lemay's previous bestseller, *Teach Yourself Web Publishing with HTML in 14 Days, Premier Edition*. In it, readers will find all the advanced topics and updates—including audio, video, and animation—to Web page creation.

This book explores the use of CGI scripts, tables, HTML 3.0, the Netscape and Internet Explorer extensions, Java applets and JavaScript, and VRML.

Price: $59.99 USA/$81.95 CDN   *User Level: New-Casual-Accomplished*
ISBN: 1-57521-096-7   *Internet—Web Publishing*

Teach Yourself Web Publishing with HTML in 14 Days, Premier Edition

—Laura Lemay

This book teaches everything about publishing on the Web. In addition to its exhaustive coverage of HTML, it also gives readers hands-on practice in designing and writing HTML documents.

The CD-ROM is Mac- and PC-compatible and includes applications that help readers create Web pages using graphics and templates. Readers learn how to upload their pages to a server and how to advertise.

Price: $39.99 USA/$53.99 CDN   *User Level: New-Accomplished*
ISBN: 1-57521-014-2   *Internet—Web Publishing*

Teach Yourself Java in 21 Days

—Laura Lemay, et al.

Introducing the first, best, and most detailed guide to developing applications with the hot new Java language from Sun Microsystems. This book provides detailed coverage of the hottest new technology on the World Wide Web and shows readers how to develop applications using the Java language.

It also includes coverage of browsing Java applications with Netscape and other popular Web browsers. The CD-ROM includes the Java Developer's Kit.

Price: $39.99 USA/$53.99 CDN   *User Level: Casual-Accomplished-Expert*
ISBN: 1-57521-030-4   *Internet—Programming*

Add to Your Sams Library Today with the Best Books for Programming, Operating Systems, and New Technologies

The easiest way to order is to pick up the phone and call

1-800-428-5331

between 9:00 a.m. and 5:00 p.m. EST.
For faster service please have your credit card available.

ISBN	Quantity	Description of Item	Unit Cost	Total Cost
1-57521-128-9		Laura Lemay's Web Workshop: Netscape Navigator Gold 3 (Book/CD-ROM)	$39.99	
1-57521-125-4		Laura Lemay's Web Workshop: Graphics and Web Page Design (Book/CD-ROM)	$55.00	
1-57521-126-2		Laura Lemay's Web Workshop: Creating Commercial Web Pages (Book/CD-ROM)	$39.99	
1-57521-149-1		Laura Lemay's Web Workshop: Microsoft FrontPage (Book/CD-ROM)	$39.99	
1-57521-141-6		Laura Lemay's Web Workshop: 3D Graphics and VRML 2.0 (Book/CD-ROM)	$39.99	
1-57521-096-7		Teach Yourself Web Publishing with HTML 3.2 in 14 Days, Professional Reference Edition (Book/CD-ROM)	$59.99	
1-57521-014-2		Teach Yourself Web Publishing with HTML in 14 Days, Premier Edition (Book/CD-ROM)	$39.99	
1-57521-030-4		Teach Yourself Java in 21 Days (Book/CD-ROM)	$39.99	
❑ 3 ½" Disk		Shipping and Handling: See information below.		
❑ 5 ¼" Disk		TOTAL		

Shipping and Handling: $4.00 for the first book, and $1.75 for each additional book. Floppy disk: add $1.75 for shipping and handling. If you need to have it NOW, we can ship product to you in 24 hours for an additional charge of approximately $18.00, and you will receive your item overnight or in two days. Overseas shipping and handling adds $2.00 per book and $8.00 for up to three disks. Prices subject to change. Call for availability and pricing information on latest editions.

201 W. 103rd Street, Indianapolis, Indiana 46290

1-800-428-5331 — Orders   1-800-835-3202 — FAX   1-800-858-7674 — Customer Service

Book ISBN 1-57521-141-6

CD-ROM

Installing the CD-ROM

The companion CD-ROM contains all the source code and project files developed by the authors, plus an assortment of evaluation versions of third-party products. To install, please follow these steps.

Windows 95 Installation Instructions

NOTE: If you have the AutoPlay feature of Windows 95 enabled, the CD-ROM will install automatically. If you have disabled the AutoPlay feature, please follow the instructions.

1. Insert the CD-ROM into your CD-ROM drive.
2. From the Windows 95 desktop, double-click on the My Computer icon.
3. Double-click on the icon representing your CD-ROM drive.
4. Double-click on the icon titled setup.exe to run the CD-ROM installation program.

Windows 3.1/NT Installation Instructions

1. Insert the CD-ROM into your CD-ROM drive.
2. From File Manager or Program Manager, choose Run from the File menu.
3. Type `<drive>\setup` and press Enter, where `<drive>` corresponds to the drive letter of your CD-ROM. For example, if your CD-ROM is drive D:, type `D:\SETUP` and press Enter.
4. Follow the on-screen instructions.

Macintosh Installation Instructions

1. Insert the CD-ROM into your CD-ROM drive.
2. When an icon for the CD appears on your desktop, open the disc by double-clicking on its icon.
3. Double-click on the icon named Guide to the CD-ROM, and follow the directions which appear.